Bring Your Own Children:

South America!

A Family Sabbatical Handbook

Robin Malinosky-Rummell, Ph.D.

Comments by Christopher Malinosky

Book Publishers Network
P.O. Box 2256
Bothell • WA • 98041
Ph • 425-483-3040

Copyright © 2007 by Robin Malinosky-Rummell

All rights reserved. No part of this book may be reproduced, stored in, or introduced into a retrieval system, or transmitted in any form or by any means (electronic, mechanical, photocopying, recording, or otherwise) without the prior written permission of the publisher.

10 9 8 7 6 5 4 3 2

Printed in the United States of America

LCCN: 2007920245

ISBN: 1-887542-48-5

ISBN13: 978-1-887542-48-7

Editor: Julie Scandora

Cover Design: Laura Zugzda

Interior Layout: Stephanie Martindale

Contents

Acknowledgements

Of course, the first person to thank is my husband, Francis, whose love, support, patience, and willingness to carry heavy things made the trip possible. Not only did he contribute his computer savvy in generating the maps and budget, but he put up with my stress for countless hours throughout the project. I never underestimate the power of a truly great follower. The other most important contributing member is my son, Christopher, who proved that a young boy can be a delightful travel companion and a sensitive and insightful author. He gives me immense joy by challenging my perspective and expanding my horizons. We are so lucky to have the best son in the world.

Neither our trip nor this book would be possible without many inspirational and helpful people along the journey. My grandfather, Leo Rummell, engendered my passion for traveling by taking me on my first trip abroad. Adrianna fanned the flames with her engaging stories of her homeland, Venezuela. Dave, Julie, PJ, and Ben Carr opened their home to us before the big event, and even threw us a going-away party. My parents, particularly my mother, helped out tremendously by letting us take over a room for a few days, managing our finances, collecting unreliable rent checks, wiring money to a Brazilian bank account, opening pounds of mail, and dealing with all the headaches of maintaining our accounts and belongings, not to mention providing airport pickup service. My sister-in-law, Valerie Malinosky, kept an eye on our home and raked acres of leaves.

During our trip, our biggest thanks first go to Rich Baltus and Cyndi Morley. Not only did we have a great time together at so many junctures along the way, but we also are indebted to them for their multitude of travel tips and advice. If it were not for them, we probably would have missed all of the Carnival activities in Rio. We are also thankful to Dick Egan, the FUVIRESE staff, and the Silva family for making our time at FUVIRESE so special, and especially Alfonso Morales, our *amigo del corazón*, for showing us the real Ecuador and introducing us to the rain-forest. He is an inspirational role model to us all, especially Christopher. We really appreciated the gang at the Sundown Inn, Juan Carlos, Maria Elena, and Jaime Jaramillo, who patiently nurtured our budding Spanish and our spirits. Every time we play Risk we are reminded of the fun we had with them. We cherished our time with the Rurrenabaque group, particularly nature's child Sven whose travels continue to inspire us to this day. Our fellow CIWY volunteers, Murray, Frank and Alma, Kate and James, Hadar, and Suzanna and Dan, helped us survive 15 days of tough work. Our relationships there bind us forever. Thanks to Mama Vicky Hernaiz and her warm family for opening up their home to us and involving us in one of the most special holiday celebrations ever. Our welcoming hosts, Eduardo and Veronica, at the Hostal Independencia in Punta Arenas helped us navigate Patagonia, as did Azu at the Altos de Ushuaia. Finally, cheers to the Traveling Bastards, George Mickey, Mark Roberts, Brenda Robertson, and Dilip and Raj Chandran, for convincing us to go to Rio and keeping the partying spirit alive.

Several people deserve special thanks for their contributions to this project. In a class all by himself, Daveed (David de Jel) shared his wit and companionship with us throughout the trip, and provided excellent insights in developing this manuscript. Bonnie Michaels gave me invaluable encouragement and support in my budding career as a travel writer. I am forever indebted to fellow author Julie Carr who provided desperately needed leadership through the icy literary waters. Thanks also to my father for commenting on a draft of the book, and to Peter Mortola for his kind words about my writing. Lastly, I want to acknowledge all of the fabulous folks at the Book Publisher's Network, including Sheryn Hara, Stephanie Martindale, Laura Zugzda, and Julie Scandora, without whose assistance this project would never have come to fruition. You all are great!

Chapter 10
Trinidad and Tobago
Venezuela
Guyana
Suriname
French Guiana
Chapter 2
Galápagos Islands
(Ecuador)
Columbia
Ecuador
Chapter 3
Peru
Brazil
Chapter 7
Chapter 4
Bolivia
Chapter 5
Paraguay
Chapter 9
Chapter 8
Chile
Argentina
Uruguay
Chapter 6

How to Use This Book/Disclaimer

Due to the lack of materials on the market for families traveling to South America, this book provides detailed resources in combination with a travel narrative to give readers a sense of what they might encounter on the road. Furthermore, we want to encourage families to consider extended travel together by describing exactly how to make this happen. For those brave families willing to take the plunge, we hope that they can benefit from our experience by understanding and preparing for the pros and cons of spending a long-term sabbatical together.

The book is divided by region into chapters that correspond to the boxes drawn on the map on the opposite page. We realize that many families may not want to go to all countries in South America, and therefore relevant resources are listed at the end of each chapter for easy portability. Readers can simply remove the chapters that they need before they leave home or while on the road.

Specific prices are given to help create a budget and develop an awareness of the cost of items and services. However, the reader must take into account that prices change and plan accordingly.

As pointed out in this book, the political climate can also shift, and readers are consistently encouraged to seek out up-to-date information about the safety of all places to which they are planning to journey.

Therefore, although we strove to make the information in this book as accurate as possible, we accept no liability or responsibility for any loss, injury, or inconvenience sustained by anyone using this book.

Our Route
To Home
Trinidad and Tobago
From Home
Venezuela
Guyana
Suriname
French Guiana
Columbia
Ecuador
Galápagos
Islands
(Ecuador)
Peru
Brazil
Bolivia
Paraguay
Chile
Argentina
Uruguay

Chapter 1

How Did We Get Here?

I'm sitting wedged into the back seat of a Surinamese "bus" between a woman breastfeeding her baby and a sassy young man smoking a cigarette and fiddling with his radio. The "bus" is a minivan crammed full of dark-skinned folks, four or five to a seat, smoking, drinking shots, slapping each other, laughing, and arguing. Our light skin advertises our status as foreigners, as does our total inability to participate in the conversation. The minivan lurches back and forth along a bright red mud road full of potholes, which contrasts dramatically with the sapphire blue sky overhead and dense green tropical rainforest surrounding us. I'm straddling the spare tire and struggling to stay upright as the bus lurches precariously to the left. The baby, whose tiny limbs are covered with small white pustules, falls asleep with its head in my lap. The guy on my right jostles my arm as he ducks to avoid being hit by the older jokester in front of him. I sneak a glance between the crowded passengers at my husband, Fran, who is trying somewhat unsuccessfully to stake a claim on a small slice of seat with my eight-year-old son, Christopher, on his lap. I catch his eye and we burst out laughing. How in the world did we end up here?

Like many other Americans, my husband and I had fantasized for years about "getting away from it all" on an extended journey without ever really believing that it would happen. The dream began in earnest six years beforehand in the middle of a district-wide school staff meeting. Bored with the same old "do more with less" message, I decided to use my time constructively by reading my employee handbook. Partway through the booklet, the phrase "unpaid leave of absence" grabbed my attention. Apparently, after five years, my new employer was willing to give me a year of unpaid leave in order to pursue something relevant, such as higher education or military duty. As I began to imagine the myriad of travel possibilities, I wondered how I would legitimize the experience to my new employers.

Finally freed from the staff meeting, I raced home and thrust the handbook into the face of my unsuspecting and unemployed husband, Fran. Upon hearing my idea to take a year-long sabbatical, he laughed, rolled his eyes, and adopted that tolerant look that he gets whenever I start planning too far in advance. We certainly weren't in any position to take a year of unpaid leave. Fran had recently been laid off, and I had just taken on a new job as a school psychologist working with emotionally disturbed kids. But soon he found employment with a small engineering firm, and he began warming up to the idea. We started saving for the big vacation.

In my early years as a school psychologist, I realized that the Hispanic population in Washington County, Oregon, was critically underserved with very few culturally and linguistically competent professionals available to work with them. I began attending workshops and eventually found myself taking Spanish lessons. Through this process, I decided that I needed to spend some extended time in a Spanish-speaking country to improve my language skills.

At the same time, we befriended Adrianna, a Venezuelan woman who intrigued us with stories about the natural beauty of her country. We had already traveled several times to Europe, Southeast Asia, and Australia, but we had little interest in going south of the border. We unfairly based our image of Central and South America on years of negative media coverage, as well as our experiences in Tijuana, Mexico, the only Latino city we knew. We regarded the entire region as a dirty, dangerous, and poverty-stricken part of the world. Adrianna convinced us to move past this bias, so we planned a rendezvous in her homeland for Christmas. However, right before we left, she called from the

Venezuelan capital of Caracas in a panic due to a city-wide garbage strike. This certainly did not alleviate our fears about going to South America! Fortunately, upon arrival, our initial apprehension quickly dissipated, as did most of our negative stereotypes. The country lived up to Adrianna's glowing descriptions of abundant, unspoiled nature and wildlife, delicious food, and friendly, welcoming people who eagerly helped me muddle through my botched attempts at the language. We were quite surprised to discover the comfort and safety in which we could travel with a child, and the prices were a fraction of what we typically spent in Europe. Ultimately the trip was a success, and we began to view the entire continent in a totally different light.

Creating a Customized Itinerary and Budget

After agreeing on South America for at least part of our year-long itinerary, Fran and I began exploring other potential destinations. So many wonderful, exotic places in the world to choose from! We raided the local library (see the Resources list at the end of this chapter) and took out numerous guidebooks, travel narratives, videos, and picture books, especially for Christopher. We hung a large map of the continent on our wall for inspiration. We spent many hours on the Internet researching Spanish schools and volunteer opportunities, taking advantage of the new wave of interest in educational travel and working vacations. While at first a year abroad seemed quite long, once we broke it down into months and then days spent in transit and visiting various points of interest, we quickly realized that we needed to plan wisely. In order to maximize our time, we wondered if we should buy an "around-the-world ticket" or focus on one region. Should we make more effort to visit far-away, expensive sights that are difficult to access in the typical American two-week vacation, or spend more time on fewer places and really immerse ourselves in the culture? How much travel time did we need to visit remote areas? Most important, could we afford it?

To help narrow down our overwhelming options, Fran and I sat down and generated a list of sabbatical goals and a budget. Our goals included increasing our fluency in Spanish, making connections with local people and gaining insight into their culture, volunteering (e.g., in schools and/or factories) in order to learn more about job-related interests, and spending quality time as a family while experiencing some must-see highlights such as Machu Picchu and Iguaçu Falls. Next, we estimated US$100 a day in expenses for all three of us (totaling US$35,000 for the year). Would this be possible? We calculated all anticipated costs with help from Lonely Planet's *South America on a Shoestring* guidebook and decided that we could live comfortably in South America on that budget (see Appendix A). To keep costs low, we would rely on public transportation, so we gave careful consideration to weather conditions in developing a travel route. For example, some areas are completely inaccessible during the rainy season (November to March) in Bolivia, while Patagonia is best visited during that time. Once we generated a tentative itinerary, which incorporated all of our goals, the weather considerations, our finances and a reasonable pace for our family to travel, we decided to limit our trip to South America. Following the seasonal progression of the continent, we planned to arrive in Ecuador in July, journey south along the Pacific coast, experience Patagonia during their summertime, gradually weave our way back north through the central and eastern parts of the continent, and fly home from Venezuela the following year. This plan had the added advantage of minimizing the money spent on plane tickets, due to the proximity of Ecuador and Venezuela to the United States.

I cannot stress the importance of a thorough discussion of goals, pacing, and budget with your traveling partner(s) at this critical planning stage. Imagine spending valuable time and money for a "once-in-a-lifetime" trip, and then being dragged relentlessly through an ominous succession of heavily touristed sights, or sitting around impatiently waiting while your partner sleeps in until noon and then wants to hang out with the locals at a bar. Both are worthy pursuits in their own right but totally different views of a vacation, nonetheless. I thrive on the excitement of planning a trip and, once there, eagerly venture out to see the anticipated sights and revel in the new experiences. In contrast, Fran does not like to spend a lot of time developing a schedule beforehand, preferring instead to be spontaneous and spend time getting into the feel and rhythm of a place. Making compromises that satisfy everyone's needs and interests is an ongoing process throughout the journey, so be sure to lay a solid foundation right from the start. Although they can be quite stressful, these negotiations can also be fun and bring you closer together as a family by learning from each other's ideas and unique contributions to the overall experience. We frequently reviewed our goals and timelines throughout the sabbatical when facing critical decisions about the direction of our trip.

Children add a whole new dimension to travel plans and pacing. We needed to ensure ample time for child-oriented activities, a slower speed to accommodate little legs, and daily structure for home-schooling on the road. When confronted with the abstract concept of what he would like to do in South America, Christopher initially had no idea. However, as he developed an awareness of his own preferences, he was increasingly able to articulate his interests, and Fran and I strove to incorporate them into the agenda. As a result, we expanded our own horizons and greatly enriched our experience by doing things we normally would not have considered. Furthermore, Christopher provided us with an instant connection to other families, as the warm Latino people love children and often went to great lengths to include us in their lives.

Is It Safe?

The tragedy of September 11 acutely called into question whether it was really safe to travel abroad as a family, especially given ongoing terrorist activities. Our youthful, adventurous, risk-taking attitude changed when Christopher was born. While I can readily accept responsibility for getting myself into a tricky situation or becoming sick, I would be absolutely devastated if I put my son in harm's way. To address these concerns, we obtained as much information as possible about the places we were planning to visit, both before our trip and while on the road. The Internet increased the accessibility of national travel advisories (see Resources), international news coverage, and communication with people who were living and traveling in the region we were planning to see. We regularly asked locals and fellow travelers about the safety of anticipated travel routes, from the hotel surroundings to the entire country, in order to stay vigilant for our lives and our belongings. Ultimately, we made some decisions based specifically on safety concerns.

We did not visit Columbia due to the high risk of being kidnapped, and we eliminated most of our trip to Venezuela due to a military coup. On the other hand, true travelers never let fear alone stop them from achieving their goals. In fact, a certain level of fear may be mistakenly based on an isolated incident or erroneous information. For example, my father and brother both expressed concern about Argentina due to the highly publicized riots there following its financial crisis in 2002. I quickly pointed out that, despite the riots following the Rodney King verdict in 1992, my brother chose to live in Los Angeles, and we still visited him regularly. The most important point is to do your research, make informed decisions, and don't let an irrational fear keep you trapped in your comfort zone.

Staying Healthy on the Road

Next to safety, health care is probably the second biggest concern facing families traveling in developing countries. After researching the health issues of each of the South American countries we planned to visit (see Resources), we made an appointment at a travel clinic recommended by our doctor. We each received the appropriate shots (including typhoid, polio, and yellow fever) which, in combination with the office visit, totaled about US$900 for all of us and was not covered by our health insurance. The following day I became quite ill and missed work; when I returned, my students teased me about my case of "24-hour polio." In addition, we took advantage of the Hepatitis A and B vaccination clinics regularly provided by my employer. Be sure to count on several months for this process; many vaccinations cannot be done at the last minute. Interestingly, despite over 30 border crossings, we were required to show our yellow immunization booklets only once, when extending our Suriname visas.

Next we took inventory of all the medications we might need, not knowing what would be available abroad. Better safe than sorry! We stocked up on all of our prescriptions and made sure to carry printed copies with us. These documents proved essential at one border crossing (from Bolivia into Argentina) where officials held up our entire bus to check our medications against our prescriptions. The immense quantity of pill bottles caused the border guards to look at me with concern and ask if I had a serious illness. Perhaps they were taking some measures to keep people with communicable diseases, such as AIDS, out of the country. Fran found it humorous that so many of our medications were for my nose, while Christopher cracked up when a guard sniffed one of my tampons! At any rate, we made it through, and Fran no longer gave me a hard time about lugging around all those prescription copies.

To cut costs, it is also essential to call around or surf the Net for the best rates on medication and insurance. Costco gave us the cheapest price on the anti-malarial prophylactics, Lariam, which still cost us US$10 each. Council Travel gave us the best deal on travel insurance, and can also provide Student and Teacher Identification cards (although we found their Teacher Identification card worthless in South America). My mother, a nurse, noted that while the company would provide a medical evacuation if we needed it, we were not covered for medical care upon returning to the United States. At her suggestion, we bought a catastrophic coverage plan from the health insurance agent through Fran's work for under US$200 a month for the three of us. Fortunately, we were healthier during our year abroad than we had been the previous year in the States!

Specific medical concerns, such as vision care and birth control, also take some special consideration for a year on the road. While I have always strongly preferred contacts to glasses, I was unsure if I would have access twice daily to clean water, nor did I want to lug around all the contact solution paraphernalia. Consequently, I made the switch to glasses a few months before we left and was extremely glad that I did. It is so much easier to put on and take off a pair of glasses, particularly in planes or long overnight bus rides with no bathrooms. Invest in a comfortable pair that you really like, and make sure to adequately address sun glare by purchasing suitable lenses. If you will be traipsing around in the jungle or a humid place, consider buying plastic frames, as the coating began peeling off my expensive designer metal frames after a few months. Additionally, a sports strap or just a string to secure your glasses can prove helpful, especially when hanging out with inquisitive primates. You may still want to bring a couple pair of disposable contacts for those really adventurous times when glasses might become steamed up, get soaked, or fall off your face (e.g., while white-water rafting). While it is possible to obtain glasses inexpensively in towns with a local optician, you will need the prescription and may want to pack an extra pair of glasses anyway. If you are really opposed to glasses, fellow traveler Daveed wore his contacts throughout South America without any major difficulties. So it can be done!

As far as birth control, women like me who don't savor the idea of carrying around a year's supply of the pill may want to consider an IUD. Talk to your doctor and see what your options are. Again, plan in advance and test drive your options first; you certainly don't want to encounter problems a month or two into your big adventure.

Financial Ties that Bind

So how will you deal with financial matters while on the road? Some people just sell everything to pay for the trip, thus limiting ties and material worries back home. In contrast, we were committed to returning to our current jobs and lifestyle. With properties, cars, and a house full of furniture and clothes, we needed to do a lot of advance planning. We had mortgages, insurance (homeowner, auto, life, and health), taxes, and other bills that needed to be paid while we were gone. We also required international access to our savings during our trip but wanted to protect it from fraud as well. Fortunately, my mother agreed to manage our finances. In addition to helping us out tremendously, taking on this responsibility seemed to alleviate some of my parents' concerns and involved them in our trip. We added my mother's name to all of our bank accounts, ordered checks with her name on them, and gave her power of attorney on forms purchased from an office supply store. To simplify matters, we put as many regular transactions on auto deposit and withdrawal as possible. The scope of my mother's duties included keeping money in the travel accounts, collecting rent on our properties, making sure the bills got paid (such as taxes, homeowners dues, and professional licensure renewals, which could not be automatically withdrawn), and taking care of all those bothersome unexpected matters that arise, such as parking tickets on a car we no longer owned and a request from the city to fix a sidewalk square. My mother's help was crucial to the success of our adventure.

We traveled with two bank cards networked to the Plus and Cirrus systems (U.S. Bank and Citibank, respectively), linked only to a "travel account" so that if someone tried to empty the accounts they could not access all of our assets. We also carried two credit cards, one Visa and one MasterCard (also Plus and Cirrus networks). Having cards connected to each network was essential, as we frequently encountered situations during our trip where the sole machine in town was on only one of the two networks. Setting up the Citibank account from the West Coast was easier said than done, requiring multiple calls to people who each gave different answers to my questions and obviously did not know their geography. When I asked one woman how I might find out the locations of the ATMs in South America, she responded, "You mean like in France?" She eventually was able to find South America in the computer but went on to butcher the pronunciation of the countries so badly that I finally asked her to spell them for me instead.

The management of our property was another major concern. We had high hopes of returning to our home in the same shape as we left it. Fortunately, we were able to rent the bottom portion to Fran's sister, and by advertising in the local paper, we found a couple who was willing to share the house with her and her five cats. The combined rent covered the mortgage, insurance, and taxes for the year. Since we have another rental property, we felt comfortable with our ability to write a clear rental agreement (see Harriman's *Take Your Kids to Europe* for an example, or go to your local office supply store for forms). As part of the deal we used the garage to store most of our belongings and one vehicle. Our renters kept the house in good condition, but they had some difficulty paying the rent on time. Thanks to my parents' diligence, they eventually paid in full. In contrast, we heard horror stories from other travelers about rental catastrophes. Make sure to allocate some money in your budget for an "emergency" fund in case such a story becomes your own! Of course, a property management company would be happy to handle your home rental for a fee. In order to facilitate a smooth transition, we moved out and spent a month in the area after the renters moved into our house. Not only did our family and friends tolerate our freeloading for a month, but friends Dave and Julie even threw us a big going-away party! How grateful we were to have the support we needed to make our dream a reality.

Cutting through the Red Tape

Planning for a year-long trip certainly presents some unique challenges. At first, the whole task seemed so overwhelming that I did not even make a "To Do" list, which is extremely uncharacteristic for me. Instead, I would be struck by an impulse to begin work on some aspect of the project, and just go with that instinct. By the time I actually put together my final checklist, I was pleasantly surprised by how much I had already accomplished. Readers now are one step ahead of the game because, in addition to the information presented here, Bonnie Michaels' *A Journey of Work-Life Renewal* also provides invaluable checklists in preparing for a sabbatical.

About a year before take-off, we began letting people (including our employers) know about our plans. Talking about the trip finally made it seem as if it really might happen. I went through the proper paperwork channels to request the time off of work, emphasizing how long-term exposure to Spanish and different Latino cultures would be beneficial to my work in the schools. In fact, I even wrote a grant proposal to this effect, through my alma mater, Wellesley College. Although I did not receive the travel fellowship, I would encourage others to look for funding by contacting their colleges or universities (start with the Alumni Association Office). While my employers readily approved my unpaid leave, Fran's initial request for time off went a little less smoothly. His boss had generously offered him a partnership in the company, and after looking at the paperwork, Fran told him, "This all looks great, but in two years I'm going away for a year. How will that work?" His stunned boss retreated to his office for a few hours, but once he emerged, they managed to work it out. Fran had a large project that conveniently ended two months before we left, and he delegated the remaining responsibilities to the rest of his colleagues.

Plane tickets with a year between the departure and return dates seemed to throw the airlines for a loop. Most airlines will not offer them, and two travel agents suggested that we purchase one-way tickets to South America for a higher price than the round-trip airfares. After many disheartening inquiries, I happened upon a travel agency called Éxito Travel, advertised in our local Portland newspaper. Located in Oakland, CA, this office specializes in Latin American travel and has experience with long-term plans. For under US$1,000 each, we bought "open jaw" tickets from Continental Airlines, which conveniently enable passengers to fly into one city and out of another. We chose to fly into Quito, Ecuador on July 3, 2002, our 14th wedding anniversary, and planned to return to Portland from Caracas, Venezuela, the following July. Our tickets allowed us to return within a year of the departure date. However, we could only schedule a return flight 11 months from when we actually purchased the tickets. Since we bought the tickets in December 2001, we had to schedule a return trip for November 2002. Later, in South America, we changed the return date from November to the following July 2003, after the July flight schedule was available. This transaction cost us US$100 each, and the Éxito travel agent clearly explained this process up front. Much to our relief, we accomplished this task very easily at the Continental Airlines office in Guayaquil, Ecuador, and we even managed to conduct the entire interaction in Spanish.

After we had our plane tickets, we made arrangements for our arrival in Ecuador. We joined the South American Explorers Club (see Resources), which provided a wealth of information and travel support to us. We made sure to book comfortable accommodations for the first night in Quito following the long plane flight, and requested a transfer from the airport to the hotel. Based on bad past experiences, including a night spent in a Thai brothel, we strongly encourage anyone traveling abroad, particularly with children, to prearrange the first night stay, and perhaps even the second night as well, to avoid early check-out times. The extra expense is worth every penny!

Working during Our Vacation

Because our goals included learning more about job-related interests and local culture, as well as improving our Spanish, the possibility of meaningful volunteer work strongly appealed to us. However, when we began surfing the Web, we discovered that many organizations wanted **us** to pay **them** exorbitant amounts of money for the opportunity to work for free! Furthermore, because their company headquarters were often located in places such as Texas and London, we were concerned about how much of our money would be going towards overhead and management rather than to benefit the South American folks who really needed it. Later we discovered that the "gap year" concept, or taking a year off before college/university, has become very popular in Great Britain. Concerned parents would rather have their children doing something productive and supervised instead of drinking away their time on a foreign beach, so they either pony up the cash to fund a volunteer experience or host "fundraisers" to send their kids there. Thus, the number of volunteer agencies and their prices have skyrocketed due to increased demand.

Quite fortuitously for us, during an Easter Day celebration with friends we were introduced to two women who had worked for an organization in Baños, Ecuador. They connected us with Dick Egan, the United States contact for an Ecuadorian foundation called FUVIRESE (Foundation of Life, Reality, and Service; see Resources in Chapter 2). We met with Dick to learn more about the organization and the volunteer possibilities there. FUVIRESE assists physically disabled children and adults by providing physical therapy and educational opportunities in their school, as well as producing wheelchairs in part through funding from Rotary International. I wanted more experience in a Latino school setting, and Fran was looking for a way to contribute his engineering skills. Furthermore, Christopher would be able to come to school with me and have fun interacting with the children and staff there, while improving his Spanish skills too. This opportunity seemed ideal, so Dick made the necessary arrangements for us to work there and rent a nearby apartment. As luck would have it, he was also planning to go to Baños in early July with his family, and he invited us along. Things were very conveniently falling into place, and we were feeling quite encouraged indeed.

Home-schooling on the Go

We easily worked out the logistics of Christopher's second grade education. We informed the local public school of our plans, and they just treated the situation as if he was moving out of the country so that we did not need to formally register him as a home-schooled student. We obtained educational workbooks from local stores and asked Christopher's teacher to look over the material to verify that it adequately covered what he would be learning in second grade (see Resources). During the year, we sent home some of these books as evidence that he really did complete the curriculum on the road, although his school district never requested them. We often left the used books with schools and families who could benefit from them as well; we just erased the pencil marks and thus created a whole new book for the kids. We also found a wonderful Social Studies workbook specifically about South America, and while it was designed for older children, we adapted it to suit our purposes. With our help, Christopher was able to read information about each country, fill in the corresponding worksheets, and look out the bus window to see the curriculum material come alive! Talk about an educational field trip!

Packing Deliberations

Decisions regarding what to pack for a year abroad can be fairly daunting and stressful for anyone. In an effort to prepare for every eventuality, I poured through many available resources and developed my own list, which includes child-friendly ideas (see Appendix B). We bought equipment (including iodine tablets and a water purifier that we never used), reading material in English (which turned out to be extremely important), and a Spanish-English Dictionary (even more important). We also purchased an electronic Spanish-English dictionary, and while it was more lightweight than the bulky book, we found it more difficult to use and somewhat limited in scope. We carefully reviewed our clothing and bought the mandatory lightweight nylon travel pants that zipper into shorts, which I found indispensable in the rainforest. It's a very fine line between packing too much and too little, and it seems everyone

Fran carries our year's worth of worldly possessions

has his or her own opinion about what must be taken and what can be left behind. You are forced to be very selective when you have to carry supplies to last a year on your back. On the other hand, some products cannot be found in most towns (e.g., tampons, certain types of deodorant, decent dental floss and toothbrushes, camera batteries), and therefore must be brought or sent from the States. We learned this the hard way, and asked my parents to send us some much-needed items about half-way through our trip. This process in itself proved difficult and costly for us as well as my parents, so I would encourage travelers not to rely on this method and bring enough of the essentials from home. For Christopher's traveling enjoyment (as well as our own), we filled a backpack on wheels with toys and reading materials in addition to his home-schooling supplies. Children's books in English and his beloved Game Boy proved crucial for family sabbatical survival.

Countdown to Take-off!

As our departure date approached, we packed up our furniture, put the gym membership on hold, stored our second vehicle with friends, wrote up a will, finalized our insurance coverage (changing our account from residence to rental and putting our auto on inactive status), and completed about a million other little details. We opened an email account and made a list of email addresses and emergency numbers to bring with us. We copied our credit cards and important documents twice, storing one set in our safety deposit box, and adding the other to our growing luggage. With our minds running a mile a minute, we spent the last night in a hotel room near the airport, grabbed the shuttle, transferred Fran's Leatherman tool from his belt to our checked-in baggage, worked our way through the huge security lines, and boarded the plane. As we sat back in our seats, we squeezed each others' hands and, for the first time in months, took a deep breath and relaxed. Our journey had officially begun!

We're off!

CHRISTOPHER'S COMMENTS

I was feeling sad because I did not want to leave. I wanted to stay home and play with my friends. I didn't even know anything about South America except that they speak Spanish. I guess I was feeling scared about speaking Spanish because I didn't know how to speak it very well. When my Mom and Dad were talking to me about South America, I didn't listen to them because it didn't really mean anything to me. I just knew I had to go!

TRAVELER'S TIPS

1. Cut the overwhelming task of preparing for a long sabbatical into manageable chunks, and work on whatever strikes your fancy.

2. Leave plenty of time to plan. A year is really the minimum amount, especially when vaccinations are required.

3. Raid the library, rent movies, and research possibilities over the Net before investing in your own travel material.

4. Have a family discussion to generate a list of each member's goals and interests for the sabbatical. Discuss pacing preferences and expectations, and try to reach a compromise when creating possible routes.

5. Consider weather in developing your itinerary; some areas are not accessible in the rainy or winter seasons, and some parts of the world are just too uncomfortable at certain times of the year.

6. Don't try to do too much. Give yourself time to explore and be spontaneous, and allow for scheduling snafus. A year is not forever.

7. Children require a slower pace. Plan for child-friendly activities regularly.

8. Make sure to incorporate downtime every two to three months. Spend a week at a time just relaxing and recuperating from rigorous travel. Language lessons for three hours/day may be the biggest planned activity during this time.

9. Make a budget based on updated information and add about a third more than you think it will cost to be on the safe side.

10. Investigate grant possibilities through your college alma mater or other local organizations as potential funding sources for your trip.

11. Always use the most recent information possible; the Internet is probably your best resource for current information. Check travel advisories.

12. Do a trial run whenever possible. If you can't visit the area (or a similar one), investigate volunteer possibilities or other local experiences that may parallel your planned sabbatical.

13. Prepare for your trip by learning at least a few words of the local language. Invest in a dictionary.

14. Purchase travel insurance. Review the coverage carefully. Ensure that your medical costs are also covered upon returning to the United States.

15. Stock up on medications. Carry copies of your prescriptions and yellow immunization booklets. Be prepared to be ill the day after several shots.

16. Glasses are easier for traveling than contact lenses. However, you may want to bring along a few disposable pairs for adventurous days or water activities. Bring your prescription in case of loss or damage.

17. Carry two types of debit cards and credit cards (Cirrus and Plus networks). Research critical information such as the prevalence of ATMs ahead of time. Open up a travel account and keep a maximum of US$4,000 in it at a time. That way, if your card is stolen, your entire savings will not be drained.

18. Identify someone at home to handle your financial affairs. Put this person on all of your accounts and checks. Give him or her power of attorney. Pay or offer something in exchange for the help. This person will be a lifesaver!

19. Invest in a safety deposit box to store copies of all of your important documents. Give the key to your financial person, and make sure his or her name is on the account.

20. If traveling in a developing country, bring a year's supply of tampons, contraception, and other preferred products such as deodorant, dental care, hair care, and skin care. Film and batteries also can be very expensive.

21. Bring lots of English language books for young readers.

22. Consider purchasing a backpack with front panel opening for easy access and zippers that come together so that they can be locked (Eagle Creek may be a resource here). Bring along a bicycle chain to secure all bags together when stored.

23. Plan to stash your money in several places. Document these amounts. Bring along large envelopes to store your valuables in hotel safes.

RESOURCES

PRE-TRIP PLANNING RESOURCES

Note: Guidebooks and other resources are updated regularly. Always make sure that you have the most recent edition before investing in one.

Bell, Brian (Editorial Director, 2001). *Insight Guide: South America.* APA Publications.

This guidebook provides an overview with beautiful illustrations of South American highlights, as well as additional resources in each country.

Box, Ben (2002). *South American Handbook, Seventy-eighth Edition.* Footprint Handbooks.

One of our bibles throughout our journey, this guidebook contains specific details for travel in South American and a wide range of accommodations and dining options to fit any budget.

Brown, Polly Rodger, and James Read (2003). *First-Time Latin America: Everything You Need to Know Before You Go*. Rough Guides.

This book delivers the goods, just as the title suggests.

Carlstein, Andrés (2002). *Odyssey to Ushuaia: A Motorcycling Adventure from New York to Tierra del Fuego*. Chicago Review Press, Inc.

This travel narrative was written by a young American; his insights into the life of his native Columbian traveling partner influenced our decision not to go to Columbia.

Gorry, Conner (2000). *Read This First: Central and South America.* Lonely Planet Publications.

This guidebook gives extensive travel advice as well as specific information on every country in the area.

Hasbrouck, Edward (2004). *The Practical Nomad: How to Travel Around the World, 3rd Edition.* Avalon Travel Publishing.

Written by a travel agent, this book is full of insider information designed to help the independent traveler effectively plan and prepare for the trip, including how to find the cheapest airfares and remain safe abroad. See his website at www.practicalnomad.com.

Hasbrouck, Edward (2001). *The Practical Nomad: Guide to the Online Travel Marketplace, 1st Edition.* Avalon Travel Publishing.

A companion guide to *How to Travel Around the World,* this book gives detailed advice regarding how to find the best travel deals over the Internet.

Harriman, Cynthia W. (2006). *Take Your Kids to Europe: How to Travel Safely (and Sanely) in Europe with Your Children, Seventh Edition.* The Globe Pequot Press.

This guidebook gives lots of advice for inexpensive family travel in Europe, and contains some brief narrative comments.

Hubbs, Clayton A. (Ed., 2002). *Alternative Travel Directory: The Complete Guide to Traveling, Studying, and Living Overseas, Seventh Edition.* Transitions Abroad Publishing, Inc.

This travel reference book contains numerous resources including language schools and volunteer opportunities world-wide.

Kottler, Jeffrey (1997). *Travel that Can Change Your Life: How to Create a Transformative Experience.* Jossey-Bass Inc. Publishers.

The author describes how to make the most out of your vacation, including the psychological processes involved in long-term travel.

Lanigan, Cathy (2002). *Travel with Children, Fourth Edition.* Lonely Planet Publications.

This book provides in-depth advice combined with brief narratives on family travel all over the world, with a small section on South America.

Lansky, Doug. (2003). *First-Time Around the World: A Trip Planner for the Ultimate Journey*. Rough Guides.

This book is full of useful information for planning extended travel around the world, as well as some highlights of places to visit.

Lyon, James et al. (2000). *South America on a Shoestring*. Lonely Planet Publications.

Our other bible throughout our trip, this guidebook is best for maps, overviews, and cheap places to stay and eat.

McMillon, Bill, Doug Cutchins, and Anne Geissinger (2003). *Volunteer Vacations: Short-Term Adventures That Will Benefit You and Others, Eighth Edition*. Chicago Review Press, Inc.

This reference book lists short- and long-term volunteer opportunities all over the world and includes some narratives of volunteer experiences.

Meyers, Carole Terwilliger (Ed., 1995). *The Family Travel Guide: An Inspiring Collection of Family-friendly Vacations*. Carousel Press.

This guide is chock-full of helpful hints and resources for family travel, as well as descriptions of many family-friendly vacations around the world, although South America is not mentioned.

Michaels, Bonnie, and Michael Seef (2003). *A Journey of Work-Life Renewal: The Power to Recharge and Rekindle Passion in Your Life*. Managing Work & Family, Inc.

www.mwfam.com.

This book blends narrative with practical information about this couple's year-long sabbatical spent traveling, learning, and volunteering around the world.

Nichols, Jennifer, and Bill Nichols (2004). *Exotic Travel Destinations for Families*. Santa Monica Press, LLC.

This guidebook provides tips and brief narratives on short-term family travel all over the world, with a section on South America limited to Ecuador only.

Transitions Abroad Magazine
802-442-4827
www.transitionsabroad.com

This magazine is loaded with up-to-date information on traveling, volunteering, and language-learning around the world.

Tristram, Claire (1997). *Have Kid, Will Travel: 101 Survival Strategies for Vacationing with Babies and Young Children*. Andrews McMeel Publishing.

This book provides detailed suggestions for traveling with infants and young children, with a small section on international travel.

Truszkowski, Helen (2000). *Take the Kids Travelling*. Cadogan Guides: Globe Pequot Press.

This book contains many great family travel tips and ideas as well as resources all over the globe.

Young, Isabelle (2000). *Healthy Travel: Central and South America*. Lonely Planet Publications.

A very important book devoted to keeping the whole family healthy on the road.

SAFETY RESOURCES

Citizens Emergency Center
(202) 647-5225
http://travel.state.gov/travel

South American Explorers Club
www.samexplo.org

Has free safety information about travel to South American countries. For example, on a link to the British Consulate, it indicates that 800 kidnappings occurred in 2005 in Columbia.

See also Hasbrouck, Edward (2004). *The Practical Nomad: How to Travel Around the World, 3rd Edition*. Avalon Travel Publishing.

LATIN AMERICAN TRAVEL SPECIALISTS

Éxito Travel

800-655-4053
www.exitotravel.com

Specialists in Latin American travel, including long-term stays.

TRAVEL INSURANCE

Council Travel

800-2COUNCIL
www.counciltravel.com

We felt they provided the best deal with good coverage for our family. They also offer International Student Identity Cards and Teacher Identity Cards, but the latter was of very limited use for South America.

HOME-SCHOOL CURRICULUM RESOURCES

Kramme, Michael (2002). *Exploring South America.*

Continents of the World Geography Series, Mark Twain Media Publishing Company, Carson-Dellosa Publishing Company, Inc.

This workbook was an amazing educational resource for South America, giving information and written tasks related to all aspects of culture, commerce, weather patterns, and much more, geared to a fifth grade level. The publisher also has Spanish language lesson books.

Geography Unit: South America. Evan-Moor Educational Publishers.

www.evan-moor.com

McGraw-Hill Children's Publishing, now a member of the School Specialty Children's Publishing

1-800-417-3261
www.mhkids.com

This publisher has academic books for each grade level as well as Spanish language books.

Rainbow Bridge Publishing

www.summerbridgeactivities.com

This publisher has Spanish language books.

SOUTH AMERICAN CONTACTS

South American Explorers Club

126 Indian Creek Rd.
Ithaca, NY 14850
607-277-0488
www.samexplo.org

General Membership is US$50 individual, US$80 couple, which entitles members to its newsletters and access to a plethora of information via email or by visiting its clubhouses in Quito, Ecuador, Lima and Cusco, Peru, and now, Buenos Aires, Argentina (which was not open on our trip). The website also has free information, including safety information. The clubhouses offer book exchanges and guidebooks for sale, cultural events, and other nice services for travelers. At our request over the Internet, their staff special-ordered our Footprint guide and had it ready for us to pick up at the Lima clubhouse.

Locations:

Quito, Ecuador: Apartado 17-21-431, Eloy Alfaro, Quito, Ecuador
Street Address: Jorge Washington 311 y Leonidas Plaza, Mariscal Sucre
Telefax: (593-2) 2225-228

Lima, Peru: Calle Piura 135, Miraflores
Telefax: (51-1) 445 3306

Cusco, Peru: Apartado 500, Cusco, Peru
Street Address: Coquechaca 188, Buzzer 4
Telefax: (51-84) 245-484

Buenos Aires, Argentina: Jerónimo Salguero 553
Tel: +54-(9)11-4861-7571

This clubhouse was not opened during our trip.

FAVORITE SPANISH-ENGLISH DICTIONARY

Webster's New World Spanish Dictionary, Pocket Edition (1991). Harrap Books, Ltd., Macmillan, Inc.

Ecuador
From Portland, Oregon, USA
Columbia
Ibarra
Otavalo
Quito
Equator
Isla Bartolomé
Isla Baltra
Puerto Ayora
Isla Santa Cruz
Canoa
Tena
Baños
Puyo
Riobamba
Puerto López
Montañita
Galápagos Islands
Guayaquil
Alausí
Cuenca
Pacific Ocean
Loja
Peru
Vilcabamba
Piura

Chapter 2

EXTRANJEROS IN ECUADOR

The plane landed on dark, unfamiliar soil. In just a few hours, we had transformed into *extranjeros* (literally, "strangers," the Spanish word for foreigners), which was to be our new identity for the upcoming year. Jetlagged and exhausted, we worked our way through the Quito airport muttering the usual arrival mantra: luggage, currency, visitor information. We picked up the luggage and made it through customs without incident, gave the currency exchange a miss as Ecuador uses U.S. dollars, and located the information booth, which was closed. Mission accomplished! If only it were that easy.... As we walked outside, we were immediately overwhelmed by the mob just barely restrained by the metal fence surrounding the exit. The onlookers vied for our attention, shouting "taxi," "hotel," and various other services in English and Spanish. We were so thankful we had arranged a hotel with airport pickup ahead of time. Eventually we located a man with the telltale sign reading "Malinosky-Rummell." We quietly confirmed the hotel name with him, keeping in mind stories of "fakes" who copy travelers' names off these signs and lead them to unexpected and potentially disastrous outcomes. As we made our way to the minivan and then the hotel, the driver gave us some information about the city and our location, including areas that are *seguro* (safe) and *peligroso* (dangerous). The woman at L'Auberge Inn, located about equidistant between the old and new sections of town, further reinforced these safety concerns. She stressed that some visitors had been mugged after dark in the nearby park. Needless to say, we chose to eat near the hotel that evening.

The next morning, bright sunlight flooded through our tiny window, relieving our stress and illuminating a glorious view of the statue, *La Virgen* (the Virgin), perched high atop a hill like a welcoming beacon. We eagerly peered down at the narrow streets already bustling with people. Men in business suits strode hurriedly alongside indigenous women wearing bowler hats and lugging bulky colorful woven shawls, symbols of the exotic South American culture we had journeyed so far to see. Fran excitedly pointed out that just the sight of these women had already accomplished one of his goals for the trip. Bursting with enthusiasm, we quickly dressed and headed out to meld into the lively scene.

Quito is the world's second highest capital city, nestled high in the Andes at 9,500 feet. As a result, we fought a bit of altitude sickness, including headaches and some dizziness. Controlling our symptoms with some aspirin, we spent the day exploring this beautiful, surprisingly clean town. We got our bearings at the South American Explorers Club (SAEC), where we obtained a wealth of information about our recently adopted home while Christopher chatted with a new friend about the finer points of Game Boys. This organization provides its members with an extensive array of services, including constantly updated detailed descriptions about places of interest throughout South America, a book exchange and lending library, and discounts on services ranging from hotels to Spanish lessons. The cozy clubhouse also facilitates connections among independent travelers searching for potential trekking partners, tutors, or even roommates. After spending the morning at the SAEC, the Casa de la Cultura Ecuatoriana (House of Ecuadorian Culture) held our interest with its anthropology and modern art, while Christopher enjoyed playing on the unique open-air sculpture gallery. We strolled down the alluring cobbled streets of the old town, lined with gracious colonial architecture hung with wrought-iron balconies. Christopher chased the pigeons in Plaza Independencia, and then we all enjoyed some lovely chamber music in La Compañía, an impressive church full of gold. On the way to the restroom, we discovered an unusual butterfly exhibit tucked into a back room. Unfortunately, we were so absorbed by the elegant music and intricately mounted insects that we completely forgot Christopher's Game Boy in the bathroom. We had already left the building and were headed down the street when we realized it was missing. After the obligatory shouting and finger-pointing about who was at fault, we raced back to the church. Without the Game Boy we could kiss peaceful moments on the public buses goodbye! We explained the situation to the guard and he looked very discouraging when we asked to retrace our steps. Miraculously, it was still hanging up in the bathroom where Christopher had left it. *"Un milagro de la Virgen!"* ("A miracle of the Virgin!") I joyfully shouted to the guard. He looked unconvinced.

We had such a successful first day that we set out for La Mitad del Mundo (literally, "The Middle of the World," or the equator) on the next. Misjudging the distance to the bus stop, we ended up walking for many blocks. At this point we made the distressing discovery that Christopher becomes nauseous to the point of vomiting when he exercises too much in high altitudes. This awareness certainly impacted our decision-making throughout the rest of our journey. While it was overcast and chilly on the equator due to the altitude, Christopher was still able to enjoy the play structure and began to feel better. After giving him some time, we decided to go inside the monument, which was well worth the expense. Not only did it have a great view at the top, it also had many elaborate exhibits of the different native people of Ecuador.

For probably the first time in my life, I was looking forward to using the public toilet north of the monument. I had watched the water rotate clockwise in our hotel, which was located south of the equator, and I was eager to watch it go in the opposite direction (counterclockwise). To my disappointment, I saw that the water continued to rotate clockwise. Strange. Neither Fran nor I could figure out why the water rotated in the same direction both north and south of the monument at the equator. It wasn't until weeks later we learned that the whole monument is actually about 225 feet south of the true equator! At our friend Daveed's encouragement, we schlepped all the way back out to the area

One foot in the north, the other in the south

to find the true equator located at the Museo De Sitio Inti-Ñan. The hosts there gave a convincing demonstration of the gravitational force using a simple washtub and plug, pulled by our budding star, Christopher. Sure enough, the water spins counterclockwise in the northern hemisphere and clockwise in the southern hemisphere. Directly on the equator, the water goes straight down! While Fran initially scoffed at Daveed's description of this fascinating natural phenomenon, he had to eat his words after we had witnessed it firsthand.

The View from a Wheelchair

At the designated time and place in Quito we connected with Dick Egan, his son, daughter-in-law, and their one-year-old baby and headed in a private van to FUVIRESE, our volunteer placement in Baños. Ensconced in verdant mountains beneath an active volcano, Baños (literally "baths" in Spanish) derives its name from the outlying geothermal hot springs. Lush jagged peaks and waterfalls surround this small village where local culture and foreign comforts delightfully co-mingle. Young men twist large coils of taffy in front of tiny tourist shops next to women roasting stakes of cuy (pronounced "quee," or guinea pigs) over barbecue pits. We sampled this local specialty and found it quite tasty, albeit a bit challenging to get the meat off those tiny bones! We felt quite safe exploring all of the area's nooks and crannies on foot at any time of day. In the evenings, the streets come alive with children playing, women socializing, and men drinking bottles of the local brew. A shuttle rattles haphazardly through the town, whisking tourists up to the top of the volcano for a late-night party. Due to the high number of foreigners ("expats") who make Baños their home, a wide variety of excellent restaurants, bars with live music, and even little movie-houses abound. At Le Petit Restaurant, we treated ourselves twice to a fabulous French meal of lamb, steak in a pepper-cognac sauce, a dreamy chocolate dessert (made with the delicious local chocolate), and a rich South American wine all accompanied by live Andean panpipe music for US$20. What a heavenly blend of the best of both worlds!

We rented a second-floor apartment through Veronica Silva, one of the FUVIRESE directors, and her sister Paula's family lived

Barbecued cuy in Baños

downstairs. From our window, we often watched a group of teenagers playing a rousing game of soccer in the street. The roof of our apartment had a lovely view of the smoking volcano and *La Virgen*, a statue of Mary erected to protect the town from harm. Apparently *La Virgen* was holding up her end of the bargain because the last time the volcano erupted, the lava flowed in the opposite direction and wiped out a neighboring village instead. Nevertheless, the citizens of Baños conduct routine evacuation drills, just in case. During our stay there, we joined in this monthly safety precaution by assisting the FUVIRESE staff in relocating their clients to a more secure location on the outskirts of town.

Our roomy abode consisted of two bedrooms attached to a large main kitchen/dining/living area. The only drawback was that we had to walk a few steps outside to the tiny bathroom filled with a multitude of hazards. The low ceiling prevented its occupants from standing fully upright without hitting their head on its sharp edges. The intimidating electronic instant water heater in the shower alternated between shocking and scalding the bathers. But the worst problem was the water situation. Whenever anyone used the water downstairs, there was absolutely no water upstairs. We quickly learned that there would be no water on Monday mornings when Paula washed her dog, as well as Wednesday and Saturday mornings when another woman came to do laundry. Cooking and other water uses downstairs also resulted in a very unpredictable flow in our apartment on the other mornings, not to mention the days that the entire town had no water due to pipe cleaning or some mysterious difficulty. We ultimately ended up taking showers at night, but even so, I was often caught mid-shampoo with no water. No wonder so many local people use the hot springs for bathing!

But the small inconveniences did little to dampen our spirits, and for a total of US$200 for the month, it was great for our budget. To keep our costs low, we typically bought produce at the nearby market, such as meat, cheese, eggs, fruits, veggies, and numerous kinds of potatoes, all sold by women in their traditional heavy skirts and bowler hats. Fran especially enjoys forays into open-air markets and grocery stores to learn about the agriculture and eating habits of the local people, and he always makes a point of visiting them whenever we find ourselves in a new environment. He carefully prepared our purchases using sterilized water and then cooked our meals over the propane-powered stovetop. Paula also frequently sent up tasty home-cooked dishes, prompting Fran to ask her how to prepare her specialty of rice, egg, sausage, and potato cakes. Although a bit surprised to be teaching a man to cook, she was a great sport, and we all enjoyed the fruits of their labors.

To save money in restaurants, we regularly ordered the traditional meal by asking for an *almuerzo* (lunch), which, without fail, consisted of chicken, potato soup, rice, and juice, for approximately US$1.50. Breakfast (*desayuno*) usually consisted of stale bread and unappetizing instant coffee, a sadly ironic twist of fate considering Ecuador is renowned for its marvelous coffee beans. The instant grounds were typically premixed in just enough water to dissolve them, and then poured into a glass container, sometimes even a recycled coke bottle. Placed alongside the salt and pepper on the table, the coffee was easily mistaken for some type of odd condiment, or worse, someone's leftover garbage. To make it more palatable, I always ordered *café con leche* (coffee with milk), but quite disappointingly, I often received a cup of heated milk with a layer of goo on top (like the creamy skin on top of hot pudding) into which I was expected to add the instant coffee. I dreaded accidentally sucking up this lumpy goo early in the morning. The goo was so notorious that the Ecuadorians even had a name for it, called *la nata*. Towards the end of our stay in Baños, we found a touristy place advertising the best Italian coffee in the country. The coffee was truly divine, but it was disheartening that they had to import the beans all the way from Italy rather than investing in the locally grown resources instead.

Dick helped us get settled and begin our one-month volunteer assignment at FUVIRESE, an organization that serves disabled (primarily physically handicapped) children and adults. Christopher and I assisted the teachers at the school, serving children aged five and up who had a wide range of physical and cognitive limitations. While we struggled with the language barrier, we found Ecuadorian Spanish to be quite understandable, and people were very patient and willing to communicate with us. Furthermore, because the teaching staff was accustomed to speaking in simple, basic phrases to the students, Christopher and I could usually comprehend them. Our Spanish quickly improved, especially our commands to the children such as "*¡Siéntate!*" ("Sit down!"), "*¡Espera!*" ("Wait!"), and "*¡Silencio!*" (self-explanatory). We spent our days involved in their academic and functional living skills activities, which included trips to the grocery store, making soup, and swimming lessons. Once a week we loaded everybody up in the van and took them to the *baños*, or hot springs. The *campesinos* (i.e., the native subsistence farmers living in the country) use the springs to bathe themselves. I found the hair and other unidentifiable bits floating in them somewhat disconcerting, but Christopher and the other kids had so much fun splashing around in the water that any unpleasantness was easily overlooked. We were thrilled to contribute much needed curriculum material (e.g., Christopher's home-school books) to the school. I also subbed for one of the teachers when she had a family emergency, and eventually I suggested some simple visual aids and behavior management strategies, my area of clinical expertise. Down the street, Fran volunteered his engineering skills by making wheelchairs in the *taller* (workshop). Supported by a grant from Rotary International, the goal was for the agency to become self-sufficient through wheelchair sales.

Ironically, despite trying to avoid the day-to-day monotony by taking a "year off," we quickly fell into routines in Ecuador. We discovered the need for predictability in order to meet our scheduling demands, to find items, and to eliminate wasted time and frustration, especially further on when we had several stretches of daily packing and unpacking with lots of movement in between. Christopher, in particular, really relied on this structure. As a child psychologist, I often advocate to parents and teachers the need for predictability to develop a child's sense of security and overall mental health, but Christopher demonstrated daily how essential this concept truly is. Without it, he constantly asked questions about our upcoming plans and became increasingly stressed. Normally a very amicable, easy-going child, he grew irritable, unhappy, and downright defiant when pushed to pursue our schedule with no child-oriented event or apparent end in sight. To avoid these problems, we frequently relayed our short- and long-term plans, describing and even demonstrating visually through pictures how Christopher would be spending each day. Details such as what type of transportation we would take, the trip's duration, and what the next sleeping arrangements might be were of utmost importance to him. We also made sure to emphasize and build in activities of potential interest to a seven-year-old boy. Even small things, such as choosing a special snack at the bus stop or at the end of a long day spent volunteering, could buy hours of contentment.

Furthermore, during our time at FUVIRESE, we also began to develop some of the same work habits that we had at home, with a concurrent rise in stress level. One morning I was rushing to work, and my foot missed the curb, raised about a foot above the street. I fell and ripped a hole in one of the two pairs of jeans that were supposed to last me all year. I already felt grubby without my morning shower and lacked my usual jolt of caffeine, and the accumulated pressure of being late and ruining my pants, combined with months of working and scrambling to prepare for the trip, caused me to burst out crying. What a lousy way to start the day! I became irritated by the kids who were testing my authority as a substitute teacher, and resentful of the strain of the job as well as Fran's increasing involvement in his wheelchair projects. The last week of our stay, we realized that there were still some sights, such as the *zoológico* (zoo), that we wanted to see. Fran felt obligated to complete his wheelchair project, rather than go with me and Christopher. I got angry about his decision to prioritize work commitments over family time, and we ended up having an argument that was quite similar to any number of previous disagreements back home. To top it off, the weather in Baños was cold, rainy, and dark due to its location on the equator, where 12 hours of daylight is a year-round reality. We had just survived winter in the equally cold, rainy, and dark Pacific Northwest and by July, I was desperate for sunlight. After our month in Baños, we realized that we needed to pursue volunteer experiences that were drastically different from our jobs at home to really get a break from "the daily grind," in addition to opening up novel opportunities for mental stimulation and growth. We also recognized the importance of being ready, both mentally and emotionally, to fully commit to the demands of the project, instead of perceiving it as a vacation. Finally, location and climate would play a huge factor in determining where we would settle down in the months to come.

On the other hand, the biggest advantage to volunteering was the lasting relationships we formed with our coworkers. Alfonso Morales, one of the directors and founder of FUVIRESE, took us under his wing, and together we explored the unique offerings of his country. Gregarious and outgoing, Alfonso has friends all over the world and is truly inspirational. While serving in compulsory military duty he was injured and became paraplegic. Instead of sitting on a street corner with his hand out, Alfonso took action. He refused to allow his wheelchair to limit his mobility, so he created FUVIRESE and built wheelchair ramps into the sidewalks of Baños. He continued traveling within and even outside of Ecuador, developing local and international partnerships to support his work at the foundation. Spending time with Alfonso really opened our eyes to the struggles and barriers that a handicapped person must overcome, particularly in a country with minimal resources. But Alfonso never let anything stop him. What a wonderful role model he provided for Christopher, and the two developed a tight bond. Alfonso still affectionately calls him his *amigo de mi corazón*, his friend of the heart.

Our adventures with Alfonso usually began at the bus station, surrounded by stalls selling *caña*, or sugar cane cut into chunks or freshly squeezed into juice. Unlike many other countries in Central and South America, most towns in Ecuador coordinate their bus companies so that they all reside in one building (called the *terminal terrestre*). As a result, the buses all conveniently arrive and depart from the same place. Travelers simply go to the *terminal terrestre*, tell their destination to one of the men working there, and usually find themselves on a bus heading in that direction within the hour. We never needed to buy tickets in advance. Furthermore, the small country contains some of the greatest biodiversity on the planet so that an incredible array of cultures and ecosystems can easily be reached in one day. The only downside is that most of the buses are run down and slow, as they stop frequently along the way to pick up and drop off passengers. Alfonso was fond of pointing out that these buses are the typical mode of transportation used by Ecuadorians, and we often saw people in local dress boarding the buses with livestock in tow. Chickens and roosters were most popular. Through a curious blend of English and

On the road outside Baños

Spanish, Alfonso lovingly shared his country with us, giving us lessons ranging from the history and different ethnic cultures to the local foods (including the six different types of Ecuadorian bananas) and traditional medicines of the land.

Traveling throughout Ecuador within the confines of a wheelchair required Alfonso to be resourceful and assertive, and to rely on the good-natured assistance of the Ecuadorian people. Whenever he boarded a bus, he had to ask the bus driver or the assistant to pick him up and put him in an appropriate seat and then depend on someone to take care in packing up his wheelchair and putting it on top of the bus. When he arrived at his destination, he needed to sound the alarm and go through the reverse process. Most Ecuadorian cities are not very wheelchair accessible due to the high sidewalks without ramps, as well as the deteriorated nature of the walkways, so we were often limited to rolling down the streets and peering into stores from a distance. When we sought out hotels, Alfonso sent the taxi driver in first to check if they had rooms for a "disabled person," which typically entailed an easily accessible room on the first floor with adequate bathing facilities. Furthermore, the crumbling roads often caused Alfonso's tires to give out, necessitating a search for someplace to repair them. Because all kinds of vehicles encountered these problems, an appropriate bicycle or tire *taller* was fairly easy to find and provided an interesting way to connect with people and watch them use their ingenuity to splice together discarded objects into workable parts. We certainly applauded Alfonso's persistence in remaining mobile despite these types of setbacks, and considered ourselves very lucky that we did not have to deal with these daily challenges as he did.

On our first trip with Alfonso, we visited his friend, Rolando, president of ASODICH (Asociación de Parapléjicos y Minusválidos de Chimborazo), an organization for the physically handicapped similar to FUVIRESE. Also paraplegic, Rolando picked us up at the crowded market in Riobamba and graciously began showing us around his hometown. However, our pleasant excursion suddenly transformed into one of the most frightening incidents of our entire trip. A little boy darted out in front of the van, and although he tried to swerve, Rolando hit him. I felt physically ill hearing the thump of the little body connecting with the van. As he slammed on the brakes, a large group of the boy's friends, relatives, and neighbors quickly surrounded us and began shouting and hitting the van. Too afraid to get out, we watched in horror as his father carried the boy in front of our vehicle and shook him at us. The boy's mouth hung open, dripping with an unidentifiable white substance. Upon observing his gaping jaw, Fran and Christopher feared that the child's head was crushed. Out of the corner of my eye I caught sight of the boy's mother racing out of a house nearby. She charged at the van, screaming and punching Rolando through the open window. Terrified, I froze in my seat, wondering how we were ever going to extricate ourselves safely from our precarious predicament. Our little group of two paraplegic men, two *extranjeros*, and a seven-year-old boy was no match for the large, irate mob.

With the situation rapidly deteriorating, Alfonso managed to take charge and save the day. Urging the family to calm down with his famous "*¡Tranquilo! ¡Tranquilo!*" he emphasized that we needed to get the child to the hospital first and worry about the conflict later. The furious family asked how they were going to pay for the medical care, but Alfonso reassured them that we would find a way. The family got into the van and Rolando drove us all to the nearest military hospital. Sitting directly opposite the boy's distressed mother, we cringed as she focused her rage on her husband, intermittently yelling and hitting him for not watching their child. Fortunately, what had looked like white foam coming out of the child's mouth was really just *choclo* (corn remnants), and only his leg was damaged. The hospital fee was US$40, and Alfonso, Fran, and I pitched in to fix the broken appendage. By constantly reiterating that the accident was not Rolando's fault, Alfonso diffused the situation and the atmosphere dramatically improved. Much to Rolando's relief, the family agreed not to notify the police. Apparently, the legal system in Ecuador differs from the U.S. in that the driver can be imprisoned for an indefinite period of time, whether or not the accident is his or her fault. In fact, if the victim dies, the driver can be charged with murder. In *The Practical Nomad*, Ed Hasbrouck indicates that this scenario is true for many countries around the world. Understandably shaken, Rolando returned home, and we all decided to call it a day, extremely thankful that the little boy wasn't more seriously hurt.

Our next journey was quite calm by comparison. Alfonso suggested that we travel to the jungle to visit his friends in Tena. On the first night of our arrival, the biggest butterfly we had ever seen flew into the restaurant where we were eating dinner. It was about as big as my hand, so at first we mistook it for a small bird. As it landed softly on a table near us, we cautiously approached it, astounded by its size. Christopher was devastated that we did not have the camera. In an effort to appease him, we returned the next day in hopes of taking a picture, but the butterfly was long gone. We continued on across a thatched footbridge to the Parque Amazonica, a little island brimming with more exotic butterflies, including blue morphos, insects, birds, turtles, and monkeys. As we meandered through the tropical foliage, Alfonso plucked part of a plant off the ground and stuck it on his nose. Christopher followed suit, and they both started cackling like a pair of parrots. Soon distracted by some leaf-cutting ants, we followed their trail to a spider monkey chained to a tree. Feeling bold, we slowly drew near the monkey. Eager for company, the monkey rapidly advanced on us and tried to grab Christopher's leg! While the monkey was probably just lonely and trying to play, I freaked out anyway, screaming with fear as I beat a hasty retreat, dragging my surprised son behind me. After that, Alfonso tirelessly teased me about scaring that poor monkey with my loud shrieking.

Accompanied by Alfonso's delightful friends, we later relaxed on a sandy beach in Misahuallí at the edge of the Napo River. We pulled some snacks out of our bag, and while our attention was diverted, a troop of daring monkeys stole our cookies and darted up into a tree. We didn't even notice until they tried to open the package and instead only succeeded in dropping them onto some unsuspecting tourists. We promptly retrieved the treats and then proceeded to fend off the insistent little beggars as they tried to grab them right out of our hands while we were eating. Their antics simply served in endearing them to us, and we suddenly realized that we had fallen in love with the rainforest. Before leaving for South America, we had informed our travel doctor that we did not plan to go for fear of catching malaria or some other strange disease. He had encouraged us to rethink this decision, and now we understood why. After Alfonso and his friends had treated us to the

Christopher and Alfonso clowning around in the jungle

magic of the jungle, we were absolutely hooked and sought to immerse ourselves in its captivating presence whenever possible.

Perhaps our favorite outing with Alfonso was a bike ride through the mountains surrounding Baños on the road towards Tena. The rainy season had begun, and my coworkers warned me that a house had been swept away along the very same road, killing its resident in the process. Of course, Alfonso was certainly not going to let a little precipitation deter us! So he helped us rent some bikes in town, and we set out on our adventure. Alfonso led the way in his specialized wheelchair and trailer, Fran followed him with Christopher squeezed into a small seat directly over the back wheel, and I brought up the rear. Making quite a spectacle, we attracted so much attention as we rode through the small towns that I felt like a celebrity! Bouncing and sliding over the muddy, rocky road, we passed spectacular views of sharp volcanic mountains covered with jungle foliage and waterfalls plunging down into a deep gorge below. We pedaled by the sobering remains of the flooded house, reduced to a jumble of boards and mud. The light drizzle became heavier throughout the trip, creating a surreal haze on the landscape around us. Further on, we had to stop for about an hour beside a waterfall cascading directly onto the road while a bulldozer cleared a path for us through a huge landslide. About ten miles out of town, we stopped at a basket suspended on a cable crossing from one side of the gorge to the other. After Alfonso assured us that many locals use this method of transportation daily to go to and from their jobs, we tentatively boarded the basket. Feeling simultaneously frightened and exhilarated, we zipped through the mist across the deep crevasse and then hiked to the waterfall below, taking care to avoid donkeys laden with wooden crates struggling up the path beside us. After a full day of biking, hiking, and basket-riding, we happily caught a lift back into town in a tarp-covered truck and let someone else brave the slippery, mucky streets for a while.

As volunteers, we participated in Ecuadorian life in a way that we never would have experienced as solo travelers. We joined Alfonso and his relatives for a *peña*, an Ecuadorian gathering in which a band somewhat spontaneously decides to play in a local bar for the night. News of the show travels by word of mouth, and with all of his connections, Alfonso got wind of such an event and invited us along. His sweet mother even

The boys (Daveed, Fran, and Christopher) hard at work in the taller

Christopher goes native in Ecuador

offered to babysit Christopher so that we could really enjoy an adults-only evening. Alfonso and I danced together, rocking and rolling in his wheelchair, and his cousin also showed me some dance steps. After the band finished, a DJ began playing songs from the Grease soundtrack, and I started lip-synching the words. His cousin then tried to copy me despite my protests that I did NOT know any hip new American moves! Another night, my coworker put together a private showing of special Ecuadorian folk dances, complete with several costumes from different areas of the country. She even dressed Fran, Christopher, and me in the traditional outfits for some great photos. We certainly learned more about Ecuador from an insider's view than we ever would have gotten on our own.

The Traveler's Counterculture

In addition to our valued relationships with Alfonso and other Ecuadorians, we discovered an unexpected source of friendship through fellow travelers. Because U.S. citizens generally do not vacation in South America, we had ignorantly assumed that we would not encounter many other foreigners there at all. We were therefore surprised and delighted to meet people from all over the world (including Brits, Dutch, Germans, Italians, Spaniards, Israelis, and Aussies). Sharing the common bond of being English-speaking *extranjeros*, we connected with others in a way that Fran and I had not experienced on our previous trips abroad. We had fascinating conversations about such topics as growing up in Eastern Germany and watching the wall come down, living through the war and its aftermath in Bosnia and Croatia, and surviving mandatory military duty in Israel. Tapping into this counter-culture of travelers was not only very fun and educational, but it also served as a vital lifeline to information about places that we were planning to visit. During our month at FUVIRESE, Fran befriended Daveed while working together on wheelchairs in the *taller*. (His name is actually David but pronounced "Daveed" in the local tongue, so the name stuck.) A tall dreadlocked Dutchman with a biting, cynical wit and a shared love of travel, Daveed's unique blend of humor and pessimism always kept us in stitches. Directly resulting from our volunteer work, our friendship with Daveed is truly one of the most cherished outcomes of our journey.

Despite our previous mishap, we all decided to brave another ride with Rolando to Otavalo, a tiny northern town. Alfonso arranged for us to meet Rolando at a central location in Ambato, a city along the main highway towards Otavalo. We took a bus from Baños to the designated meeting point, sat down, and waited for Rolando. Still new to South America, my U.S. time clock kicked in after about an hour, and I sent Fran and Daveed off to call Alfonso. Fran came back with the usual message, "*¡Tranquilo, tranquilo!*" Sure enough, a couple hours later Rolando arrived, and we climbed into the crowded van. This time, the trip was interrupted only for a perfect photo of cone-shaped, snow-topped Cotopaxi. We arrived in Otavalo around 9:00 p.m., and Rolando kindly drove us around until we found a hotel that fit our budget. After checking in to our basic accommodations, we choked down some pizza while chuckling at the "entertainment" provided by a group of young kids banging away on some percussion instruments. Later, Fran and Daveed giggled some more at my swearing over the shocks provided by the hot water heater in the shared bath. But ultimately, Fran and I had the last laugh at Daveed after he retired to his room, very eager to listen to a tape he had just purchased of some "local music." Following a few moments of silence, some angry muttering penetrated through the thin wall. It turned out the tape actually had been produced in Holland, not far from his home town!

The next morning we went to the Otavalo market, famous for its elaborate handicrafts and the distinctive indigo-blue clothing worn by its inhabitants. We marveled at the industriousness of the people, whose deeply lined faces and calloused hands revealed lives full of hard work and determination. Men shouldered huge bales of hay three times their size using only a strap around their foreheads, while women carried live chickens and pigs tied up in blue shawls stretched across their backs. As quick as you can say "*¿Cuántos cuesta* (how much)?" we immediately broke one of our travel rules. Prior to the trip, we had decided not to buy anything or save mementos (e.g., programs, cards, etc.) because we did not want to lug them around. Well, one look at the beautiful items hand-crafted out of wood, stone, and wool, being offered by the friendly artisans themselves, and we couldn't resist buying just one, then two, then numerous souvenirs. We reassured ourselves that we could send our *recuerdos* (literally, mementos) back home in the mail. After buying way too much at the market, we took a long hike in the highlands around Otavalo, taking in peaceful views of women spreading out their colorful textiles to dry by sparkling blue streams, children driving cattle around a crystal clear lake, and *campesinos* going about their daily life in the country. Christopher began complaining about the walk so we hopped on a local bus back to town, where he miraculously found the energy to play soccer with some local kids. The next day Daveed befriended an artisan on another local bus ride who invited us to his *taller*, in Ibarra, a village renowned for its intricate weaving. After watching him proudly demonstrate the production of his versatile handbags, Christopher eagerly chose one to carry his mandatory travel accessories: the indispensable Game Boy, a deck of cards, and a small book. He used the handbag daily throughout the entire trip, and it held up beautifully.

Sharpening Our Spanish Skills in Canoa

As our month in Baños drew to an end, we tearfully bid goodbye to our new friends and ventured out on our own. Over the Internet, we arranged to take two weeks of Spanish lessons at the Canoa Spanish School on the Pacific coast. During a brief return to Quito beforehand to do some errands, we struggled to make sense of our map and a woman stopped to offer assistance. Not only did she give us directions to the post office, she drove us there herself and helped us mail home our package full of the souvenirs from Otavalo. She then proceeded to take us sightseeing around the city and eventually brought us back to her house to meet her family! Yet another testimony to the generosity of the Ecuadorian people.

The bus ride out to the coast wound through the dramatically steep, brown Andes Mountains and then dropped down into steamy green foliage. Whenever the bus stopped, venders got on selling exotic fruits, breads, and soda. We arrived in the coastal town of Bahía de Caráquez too late to catch a boat on towards Canoa. Trying to save a buck, we

Laundry day outside Otavalo

ignored the bright neon sign over a hotel close to the stop and instead trudged into town. We inquired first at the Hotel Vera, which according to our guidebook had some rooms with private bath, and I climbed upstairs to check out the options. Upon seeing half-naked women roaming the halls and men hurriedly zipping up their pants, a broken communal sink in the stairwell, and a "shower" in the room half black with filth, I decided to press on. At Pension Miriam, also suggested by the guidebook, the only remaining room contained two beds with half of the baseboards missing. Too tired to continue searching, we took the room and spread out what we could (sarongs, towels, and Christopher's blanket) over the questionable sheets. Throughout the night, whenever we moved, more boards would fall out from beneath us onto the floor. Between the swearing and giggling we got very little sleep! The next day, we discovered that someone's discarded chicken dinner had attracted a wide assortment of insects to the communal bathroom. The saga continued during breakfast, which consisted of bread and *café con leche* with plenty of *la nata*. Fortunately, our bad experience was not totally in vain. As we were walking out of the hotel, three *extranjeros* stopped us to see if it was a good place to stay. We took great satisfaction in recounting our ordeal there, being sure to give them an adequate account of the Hotel Vera as well!

Eager to escape Bahía de Caráquez, we impatiently crossed the bay to San Vicente, and then boarded a bus onward to Canoa. Still obviously green to South America, we had mistakenly assumed that once we got to Canoa we would easily find the Canoa Spanish School. We specifically asked the bus driver to take us there, and he assured us that he knew right where it was. However, as Daveed says, "Asking is not the way to get information." The Latino culture is such that locals will usually gesture in a direction, point at a building, nod, or make something up rather than admit that they do not know the answer to your question. It is therefore important not to rely on a single point of information, but to consult as many official and/or seemingly knowledgeable sources as possible and try to go by the general consensus. Not having done this, we walked around town with all our stuff for about three hours, inquiring about the school. We attempted to access the one available Internet connection, but there wasn't enough electricity at the hotel to

The view from our "classroom" at Canoa Beach

sustain it. These Internet problems foreshadowed more to come; twice we spent two hours round trip to Bahía de Caráquez via bus and boat just as the electricity went out, or *apagó la luz* (the lights went out), so that the Internet was not available. Finally someone suggested that the Spanish School might be at the Sundown Inn, which we had passed on the bus about two miles down the road. A shopowner allowed us to call them for a small fee. Sure enough, it turned out to be the right place, but because it was too far to carry all of our stuff, we boarded the very same bus with the very same driver who wanted to charge us the very same amount. We protested that he should have let us off when he sped by the first time, and he grudgingly took us *gratis* (free) to the school.

Luckily, our experience at the Canoa Spanish School/Sundown Inn more than made up for the struggles to get there. The beach was totally private, clean and white, lined with palm trees and teeming with a variety of wildlife. Thousands of bright red crabs scurried around digging holes and fighting with their neighbors. We watched the local dogs playing with them until inevitably one died, and then the other crabs fought over their dead mate until the victor dragged it down into a sandy grave. Birds flocked overhead, eyeing the moving meals. Huge sea turtles and fish occasionally washed up on shore. Despite the cool weather the water remained very warm and inviting, and we played in the waves and taught Christopher how to boogie-board. The food at the Inn was scrumptious and plentiful, featuring lots of tasty seafood. After raving about the local dishes during one of Fran's Spanish lessons, his teacher, Juan Carlos, arranged for us to try the special meal of small lobsters. Even the coffee did not have *la nata*. When I asked the owner, Jaime, how they managed such good coffee, he told me that no one likes *la nata* so they take special care to remove it for their guests. I beamed with gratitude! Perhaps best of all, we befriended the family (Jaime's son, Juan Carlos, and his wife, Maria Elena) who ran the Inn and spent many hours with them playing the board game Risk, watching movies, and generally hanging out. Our Spanish improved as we picked up such expressions as *yo gané* (I won) and *te toca* (your turn) and *dados* (dice). Christopher even tried to teach them to play his favorite card game, "Harry Potter." We enjoyed ourselves so much that we extended our stay twice before finally building up the momentum to leave after two and a half weeks.

Amidst all the fun, Fran and I attended four hours of private Spanish lessons daily. Imagine doing homework while relaxing in a hammock, looking out over the waves and breathing in the salt air! We worked out of grammar books but spent hours conversing with our teachers as well. I asked my instructor, Jaime, to define any word I did not know, and he took the time to slowly describe the word in Spanish until I understood it. I had heard stories from other travelers about Spanish classes with little emphasis on conversation, or groups that were too large or too mixed in terms of ability level, resulting in a poor experience. In contrast, our lessons were excellent, but while our Spanish was improving, we still made some hilarious mistakes. On one trip into town, I was searching for something to patch the rapidly expanding hole in my jeans. I approached several shopkeepers, stating that I had *suecos en mi pantalones*, and was met with some curious looks. Imagine my embarrassment when I talked to Jaime about my unsuccessful quest, and he told me that the correct word for holes is *huecos*, and *Suecos* meant "Swiss men." Apparently, I was telling people that I had "Swiss men in my pants." Christopher got a particular kick out of that little faux pas!

Exploring the Pacific Coast

Visitors to Ecuador do not have to go to the Galápagos to experience wonderful islands packed with exotic wildlife. Just a few miles from Canoa, a lovely canoe ride will transport bird-watchers to Isla Corazón to witness the mating calls of the frigates. The male birds puff up their unusually large chests like bright red balloons and produce a deep humming that collectively sounds just like a boat motor. South of Bahía de Caráquez, boat trips are available from the town of Puerto López to a larger island called Isla de la Plata, home to a larger array of feathered friends. Hundreds of blue footed boobies dance their well-choreographed mating ritual. Masked boobies sit on nests filled with eggs and small chicks, and occasionally even an adolescent bird that refuses to leave its safe haven. Depending on the time of the year, the boat trip out to the island may also involve some amazing whale-watching as the humpbacks come to these waters to breed. We watched them raise their mighty fins and tails out of the water, breach, and frolic with their families. Seeing three of these graceful giants moving in unison was so exciting that I struggled to suppress my enthusiasm until the boat captain tossed me a look that quieted me down.

Unfortunately, we found the town of Puerto López to be unpleasant. Garbage littered the beaches from the daily tasks of fishermen. Furthermore, as we were checking out of our hotel, the Hostal Frigata, we left Christopher's all-important Game Boy on the counter. We discovered its absence about a block down the street and headed back to the hotel. The owner insisted that they did not have it, that perhaps someone from next door had taken it. We sat down making no motion to leave, and I continued to press her, asking if any child might have it or know its whereabouts. After looking around our room, the chairs, and the lobby area, I asked again about questioning some local children, or perhaps the police. The owner suddenly called to another woman in the building. Lo and behold, she came out holding the missing Game Boy. She then proceeded to create an elaborate story about how Christopher had allowed another child to play with it. Of course, Christopher had not spoken to anyone else that day. Rather than stay and argue with the owner, we grabbed the elusive toy and left. Another Game Boy catastrophe averted!

In search of nicer beaches, we found ourselves in the small laid-back coastal town of Montañita. Our rustic three-story hotel, topped with bamboo thatching and palm fronds, overlooked the long stretch of white sandy beach lined with bungalows and palm trees. At night we hung out on the balcony with some energetic travelers who taught Christopher the British card game, Snap, in an effort to avoid the more difficult card game, "Harry Potter." We spent our days eating, sleeping, and languishing on the beach, and commemorated our hedonistic experience by purchasing a custom-made bathing suit for Christopher with "Montañita" stitched up the side. Next door at Darwin's Café, the youthful owner served the best Venezuelan *arepas* (a kind of fried cornmeal biscuit) outside of Venezuela that I have ever tried. When it was

Blue-footed boobies engaged in their highly ritualized mating dance

time to drag ourselves to the bus stop, Darwin himself accompanied us until our ride to Guayaquil carried us away.

Guayaquil, a large city rivaling Quito as Ecuador's center of commerce, constituted our final destination on the coast. In an effort to attract business, including tourism, the local government has worked hard to overcome its negative reputation. The brand new waterfront contains huge colorful play structures for kids and adults, and security guards search backpacks upon entry to ensure the safety of its visitors. We wandered through the winding cobblestone pathways of the recently renovated historic district of Las Peñas, admiring the pastel-colored colonial townhouses and beautiful river views. Christopher particularly enjoyed Parque Bolívar, a city park overrun with giant iguanas, hanging off trees overhead and meandering about the walkways below. Fran and I easily took care of some necessary business, including changing the return date on our plane tickets and making arrangements to fly to our next stop, the enchanting Galápagos Islands.

Heaven on Earth: The Galápagos

With its crystal clear turquoise water, chunky black lava rock, and ubiquitous wildlife, the Galápagos Islands surpassed our highest expectations. We hadn't originally planned to go there due to the expense (US$350 per person for the flight and another US$100 per person to enter the national park upon landing), especially so early in the trip. However, everyone who had traveled there absolutely insisted that we go, especially given Christopher's growing passion for the animals we had encountered during our earlier island excursions. Our guidebook was not very encouraging about affordable options for touring the islands, but we decided to go ahead anyway, primarily for Christopher's benefit. We were so glad we did! The Galápagos turned out to be a truly magical place and a real highlight of the entire trip for all of us. Furthermore, we were able to do it much more economically than our guidebook had led us to believe.

Upon landing at the airport on Isla Baltra, we boarded the readily available public transportation via bus and boat to Puerto Ayora, the main settlement on Isla Santa Cruz. Puerto Ayora proved to be an

Christopher meets a wild Galápagos turtle

adorable, very clean little town right on the ocean with a wide variety of accommodations and restaurant options. After looking at a couple of rooms, we decided on one with private bath at the Hotel Darwin. One block inland from the pricey main street on the waterfront, we discovered an alleyway full of kiosks selling delicious food to the locals. Our favorite, the family-run Familiar Williams, served fresh lobster dinners for only US$7 a plate. That soon became a habit!

From our vantage point in Puerto Ayora we had access to all of the wonderful wildlife that everyone flies to the Galápagos to see. The famous animals are everywhere, and they are so tame that at times we had to actively avoid making physical contact with them. From the main harbor we watched blue-footed boobies and pelicans diving for fish, and sea lions playing by the boats. The excellent visibility of the water, totally devoid of the usual trash found along the shores of most port towns, enabled us to observe much of the sea life. Christopher and I laughed at the marine iguanas doing "pushups" as they tore algae off the rocks just below the water's surface. A short walk away, the Charles Darwin Research Station is free to tourists, and we spent hours amidst the massive tortoises. Christopher was fascinated by the incubation process of the eggs, as well as the tracking system for the babies, while I appreciated the opportunity to get close to the huge, centuries-old creatures. We saw many more of these giants in the wild by organizing a tour to a sunken crater further inland. We also hiked to Turtle Bay, where we watched marine turtles floating in the waves, and large extended families of the sinister-looking black iguanas sunning themselves on land. We gingerly stepped over these creatures as we followed the walking path, taking care to avoid their spit as they marked their territory! Perhaps best of all, during a boat trip around the bay, we paused to swim with the sea lions. I actually looked one right in the eyes as it surfaced less than a foot away from me. I could have stayed there forever, admiring my graceful new friend, but the boat called and it was time to leave.

Towards the end of the week, we investigated various boat trips to some of the neighboring islands. Because no day trips were available the week of our stay, we instead booked a three-day "cruise" to Isla Bartolomé, Isla Rábida, and Isla Seymour. Christopher and I tend to have motion sickness, but we took some Bonine and did not have any problems. Many visitors to the Galápagos immediately get on a boat after landing at Isla Baltra, spend seven days on board, and then fly out of the same airport. We would not recommend this. When we embarked, some fellow passengers were in the middle of such a trip. While we were very excited about the flora and fauna of each island, and had made an extra effort to go to Isla Bartolomé specifically to see the penguins, these passengers had grown somewhat blasé. Comments such as "I know it will be great, but it's hard to get psyched up for more snorkeling" and "What island is this one again?" peppered their conversation. Conversely, by spending a chunk of time just sitting quietly amongst the animals in Puerto Ayora, we internalized the natural rhythms of the island, and our short boat trip was the perfect way to round out the experience.

Furthermore, if at all possible, it is probably best to arrange a boat trip with a local agency upon arrival. We may have had better luck and more options because we were there during the shoulder season (September). In any case, make sure to deal as closely as possible with the people who will actually be providing the service, and get everything written down in a contract. We heard some horror stories of people paying for trips over the Internet only to discover upon arrival that no such company existed. One woman showed us a copy of a paid contract she obtained from an office in the capital. When she provided it to the company in Puerto Ayora, they tried to back out of the commitment to supply snorkeling equipment by whiting out that part of the document! Luckily, she had a copy of the unaltered contract and held them to it. On our boat, one couple told us that they had arranged a diving trip through an agency in Quito. However, they had to switch boats mid-trip and the second boat refused to acknowledge that they had paid for diving excursions. The angry couple did not want to pay any extra money for the dives, so they ultimately missed out on three days of diving with no hope of a refund from the Quito-based organization. In contrast, we worked directly with a travel agency in Puerto Ayora and obtained a detailed contract for the entire trip. The contract included an itinerary of the island stops, the exact length of stay, food and equipment provided, any taxes and entrance fee costs, and the payment of the guide. We asked a lot of questions about what would and would not be covered by our payment. We double-checked this information against that provided in the guidebooks to make sure that we had considered all possible fees, etc. We closely examined the pictures of the boat and asked about accommodations (e.g., showers, hot water, etc.) on board. We felt quite reassured when the representative willingly answered all of our questions and provided ample documentation to cover the trip.

That said, we would highly recommend spending some time visiting the remarkable islands surrounding Isla Santa Cruz. On Isla Bartolomé, chunks of black frothy rock twist the desert landscapes into bizarre vistas. Making our way carefully through the lava fields, we marveled at the swirls and bubbles of the black substance preserved exactly as it spewed from the earth 100 years ago. We sunbathed on black and red sand beaches, taking frequent breaks for some fabulous snorkeling. In addition to seeing large schools (50 or more) of colorful, foot-long fish, we swam next to a stingray, a marine turtle, a marine iguana, and more sea lions. We hiked on trails surrounded by newborn sea lion babies, so cute and curious that it was hard to avoid touching them (although to do so would risk their being rejected by their mother). Pausing to watch one frisky pair, we all began laughing as a particularly impish baby bit the tail of a slightly irritated marine iguana! Besides observing frigates, boobies, and other birds, we had the rare opportunity to watch young pelicans extract regurgitated food right out of their mother's beaks. We were especially thrilled to catch our first glimpse of penguins swimming around and resting on some rocks, justifying our decision to visit Isla Bartolomé. But perhaps the highlight of the trip occurred right on board the boat. Just like a scene from a movie (e.g., *Titanic*, although luckily, our boat fared better than that one), about eight dolphins suddenly surrounded the front of our boat, racing up alongside us and leaping into the air at the last minute. They played next to us for about 15 minutes and then gradually swam away, jumping and splashing off into the sunset. Incredible!!! Fran and I certainly owed Christopher our gratitude for bringing us to this captivating place.

Despite diligent conservation efforts to preserve the Galápagos Islands, human impact was definitely visible throughout our ten-day stay there. We saw a sea lion with a clear ring-like scar around its neck due to plastic waste. Imported goats have wiped out many of the indigenous

Christopher hides out in a lava hole

plants and animals. Because turtles constituted such a good source of protein on long boat trips (rumored to live up to a year on their back), pirates decimated much of that population. As a constant reminder, one tortoise aptly named Lonesome George remains the last of his kind despite attempts to mate him with females of similar species. Perhaps the most poignant example of human destruction lies on Isla Rábida, once famous for its flocks of bright pink flamingos. In order for the tourists to better view the flamingos, the islanders cut back the bushes surrounding the lake frequented by these birds. The new pathway enabled the sea lions to access the lake from the ocean shore. Preferring the lake, more and more sea lions took over until their waste forced the flamingos to find other bathing places. Now, because of the tourist path, there are no longer flamingos for the tourists to see. The devastating consequences of human short-sightedness were very significant for Christopher, who vowed to return to the Galápagos Islands as an adult and help the animals there.

Heading South

After tearing ourselves away from the Galápagos and returning to real life on the mainland, we continued to head south towards Peru. By this time, we had spent almost three months in Ecuador and our visas were about to expire, so we had to pick up the pace. In Cuenca, a comfortable, family-friendly colonial town known for its fine architecture, we met up with Mariela, a friend from Canoa beach. Munching on the deliciously airy yet chewy traditional bread, we climbed with her to a viewpoint overlooking the lovely city. We also took a day trip to El Cajas National Park to experience some beautiful lakes and interesting sierra landscape. However, the altitude (over 12,000 feet) took its toll on all of us, especially Christopher, so we cut our hike short. From Cuenca we moved on to Alausí to brave the Nariz del Diablo (literally, Devil's Nose), a popular ride in which tourists can sit on the top of a train while it rumbles through some harrowing switchbacks high in the Andes Mountains. Fran really enjoyed riding outdoors, but I felt that the views from some of our buses had been at least as hair-raising as the Nariz and certainly constituted more authentic experiences. After the train trip, a bus conveniently brought us directly to our first Incan ruins at Ingapirca, a small, comfortable site providing the perfect backdrop for a picnic. Llamas roamed the picturesque grounds, and behind the ancient stone structures a short trail led up to a large sacrificial rock overlooking a deep valley. While no match for the much larger Incan ruins in Peru, Ingapirca definitely whetted our appetite for more to come.

Near the Peruvian border lies the village of Vilcabamba, famous for its inhabitants who often live for over 100 years. But perhaps even more renowned among travelers was our fantastic hostel, called Las Ruinas de Quinara. This small slice of paradise boasted a pool, sauna, hot tub, movies, pool table, spa treatments, and delicious buffet meals, all at reasonable prices. The first evening we exchanged travel stories with an intriguing Canadian couple, named Rich and Cyndi, over a delicious vegetarian dinner. We raved about our recent trip to the Galápagos, while they described their experiences teaching English in Japan. Little did we know that this short interchange would develop into one of the most important relationships of our trip. After taking full advantage of the hostel's many services, we all signed up for Christopher's first horseback ride to a working sugar mill in the mountains. We watched donkeys carry the freshly cut sugar cane into the barn, and then, harnessed to a room-sized wooden crank, they crushed the cane to extract the fluid. In the lower part of the building, the juice drained into six-foot long cement vats to be boiled and, ultimately, to produce brick-sized blocks of raw brown sugar. What an educational and relaxing way to end our Ecuador experience. We certainly felt as if we could continue in that mode for 100 years!

As we boarded our final Ecuadorian bus, we hardly noticed one of the passengers with a chicken under his arm until he tried to sell it to us. We laughed and marveled at how we had transformed from naïve *extranjeros* to more seasoned Latin American travelers, taking livestock on buses in stride and so easily fitting into the culture of these hospitable people that we were being offered a chicken. Maybe in another three months we might even consider buying it!

CHRISTOPHER'S COMMENTS

I liked volunteering in FUVIRESE with Alfonso. I went to the school and helped with the kids. There was a little girl there that would order everybody around. It was funny! I also liked taking the kids to the baths (hot springs). It was fun swimming in them because at that time I didn't know how to swim and it was easy to float on top and under the water because of all the bubbles.

I really liked being with Alfonso. He wasn't that different from any of our other friends. He could do the same things, except maybe a few sports like soccer, but he could play board games and ride bikes like everybody else. I didn't know Spanish very well but we could still communicate. I'm not sure how. When we were on the jungle trip, Alfonso found a special type of flower. He put it on his nose and I put one on mine, and we looked like we were parrots. I still have a picture of it. During the same trip, there were some monkeys that stole these cookie-like crackers. They took them up into the trees and dropped them down. It was funny! We did a bike trip with Alfonso. Alfonso had his own bike, Mom had her own bike, and me and Dad had a double-seater bike because I didn't know how to ride a normal bike. Once we stopped at a waterfall coming straight down on the road. There was a spot where the drips would come, and I put my whole arm in. I got soaked! During that trip we were stopped by a big mudslide while we were riding on our bikes. We had to wait for a long time so that the bulldozer could push the mud away. Then the bikers could go through the mud and we started riding again.

We made another friend named Daveed. He was from Holland. His email was "Monkey Face" so every time we thought of him, we thought of him as "Monkey Face" and "Daveed" because that's what Alfonso called him. But I think his real name is David. I liked Daveed because he would play chess with me. He was a nice, good friend. Daveed doesn't like roosters, but we stayed together at a place with roosters in Otavalo. In Otavalo we bought good luck charms carved out of stone. Dad had a moon, which means we will have a good sleep. Mom's was a sun which means we will have good weather. Mine was a turtle which means we will see a lot of animals, but hopefully not roosters because Daveed doesn't like them.

We went to a Spanish school. We had a nice hotel and a pretty nice beach with lots of crabbies. I didn't like the wormy things in the sand so much. There was a kid there doing Spanish lessons just like me; actually we weren't doing the lessons, just our parents were. He knew where there were some boogie boards and I learned how to boogie board. The water would start out cool and get really warm and hot. It was fun but then he left. But Juan Carlos and Maria Elena (the owners) were still there. They had a baby and taught us how to play "Risk" in Spanish. Later we figured out how to play it in English and we played it a lot. I won once, but usually Maria Elena would win because she had a good strategy. We liked the game so much we asked Santa to get it for us in the United States. There were also three girls at the beach that taught me some fun card tricks. I forgot most of them but I remember one of them and it works really good. Later we went to see one of the three girls named Mariela. We went to her house in Cuenca. She had lots and lots of snakes, frogs, and turtles there. It was really cool. Then we went to the mountains and climbed one that was really high. I got really sick because of the altitude. Mom and Dad dropped me off and looked to see if the top was a little farther. It wasn't so they came right back and we went down the mountain. I really, really tried my best to get up to the top but I was too sick to do it.

One day we walked by a store in Loja. I looked into the window and it was a Game Boy shop. It was the only Game Boy shop I saw in South America. So I asked Mom and Dad if we could go inside. So we went inside and I asked the lady how much one of the games was. She said it was US$40. That's a lot of money, right? Mom and Dad said it was too expensive, so we left the shop and went to a restaurant to eat. I went into the bathroom to wash my hands, and I'm guessing Mom and Dad were talking about the games. They probably stopped talking about it like a minute before I came out. Then, after dinner, Mom said Dad was going to get something from the bank, I think. Dad was the only one going and I'm guessing that Dad bought the game then. But I didn't know it.

The next day when I woke up, I went to go find my Game Boy bag to get my Game Boy and play some games. When I found my Game Boy, I picked it up and turned it on. The game started but it was in a different color. I thought maybe it was just in a different light. But then all these words and pictures came by that I didn't recognize. Then a title came up that said "Monsters Inc." That was one of the two games that I wanted from the store! So I turned off my Game Boy because I thought that I had wanted the game so bad that in the night I sleep-walked and stole it from the store! I was scared that Mom and Dad would make me return it. I didn't want them to find out about the game until after we got on our bus and it left, because then we couldn't take the game back to the store. But in the taxi on the way to the bus, Mom said, "Why don't you play your Game Boy?" I said, "No." She asked why, and I said "Because I don't want to." I was still scared that they would make me take it back. But Mom reached over and grabbed my Game Boy and turned it on and said "What's that?!" I told her all about the thing I thought I did. She told me that Dad had got the game for me at the store. I felt relieved! Then I played that game the whole day!

The really, really, really fun place in Ecuador was called the Galápagos Islands. They have lots and lots of animals. There were a ton of sea turtles. We went to the

Sea lion pups play with an indifferent Galápagos iguana

Catch an iguana by the tail

pier every day and saw lots of iguanas on the pier and underwater doing pushups to get their food (algae) off the rocks. There was a reserve for all these huge turtles, and they had turtle eggs with little "X's" on them. The "X's" were to show what position to keep them in so you wouldn't roll them around and kill the babies inside. We took a boat trip and saw baby sea lions. You couldn't touch the baby sea lions because their mother would abandon them. The mother could tell which one was her kid by her sense of smell, so if the baby smelled like a human, the mother couldn't figure out which one was her kid. We saw a little sea lion chewing an iguana's tail. He had no teeth so the iguana didn't even notice. Another came up and they kept playing with the iguana's tail until it walked away. It was very funny! On the cruise we went to lots of beaches. You could see movies on the ship and bottlenose dolphins playing by the side.

Before I went to the Galápagos I only had a few things I wanted to be. I wanted to be an archaeologist or an engineer like my Dad. But when I went there, I thought, "Hmmm, maybe I want to be a veterinarian," because I found out that I like animals so much. Now it is on the list of what I want to be when I grow up. I even told my

Mom and Dad that I wanted to live there. I said I would buy a house so we could all live there together, but they would have to pay rent or it wouldn't be fair. I really hope I can go back to the Galápagos some day.

Because this was the first or second time I ever traveled to so many places in one trip, I thought it was pretty fast and a little tiring. I didn't like doing my homework because my Mom and Dad would make me write three sentences and if I got one word wrong I would have to write it five times. I also didn't like leaving. Whenever I had to leave a friend, I would be sad. I liked it when we stopped and stayed with people for a longer amount of time. I liked knowing what we would do every day, and I liked having the same schedule. When I didn't know what we would do or what would happen next, I felt confused, and that wasn't a good feeling. I always asked Mommy, "What time is it?" and "What are we doing?" So every day Mom would tell me what we were going to do, and that made me feel better. But mostly I liked Ecuador because it was fun!

TRAVELER'S TIPS

1. Make arrangements for at least your first two nights in a foreign country. Splurge on the airport pickup. You won't regret it!

2. Check identification and clarify the hotel or agency name with the representative at the airport before providing any information.

3. Build in time to acclimatize. Bring plenty of aspirin. Don't push it!

4. Ease your transition into a new culture by setting up a language school program or volunteer experience ahead of time. The connections made will assist you in a variety of ways, from cutting the language barrier to finding inexpensive lodging.

5. When considering language school or volunteer options, choose a location that your entire family will enjoy. Look into the activities available in the area and make sure to build in some time to do them.

6. Ask about safety concerns in the local area and beyond. Make sure you know which areas are dangerous and avoid them.

7. Be realistic about your housing needs. You may all be too tired to interact with a host family and need the privacy that an apartment can offer. Be aware that children don't always know and follow social norms and therefore may do something that can embarrass you (e.g., complain and refuse to eat the host family's food).

8. Apartments also may work out better for families so that meals can be prepared at home. Shopping at the local market can be an informative cultural field trip.

9. Children need schedules and routines, especially when adjusting to a foreign culture. Take care to build in some predictability (e.g., a regular time for home-schooling). Talk and write out each day's schedule in a way your child can understand. Emphasize the fun things she or he will see and do!

10. Always inspect the room and bathroom facilities before committing. If you do not like the first room you see, you can request to see another. For longer stays, you may negotiate a better rate.

11. Plan some child-friendly item or activity every day. Purchasing a special treat on a long bus ride often does the trick!

12. When dining out in Latin America, ask for the standard menu, often known simply as breakfast (*desayuno*), lunch (*almuerzo*), or dinner (*cena*).

13. Treat volunteering as work. If you want a holiday, pursue something very different from what you do professionally. Make sure you have the energy required for the commitment.

14. If volunteering for a school, consider bringing much needed curriculum and books.

15. Carefully consider the disadvantages of driving in a foreign country! Be aware that the local laws may be very different from those back home.

16. You will purchase treasures along the road, no matter how steadfast your resolve to avoid this. Budget for mailing them home.

17. Use local travel agencies to arrange trips as a more affordable option. Get everything in writing and determine whom to contact if something goes amiss.

Note: All room rates are reported for a double unless otherwise indicated.

QUITO

L'Auberge Inn Hostal

Av. Colombia 1138 y Yaguachi
Tel: 02 552 912
www.ioda.net/auberge-inn
auberge@uio.satnet.net

Located halfway between new and old town, pretty courtyard, clean, double with shared bath for US$13 a night. Adjacent restaurant with good food, airport pickup available.

South American Explorers Clubhouse

Apartado 17-21-431, Eloy Alfaro, Quito, Ecuador
Street Address: Jorge Washington 311 y Leonidas Plaza, Mariscal Sucre
T/F: (593-2) 2225-228

Great resource for members, including a book exchange. See Chapter 1 Resources section for more details.

Museo de Sitio Inti-Ñan

Instituto Nacional de Patrimonio Cultural del Ecuador
Registro No. 200 CETUR
Tel: (593-2) 2395-122
museo_intinan@yahoo.ec/hotmail.com

Located at the true equator, near La Mitad del Mundo, this museum has a fascinating interactive demonstration of the gravitational forces surrounding the equator, as well as native objects including a blow-dart gun and a real shrunken head.

Other Quito highlights include:

La Mitad del Mundo, the monument dedicated to the equator located 22 miles north of Quito. Be sure to visit the Ethnographic Museum inside the monument, which includes several displays of the many different indigenous tribes throughout the country.

Casa de la Cultura Ecuatoriana, Av 12 de Octubre 555 at Patria. Great sculpture garden for the kids to explore, and a delightful collection of modern art and anthropological exhibits inside.

Walking tour of the old town, including **La Compañia Church** with its altar of gold.

BAÑOS

FUVIRESE (Fundación de Vida, Realidad y Servicio [Foundation of Life, Reality, and Service])
Alfonso Morales, Founder and Coordinator
Calle Rafael Vieira y Luis Martínez
Antiguo Hospital de Baños
Tel: (03) 741-061
fuvireseb@andinanet.net

U.S. Contact: Dick Egan
P.O. Box 13563
Green Bay, WI USA 54307-3563
Tel: 303-722-5912
www.fuvirese.org
fuvirese@aol.com

Nonprofit organization serving the handicapped through wheelchair and sidewalk ramp construction, education, and physical therapy. Volunteer opportunities are available in the workshop (*taller*) constructing wheelchairs as well as in the school assisting the teaching staff and their students. The staff kindly arranged a private apartment for us; rent was US$200 for the month.

Other favorites in Baños include:

Le Petit Restaurant, with amazing French food for a fair price.

Café Hood, with great vegetarian food and afternoon yoga classes.

Zoológico in the hills outside of town.

Hike to ***La Virgen***, soak in the **hot springs**, and take a **bike ride** on the road to Tena.

RIOBAMBA

ASODICH (Asociación de Parapléjicos y Minusválidos de Chimborazo [Association of Paraplegics and Handicapped of Chimborazo])

Rolando Gomez Montalvo, President
Los Alamos 1
Av. Sesquicentenario y Calle H
Tel: 968114

TENA

Residencial Austria

Tarqui y Díaz de Pineda, *a pocos pasos* (a few steps from) Coop. Tena Ltda.
Tel: 06-887205

Very clean, private hot baths, US$10 per night, wheelchair accessible.

Highlights include:

Parque Amazonica, a jungle park with walking trails on a little island connected to the city by a thatched footbridge.

Beach in **Misahuallí**, a small village on the bank of the Río Napo (Napo River). Guard your cookies carefully from the bands of mischievous monkeys!

OTAVALO

Visitors to Ecuador cannot miss the **Saturday Market**, with an extensive array of elaborate handicrafts and locals with their distinctive indigo-blue clothing. We met a local artisan on the bus to the nearby colonial town of **Ibarra**, and he welcomed us into his textile workshop there.

CANOA

Canoa Spanish School/Sundown Inn

Juan Carlos Jaramillo
Quito: (593)-2 2342955
Canoa: (593)-5 616359
www.ecuadorbeach.com
sundown_inn@hotmail.com

Hotel on private, clean beach near the town of Canoa, double with private bath and three full delicious meals a day for US$60 a night, as well as four hours of private Spanish lessons for Fran and me five days a week. We highly recommend the canoe trip to **Isla de Corazón** to see the frigate birds at mating season.

If you are forced to stay in **Bahía de Caráquez** on your way to Canoa, don't stay in these hotels:

Hotel Vera, unless you like brothels.

Pension Miriam, unless you like dirty, broken beds and buggy bathrooms.

PUERTO LÓPEZ

Don't Stay at Hostal Fragata, unless you make sure to keep track of your stuff!

Machalilla Tours
Malecón (Julio Izurieta)
Casilla No. 759
Tel: (05) 604-206
Randolfo15@hotmail.com

Can organize a boat tour for whale watching and to Parque Nacional Machalilla on Isla de la Plata, an island off the coast with frigates, boobies, and other wildlife.

MONTAÑITA

We stayed in a large, wooden, three-story hotel with a thatched roof right on the beach, double with an ocean view and shared bath for US$7 a night.

Darwin's Café next door has fabulous food, including the best Venezuelan *arepas* outside of Venezuela.

GUAYAQUIL

Hotel Regina
Lorenzo de Garaicoa No. 421 y P. Solano
Frente al (Across from the) Parque de la Madre
Tel: 593-04-2305401
www.hregina@yahoo.com

Relatively clean rooms with private bath, AC, and cable TV for US$14 a night.

Highlights include:

Parque Bolívar, between Ballén and 10 de Agosto, with dozens of iguanas on the grounds and in the flowering trees overhead.

A walk along the **waterfront**, with its newly constructed play structures for kids and adults, as well as the **Las Peñas** district at its northern end, a delightful collection of colorfully renovated colonial houses, wrought-iron balconies, steep stairways, and great views.

GALÁPAGOS ISLANDS

Hotel Darwin

Puerto Ayora, Isla Santa Cruz
Tel: 05-526193

Clean rooms with private bath for US$10 a night; ask to see other available rooms if the first are not to your liking.

Albatros Tours Travel Agency

Charles Darwin Avenue opposite the port
Tel: (593-5) 526657
albatrostours@yahoo.com

Offers reasonable prices on boat tours to surrounding islands. We paid US$250 per person for a three-day trip to Isla Rábida, Isla Bartolomé, Isla Seymour, and to the airport on Isla Baltra to return to the mainland. Price included comfortable room with private bath, all meals, guided tours of the islands to view iguanas, sea lions, penguins, boobies, frigates, marine turtles, and dolphins, and snorkeling opportunities and equipment. They helped organize a day trip to a private ranch to see the giant tortoises wandering around in the wild.

While in **Puerto Ayora**, on Santa Cruz Island, take advantage of the many free opportunities to view animals, including the **Charles Darwin Research Station** with its giant tortoises, babies, and Lonesome George; the walking trail to **Bahía Tortuga (Turtle Bay)** to watch the sea turtles surfing the waves; and just hanging out at the pristine **port** to view sea lions, iguanas, and sea birds.

CUENCA

Hotel Milan

Presidente Cordova 9-89
Tel: 831-104/ 835-351

Clean rooms with private bath and full breakfast with a great view for US$20 a night.

Parque Nacional El Cajas (El Cajas National Park)

This national park, 20 miles west of Cuenca, has beautiful lake views with interesting flora and fauna and well-marked trails, but the altitude of over 12,000 feet was a struggle for Christopher.

From Cuenca, we headed north to Alausí to ride on the top of the touristy train to the famous **Nariz del Diablo** and then backtracked to the small but well-kept Incan ruins of **Ingapirca** (about 35 miles north of Cuenca).

VILCABAMBA

Hosteria Las Ruinas de Quinara

Via a Yamburara
Tel: (00593-7) 580314/ 580301
From Loja: Imbabura 16-39
Ave Universitaria
Cell: 09-549576
Tel: (000593-7) 586-037
ruinasqui@hotmail.com
www.lasruinasdequinara.com

One of the most fabulous inexpensive places to stay in Ecuador. Pool, heated spa, Turkish bath, TV, movies, inexpensive spa services (e.g., massage, pedicure), and vegetarian meals available. Room with breakfast and dinner for all three of us at US$22 a night. We organized a horse tour of the surrounding area, with lovely views and a visit to a working sugar processing farm. Name might have changed to Hosteria Paraiso (see www.vilcabamba.org).

Ecuador
Columbia
Loja
Piura
Peru
Brazil
Trujillo
Lima
Aguas Callentes
Cusco
Pisco
Ica
Nazca
Bolivia
Lago Titicaca
Colca Canyon
Puno
Arequipa
Copacabana
Chile

Chapter 3

Ancient Ruins in Peru

We crossed our first border a bit sleep-deprived but sporting a new traveling partner. The previous evening, our hotel room adjoined a large central atrium with just the right acoustics to amplify the noisy, action-packed TV show designed to keep the "security" man awake. For added benefit, a rooster crowed at regular intervals throughout the night just in case he happened to nod off, or anyone else for that matter. Needless to say, we got very little sleep. As we struggled to shake ourselves out of our stupor, we stumbled into a similarly dazed traveler named Sylvia, a young Swiss German woman traveling alone. Since we were both heading in the same direction, we shared a taxi, which proceeded to run over my foot and drive away with the door hanging open. Surprisingly, we arrived all in one piece at the bus station and carried on without incident to our next South American country, Peru.

Navigating the "Gringo Trail"

Almost immediately after we entered Peru, the landscape became increasingly parched and barren until huge sand dunes surrounded us. We whizzed by clusters of dwellings flimsily put together with woven mats, bits of metal, crumbling mud bricks, and other odds and ends. Life here certainly appeared harsher than in green and typically lush

Ecuador. However, because of the sand and arid conditions, Peru is a land of many fascinating and well-preserved ruins dating back to 13,000 B.C.E. Thus, there is much to see here and a month does not come close to doing it justice.

A popular "gringo" trail runs through Peru, stretching from the Ecuadorian border down the coast to Arequipa, and then turning northeast to the Incan territory surrounding Cusco. In general, buses and roads are of better quality than those in Ecuador. While most towns do not have a central bus station, the route is so well-known that it is easy to find out where to catch the bus towards the next main city. Unfortunately, we were going at a rapid clip with little time to pause and connect with the local people. Many *viajeros* (travelers) we met were likewise trying to see several sights within two to four weeks, in contrast to travelers in Ecuador who were often there for longer periods of time. Consequently, Peruvians were frequently focused on getting the most out of the transient tourist dollar. Dishonesty in advertising was rampant, and shysters proliferated. After long bus rides, mobs of touts overwhelmed us upon arrival. Taxi drivers tried to talk us out of going to our hotel of choice, stating that it was full, closed, too expensive, or had some other problem. Paid on commission, they attempted to coerce us into a different lodging, which almost invariably turned out to be much worse than promised. One reputable agency warned us that, because tourists sought out their owner, representatives from other agencies started claiming to be him. For these reasons, it became necessary to check for identification and thoroughly investigate every situation before spending a dime. We also began to rely exclusively on recommendations from fellow travelers and trusted hostel owners, and often exchanged email addresses as well as business cards of preferred lodgings and tour companies with the people we met. Repeatedly we crossed paths with the same travelers, particularly on the pilgrimage to the mother of all Incan ruins, Machu Picchu. While the "gringo" trail provided less chance to bond meaningfully with locals, it opened up opportunities for friendships with like-minded *viajeros* from all over the world.

Fortunately, the kind hostel owner back in Vilcabamba, Ecuador, prepared us for entry into this new culture by giving us some important advice on our first Peruvian destinations. He recommended that we stay at La Casa Suiza, just outside of Trujillo in a pleasant beach town called Huanchaco. On the way, Sylvia explained that each little town in her area of Switzerland had developed its own dialect of the Swiss German language, which is exclusively an oral language as German is the written language taught in school. She was therefore astonished to find a kindred spirit in the owner of our hotel, who turned out to be from the same village in Switzerland and, therefore, spoke the very same Swiss German dialect. We all got a chuckle when, upon checking in, the staff showed us a room for the adults and another "for the children," nodding towards Christopher and Sylvia. If I had a daughter, I certainly would love to have one just like her. So I started calling her *m'hija*, the affectionate Spanish term for "my daughter."

Through the hotel, we hired a taxi for the day to see the largest pre-Columbian city in all of South America, the Chimú city of Chan Chan, as well as the Huacas del Sol y de la Luna (i.e., the Temples of the Sun and the Moon), Moche pyramids over 1,500 years old. These impressive structures have survived over the years due to the tradition of submerging everything in sand. For example, our guide explained that when a king died in Chan Chan, his subjects buried him with his wife, servants, and tons of goodies, and covered the whole palace in sand. The mourning kingdom then proceeded to build a new residence for the next ruler in a different location in the city. The unearthed palaces in this vast metropolis revealed intricate geometric designs carved in the mud walls that extended for several yards. In contrast, the Moche built a new temple on top of the old one following the death of a priest, thus creating their pyramidal shapes. Huge mosaics of colored and bas-relief decorations have been preserved for centuries inside these temples.

While the Incan and pre-Incan cultures did not have any written language, each culture depicted its way of life in its own unique handicrafts, such as pottery or textiles. In the snack shop at the base of the Huacas del Sol y de la Luna, we exchanged pleasantries with the woman behind the counter, and she in turn asked us if we wanted to see a video in English about the grisly human sacrifices that occurred there. The taped National Geographic program indicated that scenes in the Moche pottery were so horrific that scientists originally theorized that the Moche imagined them; later they were linked to ritualistic religious

Chan Chan

ceremonies conducted in temples such as the Huaca de la Luna. We were pleased that a smile and a few positive words in Spanish opened up a wealth of information about the site in such an odd place.

We sadly parted ways with *m'hija* Sylvia and somewhat apprehensively followed the trail towards Lima, another large South American city with a bad reputation among *viajeros.* Much to our delight, the big city energy felt absolutely wonderful. Residing in the Miraflores district, our very comfortable, brand new hotel was a short walk to a trendy complex of shops on a dramatic cliff overlooking the shoreline. An easy bus ride away from the suburb, downtown Lima is full of historic colonial architecture and fascinating museums, with plenty of entertainment options for the entire family. Always open to spooky experiences, we sought out the gory Museo de la Inquisición (Spanish Inquisition Museum) and the catacombs under the church of San Francisco containing thousands of elegantly displayed bones in complex patterns. We watched the Peruvian changing of the guards at the Royal Palace and had a wonderful day at the Parque de las Leyendas, an extensive zoo full of exotic animals organized into the three main regions of the country. To gain a greater understanding of Peruvian history as represented in its exquisite handicrafts, we visited the Museo de la Nación (National Museum) and the Museo Rafael Larco Herrera. Christopher was intrigued by the many life-like exhibits at the National Museum, and he insisted on opening every single one of the drawers displaying intricate textiles at the Rafael Larco Herrera Museum. While our guidebook seemed to shun large, populous Latino cities, we found it rejuvenating to be back in a thriving, modern metropolis brimming with engaging attractions, nice restaurants, and modern conveniences.

After months of being on the road, we needed to run several errands, and Miraflores served as the perfect place to accomplish these tasks. Christopher needed new shoes, for example, and we purchased another guidebook at the South American Explorers Club, located in a lovely home just ten minutes away from our hotel. Previously, we had borrowed Footprint's *South American Handbook* from our friend, Daveed, during our time together in Ecuador, and we quickly realized the limitations of relying on only one guidebook. Being long-time devotees of the Lonely Planet series, we felt that Lonely Planet's *South*

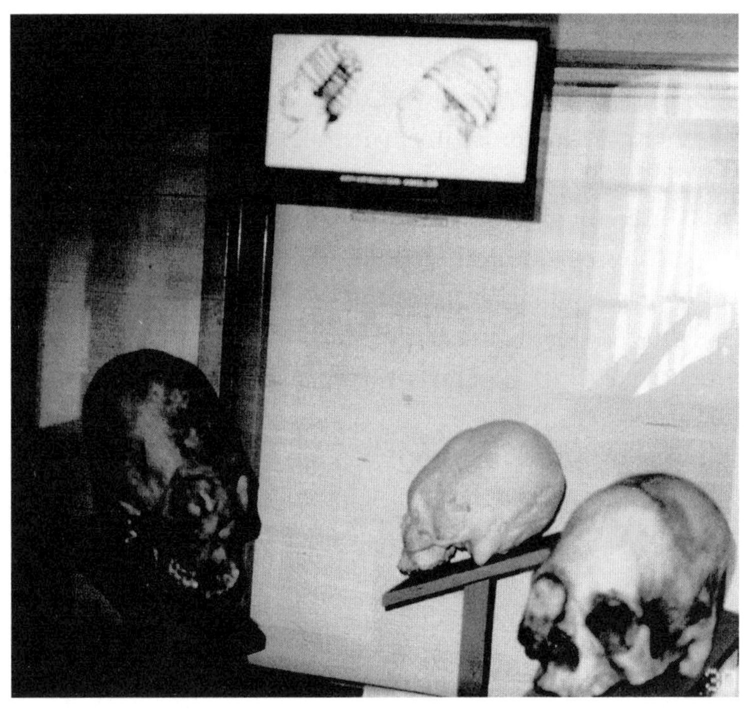

Deformed skulls as a result of head-binding

America on a Shoestring provided an excellent descriptive overview of different areas and great maps, but Footprint's *Handbook* provided more specific details as well as a broader range of accommodations and dining options. Combining the best of both, we cut out the necessary sections from each guide to carry around with us, thereby lightening our load and minimizing our appearance as *extranjeros*.

The "Poor Man's Galápagos"

We liked Lima so much we took refuge there for several days and then resumed our somewhat frenetic pace back on the "Gringo Trail" towards Pisco. Although the Chileans would disagree, this small town is reputedly the home of Pisco sours, a refreshing alcoholic drink made with a type of local brandy called pisco. Nearby, the protected Paracas Peninsula and Isla Ballesta (Ballesta Island) just off shore are known as the "poor man's Galápagos" due to the resident Humboldt penguins, sea lions, Peruvian boobies, and egrets. Accessible via a boat and bus tour, visitors must take precautions or risk getting thoroughly soaked by the waves.

Back on dry land, the Paracas Museum holds fascinating examples of deformed and "trepanned" skulls. Certain pre-Incan cultures practiced the custom of tying their babies' heads to wooden planks, forcing them to grow into an elongated form. Different shapes denoted their identity as part of separate tribes and, in some cases, their status as royalty. Early inhabitants also performed crude operations by drilling a hole into the skull, a procedure known as "trepanning." Occasionally covered with a gold plate, these wounds exist in as many as 45 percent of the exhumed skulls, and evidence of healing indicates that patients actually survived this ancient form of surgery. Researchers theorize that trepanning was performed as an early cure for mental illness, to release the "evil spirits" thought to inhabit the infected person. The process may also have relieved pressure put on the brain by the deformation resulting from the head-binding. We later saw skulls bound in a similar fashion in the small Peruvian village of Chivay, outside of Arequipa. The skulls had evolved into two distinct shapes, one tapered into a cone while the other was wider at the top like

A real-life desert mirage at Huacachina, outside Ica

an eraser. The indigenous people even wore special hats designed to fit the unique shape of their head. Our guide there explained that this practice originally differentiated between the two ethnic groups, but when the Spanish arrived, they banished the custom. While some locals reportedly still practice head-binding, they more commonly distinguish among themselves by their hat style instead.

"Sand Doesn't Melt in Your Mouth"

With our palates prepped in Pisco, we moved on to Ica for some wine-tasting and sand-boarding. The tiny hamlet of Huacachina, on the outskirts of Ica, is truly a desert oasis with a sparkling blue lake reflecting the palm trees swaying at the water's edge, sprouting up in the middle of steep sand dunes. Fran and Christopher tried boarding down those gritty mountains despite the searing heat from the midday sun. They both returned sweaty, irritated, and covered in sand. Christopher complained, "This thing doesn't work right." Fran had a little more luck with his board but commented that when he wiped out, "Sand doesn't melt in your mouth like snow does." After hearing all of that, I decided to forgo that particular experience in exchange for some serious sunbathing by the pool.

Eager to try some wine after almost four months of flavorless beer, we visited two different types of wineries. El Carmen hand-crafts pisco and sweet wines in the traditional style using an ancient wine press made out of a large tree to crush the grapes. The tasty liquid is then stored in large ceramic containers before bottling. The other, more modern winery known as El Catador, produces a wide array of wines, including some excellent dry red and white varietals. Unfortunately, a fine example of shady Peruvian business dealings threatened to cut short our wine-tasting. A manager at our hotel, Casa Arena, had arranged the tour for an all-inclusive price of 20 soles (about US$7). Halfway through the second winery visit, the taxi driver demanded another five soles because we were staying "too long." We had not even tried the wines yet and certainly had not lingered extensively in any part of the facility. I insisted that I was not going to pay, but the two younger guys with us became anxious and handed over the money. When we returned to the hotel, I

Traditional wine press in Ica

complained about the taxi driver's actions to the manager who had hired him. He dismissively responded, "Well, I hope you didn't pay him!" Two days later, I saw the same taxi driver taking some other guests out on another tour. Clearly, the management wasn't concerned about this behavior. They even urged us to attend another outing, dramatically increasing the price to include a "free" bottle of wine. Suspicious of their motives, we declined and arranged our own taxi to the winery, Bodega Vista Alegre. For a fraction of the cost, we spent as much time there as we wanted without incident.

Fortunately, we learned early to be wary of the hotel staff and their underhanded dealings. Despite our best efforts to the contrary, we got roped into their sales pitch regarding a flight over the Nazca lines, visible only by airplane. Without blinking an eye, the same shifty manager tried to convince us that most companies fly over only half of the lines, and that because their planes have three seats in the back, not everyone sits by the window. In contrast, his uncle could offer each of us a window seat over all the lines for the amazingly low price of US$60 per person. Justifiably dubious of his alleged "great deal," we did not trust him and turned him down.

Imagine our lack of astonishment when everything the manager said turned out to be a lie. We never met anyone who had sat in a middle seat on such a flight or had seen only half the lines. When we questioned reputable sources such as the airlines themselves, they informed us that a plane with three back seats did not exist in Nazca. Furthermore, if he really had an uncle with a plane, which was doubtful, his uncle's prices were excessive. In contrast, we had the good fortune to meet Pedro Guerra on the bus from Ica to Nazca. He worked directly for Aeroparacas Airlines, had identification and photographs, and encouraged us to look him up in our guidebooks. We did. For US$100 for all three of us, he offered us a room at a new hotel, transportation to and from the airlines and other local attractions, and plane flights over all the lines, with guaranteed window seats. He said that at any time we could back out if we arrived at the hotel and were not satisfied. Now this was the deal we were looking for! The hotel, Hostal Paramonga, was perfectly adequate with three beds, a private bath, and breakfast. The airline company was

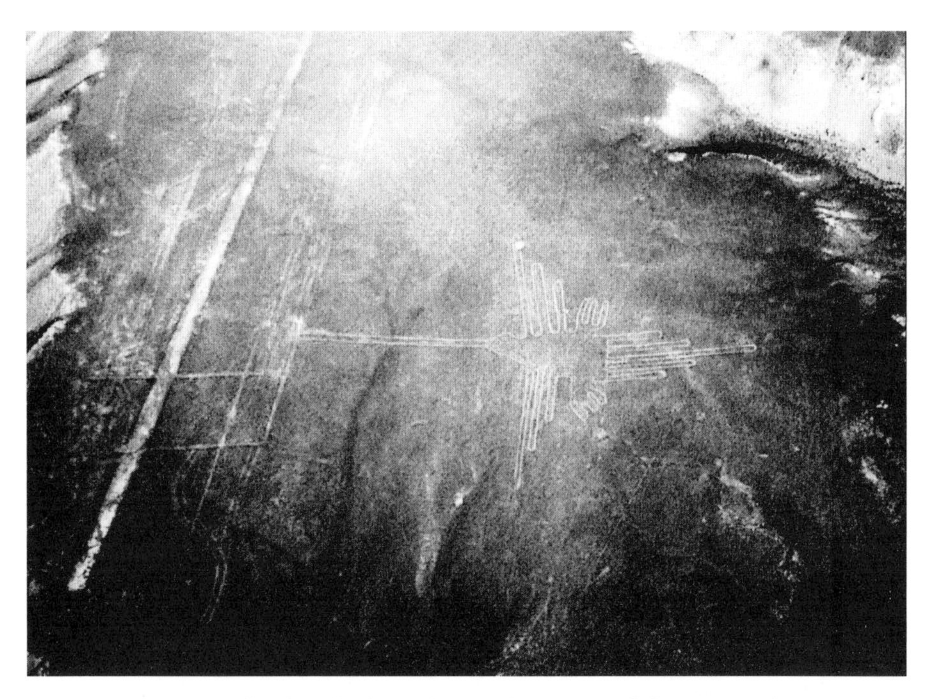

Hummingbird etched in the sand as part of the Nazca lines

very professional, and the three of us shared a plane flight over the lines. We each sat next to a window, affording an unbeatable view.

I had been eagerly anticipating our visit to the mysterious Nazca lines for years, ever since I had seen them featured on a National Geographic television program. Visible only from the air, the Nazca people created immense figures in the sand depicting many different birds and animals, including a monkey, a whale, and even a spider. These images have been preserved for over 1,000 years due to the lack of moisture; it rains only 30 minutes a year, spread out over three months. We Oregonians can't even begin to fathom that! A variety of theories abound about the purpose and creation of these magnificent geometric images, which are also reflected throughout the Nazca people's ceramics and textiles. They may have been walkways, an astronomical calendar, or symbols of desperate pleas to the gods for more rain as their water sources slowly dried up. Some theorists even suggest that they were attempts to communicate with space aliens; one of the figures is referred to as the "astronaut," and some argue that it looks like an extraterrestrial being. These incredible vestiges of an ancient culture exceeded my expectations, and our pilot was so accommodating that he actually went back over one of the figures that Christopher missed the first time around.

In addition to the famous lines, Nazca has some other fascinating attractions as well. As part of our tour, we watched traditional gold-mining and pottery-making techniques. An enthusiastic participant in arts and crafts, Christopher enjoyed playing with a piece of clay composed of earth and sand like that utilized hundreds of years ago. However, I must admit I became a bit anxious when the guide handed him a piece of pottery from the previous millennium to admire! But perhaps the most intriguing part of the tour was the Cementerio de Chanchilla (Cemetery of Chanchilla), a graveyard containing thousands of bones, pottery, textiles, and mummified bodies strewn over miles of arid land. Living Peruvians often take the skulls from the cemetery and keep them on display in their homes for protection against the tough environmental conditions, treating them lovingly like a tangible, almost living, ancestor. One section, appropriately named the "Rastafarian corner," exhibited mummies whose "dreadlocked" hair stretched up to six feet long. Pointing to a tiny wrapped bundle, our guide sadly explained that

"Rastafarian corner" of Chanchilla Cemetery

many children died in the "El Niño" years due to the harsh climate. Very curious about death and the fate of these people, Christopher repeatedly asked us, "How did the boy kill the children?" We kept trying to tell him that the weather caused the children to die until he clarified, "Then why did she say "El Niño" did it?" Translated literally, "El Niño" means "the boy." His ability to understand Spanish was certainly improving!

From Nazca we endured what Fran affectionately refers to as "the bus ride from hell" overnight to Arequipa. Lacking any other transportation options, we suffered through arguably the worst trip of the entire year. I knew we were in trouble when I kicked some poor little kid out of our reserved seats and she was covered with food. Guess what coated the seats and the floor! The bus was cramped, hot, smelly, and altogether nasty. The seats did not lean back and poor Fran had Christopher crammed onto his lap for the entire night. He still claims that the experience might have permanently damaged his knees. The route was also notorious for "lost" luggage so that at every stop I leaned out of the window to keep an eye on our belongings. Approximately once an hour, a colicky baby screamed with a cry so grating that I caught myself yearning for the prerequisite chicken. I should have heeded the warning, "Be careful what you wish for," because quite predictably, around 5:00 a.m., a rooster started crowing every two minutes from the back of the bus. I burst out laughing despite the flabbergasted looks of my traveling companions all around me. It was just too horribly ridiculous to be true. As we arrived in Arequipa I got off the bus and said, "Wow, I feel refreshed!" A German woman looked over at me as if I had lost my mind, and I tried to explain that my comment was meant to be sarcastic. Meanwhile, Fran gazed longingly as the spare driver emerged from underneath the bus after having been locked in with the luggage all night. Avoiding dirty backpacks tumbling all around him seemed a small price to pay for the opportunity to stretch out his legs under there.

Despite a lousy beginning, Arequipa turned out to be the nicest city on our journey to date, blessed with long, sunny days and refreshingly cool evenings year round. Snow-capped mountains span the horizon, and the white stately colonial architecture gives Arequipa its nickname of La Ciudad Blanca (the White City). The central plaza sports a sparkling

Arequipa sports the best plaza in South America

fountain, flowering trees, and an ornate church. Combined with the picture-perfect Andes rising majestically behind the pleasurable scene, we unanimously christened it the "Best Plaza in South America." Our beautiful old-world-style hotel, the Hostal Regis, had a little pool and bar on the rooftop with a commanding view of the city and surrounding mountains. The lovely reception area even contained an elegant chandelier and stained glass windows. Breakfast on the sunny terrace overlooking a small courtyard constituted one of our favorite daily rituals. Pampered with all of that luxury, including a private bathroom, we paid an unbelievable US$14 a night.

Located right in the heart of the city, our hotel boasted some world-renowned neighbors. Arequipa's most famous citizen, Juanita, is the mummy of a 500-year-old Incan girl sacrificed on a Peruvian mountain top. She is so well-preserved that the contents of her stomach have been analyzed to determine the Incan diet. We spent a delightful day exploring her museum of residence and the nearby Monasterio de Santa Catalina, a picturesque adobe monastery with colorful bursts of flowers at every turn. The area springs to life on the weekends when hoards of young adults and college students promenade and party in the streets. We took advantage of the festive nightlife by warming ourselves beside a bonfire on the roof of a bar and indulging in some fabulous international cuisine in the many varied restaurants. While savoring a Middle Eastern meal, Christopher suddenly cried out, "Is that Daveed?" Fran raced out of the restaurant, and sure enough, we had rediscovered our friend from FUVIRESE! We excitedly shared our recent travel adventures with Daveed over dessert, gave each other some travel tips, and made plans to reconnect later in the trip.

Near Arequipa lies the Colca Canyon, reputedly the deepest in the world at about twice the depth of the Grand Canyon. Through the Hostal Regis, we arranged an affordable guided tour of the area. Our van maneuvered along twisting roads through colorful chasms and steeply terraced green gardens. Using excellent visual aids, our informative guide taught us to distinguish among alpacas, llamas, and vicuñas. Alpacas have smaller ears and a cuter face than llamas, while vicuñas are tan with tufts of white fur on their bellies. We also observed two viscachas (rodents similar to rabbits with long fuzzy

Campesina *woman slicing cactus fruit in Colca Canyon*

tails) scooting around a high-altitude plant known as *yaceta*. Used for fuel by the *campesinos*, it grows at the rate of about a half inch a year, so that the boulder-sized specimens we observed were over 100 years old. We loved the tiny peaceful mountain hamlet of Chivay and sampled native cactus fruit prepared by a smiling local woman dressed in elaborately embroidered pastel-colored garments. Fran soothed his aching knees in the nearby thermal springs.

But perhaps the best part of the tour was our visit to a lookout point popular for sighting Andean condors. Graceful carnivorous birds similar to vultures, condors have an impressive wingspan of up to nine feet. We hiked around the canyon ledge and from a distance caught sight of two of them diving through the canyon. After about an hour, our group began assembling to board the van for our journey home. Seemingly out of nowhere, two huge condors appeared directly overhead, soaring regally only a few feet above us. Delighted at our good fortune, we enjoyed quite a show before reluctantly moving on.

The day prior to our intended departure from this delightful city, Christopher developed a frightening illness. He was running a very high temperature (104 degrees Fahrenheit) and was burning to the touch despite the Tylenol we gave him. We decided he needed medical attention and asked the manager at the Hostal Regis for a recommendation. He said that we could consult an English-speaking private doctor but that the local clinic would be less expensive and still provide comparable medical services. We went to the emergency room at the local clinic and, true to his word, the service was excellent. The health care providers gave Christopher medication and a shot in his bottom, which reduced his temperature and helped him sleep. However, the next morning, his fever was back up and accompanied by diarrhea and vomiting. Christopher could not keep down the medication, and we became quite alarmed when our thermometer showed his temperature to be 106 degrees. We brought him back into the emergency room and attempted to impress on the staff there the magnitude of our concerns in Spanish; we were afraid at that temperature that he would begin convulsing. The doctor took his temperature in Celsius, and left to consult a child specialist. During his absence, Fran examined the timeline that he had written detailing Christopher's temperatures, medications administered, and symptoms, which proved to be a very handy idea. He then converted the numbers from Fahrenheit to Celsius and compared them to the doctor's notes in the medical chart. Oddly, the charted information reported that his temperature was lower than 106 degrees. Puzzled by the discrepancy, we each measured our own temperature using our thermometer. To our surprise, Fran and I both had temperatures of 102 degrees! Our thermometer was about four degrees off. Very relieved that Christopher was not as sick as we thought, we apologized profusely to the staff for being so alarmist over this misunderstanding. They gave Christopher another shot in his bottom for good measure, and shortly after we arrived back at the hotel, he began eating, drinking, and keeping down the antibiotics. Thankfully, the crisis was resolved, but Christopher still cringes whenever we mention the "shots in his bots."

Walking in an Incan Wonderland

After this unexpected delay, we left the warm sands of the Pacific coast and headed into the jungle towards the continent's best known archaeological playground, Machu Picchu. In the heart of Incan territory, the beautiful Andean city of Cusco serves as the jumping off point to the famous ruins. Throughout the city lies evidence of the meticulous Incan stonework, huge rocks perfectly chiseled and fit together so tightly that they do not require any mortar. The exact method of construction remains a mystery and appears impossible even given our modern technologies. The construction is so solid and earthquake resistant that the Spanish conquistadors built many of their buildings directly on these indestructible Incan foundations. The Convent of Santo Domingo perfectly exemplifies this combination, a tangible reminder of the Spaniards' endeavors to superimpose the Catholic religion onto these pervasive vestiges of the resilient indigenous culture. Marveling at these structures, we spent many hours simply wandering down cobbled pathways and trying without success to push a credit card between the rocks. To commemorate the experience, we snapped a photo of Christopher next to the 12-angled stone, precisely carved to match its neighbors.

Near the convent, we watched weavers in their traditional clothing making elaborate fabrics on wooden looms at the Center for Traditional

Textiles of Cusco. Christopher sidled up to one of them and animatedly discussed the pattern of animals he was creating. Fran and I investigated the displays of the natural products used to color the yarn. I found it interesting that the Peruvian people used the cochineal bug to dye their fabrics, as did the residents of Oaxaca, Mexico. The cochineal is a small gray bug about the size of a pencil eraser that feeds on cactus and when crushed, produces a bright red permanent dye. After conquering Mexico, the Spaniards shipped billions of them to Europe. In fact, one ship reportedly held 50 tons of these bugs, which seems almost inconceivable when looking at these tiny, nearly weightless things. The British utilized them to dye their trademark redcoats when they fought against the American colonists. What an amazing amount of world history is woven into these materials.

During our meanderings around the city, we also stumbled across a children's museum, called Irq'l Yachay Museo de Arte de Niños Andinos (Art Museum of Andean Children). Through an outreach program directed at benefiting small Andean communities, volunteers introduced the children to art materials and subsequently displayed their creations in the beautiful stone museum building. Our host described the themes represented throughout the artwork and the windows they provided into the minds of these children. I was intrigued by the psychological content of the pictures, which focused on natural subjects and the ubiquitous mountains, while Christopher particularly enjoyed watching the young subjects in a short video about the project, which really made the work come alive. We all agreed that the museum was well worth a stop.

Based on the recommendation of another traveler, we stayed at a hotel with a sunny, central reception area called the Suecia II, located close to the main square of Cusco. We felt very comfortable leaving our excess belongings there during our journeys into the nearby Sacred Valley and, ultimately, Machu Picchu. We put our valuables inside a large envelope and then signed the flap. The owners wrapped the package, we signed the wrappings a few more times for safe-keeping, and then they gave us a receipt for it. We never had any problems with items being stolen. We also used locks on our backpacks, locked them together with a bicycle chain as well, and then stashed them in a little room off the reception area. The only drawback to the hotel was our mandatory daily pilgrimage through a passageway we dubbed, "The Gauntlet." A few popular restaurants, several shops, and offices lined this narrow street, and beggars and sales people besieged us whenever we braved the length of the alley. We mentally prepared ourselves to pass through that area every day, although we did find a great breakfast spot along the way for fortification. Coincidentally, we later learned that other travelers had given that walkway the very same nickname.

With a safe place to store our luggage, we evaluated our options for the journey to Machu Picchu, affectionately known as Machu Picachu, after Christopher's favorite Pokemon hero. The South American Explorers Club again provided some valuable information for this adventure. Many people hike for four days on the Inca trail, reaching altitudes of over 13,000 feet, which would be too strenuous for Christopher. Our next possibility was a two-day hike. However, the first day is spent simply getting to the original Inca trail and included an overnight stop at a reputedly hellish disco/hostel that would make the Incan leader Manco Copak turn over in his grave. Furthermore, we learned that some Incan trails are easily accessible from Machu Picchu. So, rather than spend hundreds of dollars for the two-day hike to cover expenses such as the travel agency overhead, the required guides, trail fees, etc., we decided to visit it independently and were very happy with our decision. Environmentally conscientious travelers may also want to consider the impact of tourism on the Inca trail, causing damage and resulting in recent regulations that restrict the number of hikers allowed on it.

We traveled by bus through the Sacred Valley to Ollantaytambo, a cozy little village with some Incan ruins attractively perched on a hill above the town. We stayed overnight at a B&B called Las Orquídeas, a cute whitewashed building with a beautiful flowering courtyard and a view of the ruins. While enjoying a delicious meal at a nearby restaurant, we sat back and watched the workers returning from the fields with their heavy farming tools slung over their shoulders. With the sun sinking over the ruins and casting a colorful glow on the finely chiseled stone, we sipped our wine and felt extremely privileged to be surrounded by such timeless beauty. The following day we explored the Incan site, taking special note of their innovative irrigation system that functioned so effectively it still watered the terraced gardens carved into the steep slope and filled the baths below.

From Ollantaytambo we rode the train to Aguas Calientes (literally "Warm Waters"), a small town tucked into the base of the mountain on which Machu Picchu is located. The train is the only method of transportation to Aguas Calientes as there are no roads through the dense jungle undergrowth, only well-worn Incan trails. From the town below, buses regularly ascend the steep mountain through a series of perilous switchbacks to the majestic ruins cradled delicately on its summit. Craggy peaks covered in lush green foliage encircle the site of Machu Picchu on all sides, with steep cliffs dropping hundreds of feet to a river snaking through the valley floor. Overwhelmed by the magnitude of both the architecture and its spectacular setting, we gazed at the ethereal clouds and fog floating between the mountains, giving the place a mystical feel. Llamas and alpacas roamed free throughout the Incan stonework, along with an occasional native dressed in colorful woven clothing. The sun playing on the mist graced us with an elusive rainbow, and I felt awed and humbled by the magical landscape, steeped in ancient culture and history.

We spent two full days exploring the ruins, equipped with a detailed guidebook recommended by the SAE Club, Frost's *Exploring Cusco*. We elected to go at our own pace using the book instead of hiring a guide at the entrance. Machu Picchu proved to be the pinnacle of many amazing Incan accomplishments, especially given their relatively short period of influence (only a couple hundred years) before the Spaniards conquered them in the 1500's. I wondered how they quarried and transported the huge stones, weighing hundreds of tons, so high up in the mountains and then fitted them together perfectly to create intricate shapes. The precise positioning of the stones for astrological purposes intrigued Fran, and Christopher alternated between casting imaginary spells and running after the llamas. We tried to imagine what it would be like to shower in the little baths created by the elaborate irrigation system and empathized with whoever was resigned to bathe in everyone else's run-off at the bottom.

Determined to make the most of the plentiful Incan trails, we backtracked from Machu Picchu along the most famous Inca trail to

Christopher casting a spell over Machu Picchu

the Sun Gate, a lovely archway and lookout point. While the thin paths and steep ladders may be tricky for little feet, we managed the walk with no problems and were rewarded with a perfect view of the ruins. Entering through the gate from the opposite direction, some hikers appeared looking so exhausted after their four-day ordeal that they couldn't fully enjoy their first-time experience of the magnificent site. Several *viajeros* who made the journey confirmed this impression, thus validating our decision to forgo that trek. We also walked along another trail to the Inca Gate, a very thin precipice cut in the granite mountainside with sheer drops above and below it. The engineering required to carve the narrow stone bridge out of the cliff boggled even Fran's well-trained technical mind. Not one to shy away from heights, he bravely hiked up a slippery path lacking guardrails to the top of Huayna Picchu, the most-photographed mountain adjacent to the ruins. Christopher and I decided the trip was too dangerous, so Fran generously snapped some aerial pictures from the summit for us. While we opted for the bus ride back to town after the first full day of sight-seeing, the second day we thumped down our last Incan pathway, step by painful step. A little boy in Incan clothing sprinted by us. Stopping at regular intervals to wave and sing "good-bye" to the tourists, his breathless arrival at the bottom coincided with the bus. The passengers happily reinforced his efforts with a few coins. His easy triumph over the multitude of stairs instilled in us an even deeper respect for the Incas and their hearty descendents.

As we learned at Machu Picchu, Incan trails are not for the faint of heart. In the Sacred Valley, the remains of Pisac are located high up in the mountains, overlooking the small village and traditional market. We congratulated ourselves on investing in a taxi ride to the top and then hiking down through the ruins, providing words of encouragement to the ascending hikers struggling by us. The narrow trail crumbled and, at times, dropped away down the steep side. One misstep could have sent us tumbling hundreds of feet down to the valley below. Terrified, I held Fran's hand as I gingerly inched my way around the gaps in the path, complaining about the lack of governmental safety protections. For better or worse, the fear of lawsuits due to injuries prevents these types of conditions in the U.S. After we made it to the bottom, we shared a meal with another couple we had passed on the mountain. The

Llamas explore the Incan ruins

young woman recounted a traumatic incident that occurred just after squeezing by us. She found her partner stranded next to a particularly rough pass. He was crying and she literally had to hold his hand and walk him through it. He said that after seeing us, he urged himself on by telling himself that if a child could do it, he could too. Reassuring him that Fran was the driving force behind our successful descent, I emphasized that I would not recommend that particular hike to anyone but the bravest of souls.

The Lake at the Top of the World

Our legs still sore from trudging down hundreds of steps, we proceeded on to Lake Titicaca for more Incan architecture and diverse cultures. Located about 11,500 feet above sea level, Lake Titicaca is the highest navigable lake in the world and the largest in South America. With numerous islands dotting its brilliant blue surface, the area presents plenty of interesting sight-seeing possibilities for families. Establishing a home base on the Peruvian and Bolivian sides of the border, in Puno and Copacabana, respectively, we explored the lake's offerings from two different viewpoints.

Immediately after arriving in Puno we encountered yet another example of the downside to Peruvian tourism. As we debarked from the bus, a man encouraged us to check out his new affordable hotel, assuring us of its safety and cleanliness. Luring us in with a free taxi ride, he showed us photos of the rooms in newly printed pamphlets advertising private bathrooms and televisions. We confirmed that the ride was *gratis* with the driver and piled into the car with another couple. At the hotel, the owner handed me two keys to inspect the rooms. I headed up to the first room, a dingy affair with wiring hanging out of the walls, no TV, and the adjacent bathroom consisting of a toilet with a spigot jutting out overhead. But while the first room was dumpy, the second room was worse. Upon opening the door, I encountered three open backpacks, with someone else's belongings strewn about the floor. He had given me someone else's key. I could have stolen whatever I wanted. This oversight did not bode well for the security of the building. I ran back downstairs, shook my head at Fran, and we quietly slipped past the other couple

The highest navigable lake in the world, Lake Titicaca

loudly bickering with the owner over the false promise of a television. Even if the rooms did have TV, there were absolutely no guarantees that the reception was adequate; at best, most budget hotels had only one or two barely visible channels in Spanish anyway. We asked a taxi to drive us to a hotel recommended in our guidebook. The driver persistently tried to argue us out of our requested lodging, but after such a negative experience with the first hotel, we weren't taking any more chances. We insisted on the Hostal Los Pinos Inn and agreed on a price for the taxi ride. We arrived at the hotel and handed the driver some money. He refused to give us change, claiming that we owed him twice the price, as he was charging us for the "free" ride to the first hotel from the bus station. I held my ground, becoming increasingly irate and insisting that he return our money. Finally, the hotel owner came out, and we explained the situation to her. Only after I suggested contacting the police did the taxi driver quite reluctantly return our change.

After a shaky introduction, the Hostal Los Pinos Inn turned out to be a wonderfully clean and comfortable family-run place. Although our hot water did not work initially, we spoke to the management, and they fixed it so that we benefited from some heavenly showers. We were learning to let people know when things did not seem to be functioning so they could either educate us or correct the problem. Unfortunately, we disliked the town of Puno, finding it cluttered, dirty, and overwhelming. Due to the upcoming elections, loudspeakers blared deafening propaganda in the main square day and night, adding to the chaos. We took refuge in a restaurant called La Hostería, which provided a cozy ambience and contained a large stone wood-burning pizza oven that turned out delicious meals. The owner took a particular liking to Christopher and treated us like family. We spent several hours there during our short stay in Puno, munching on tasty treats and playing card games together. At one point, we heard some commotion in the street and peered out of the window to investigate. A large crowd of about 200 *campesinos* marched proudly down the street, waving signs in support of their presidential candidate. As I noticed the smiles on many of their brown, careworn faces, I thought about the significance of their ability to publicly express their political opinion on a continent known for the oppression of its indigenous people. How fortunate we Americans are

The edible floating islands of Uros, Lake Titicaca

to have freedom of expression, and how hard these people had to work to achieve that right.

The hotel arranged a highly recommended two-day trip on the lake for us. We first stopped at the floating islands of Uros, constructed entirely from the endemic tortora reeds. The spongy, squishy feel of the island's surface felt like walking on a giant, slightly deflated balloon. Not only do the inhabitants reside on these reeds, they also use them to make boats, handicrafts, and their homes. They even eat them! Christopher ate so many of them that we had to prohibit him from doing so for fear he would become sick. One of the residents took us on a short ride in a tortora reed boat. Although some people think these islands are a bit touristy, we were enthralled by the uniqueness of the place and the friendliness of its people.

That night, we weathered a rainstorm with a local family on the island of Amantaní. Located on the second floor of a mud brick home, our comfortable bedroom was accessible by a rickety wooden staircase leading down to a muddy courtyard. Our tiny window afforded us a peaceful view of the terraced farmland sloping down to the sparkling lake. I marveled at the efficiency of the local women who managed to carry necessities on their heads, spin wool on their hand-held spools, and tread up the steep, rocky path to the town center, all at the same time. Sadly, Christopher was somewhat less enthusiastic about our stay. He did not like the dark walk outside to use the outhouse, and he quickly tired of the same meal of rice and potatoes by breakfast the next morning. To his relief, the following day we sailed to Taquile, known for its weaving. After a lovely hour-long hike around the edge of the island, we reached the main square. By that point, Christopher really needed some downtime. So instead of visiting the museum, we chatted with some other visitors while he ate a treat and then ran around the square, chasing some unsuspecting chickens. He tuckered himself out and slept through most of the voyage home.

While he napped, Fran and I enjoyed a lively conversation with our international companions, communicating in a combination of English and Spanish, with a little Portuguese and Italian thrown in for good measure. Maximo, an Italian living in England, captivated us with his stories of squatting in expensive London homes; apparently, British law enables one to legally reside in someone else's house after a short time period. He also raved about his travels through Columbia. The only problem he encountered was a border guard who insisted that he donate his CD player to the cause. Maximo told him that if he wanted the electronic device, he would have to pay for it. The guard offered him US$20 and Maximo turned over the player. We expressed surprise that Maximo settled for such a low price. "Well, he was armed!" Maximo reminded us.

As our boat docked at Puno and we prepared to leave Peru, I reflected on how adept we had become at traveling in South America. We had learned to adapt to a variety of circumstances, stand our ground against dishonest touts, and to navigate our way in several languages. Little did I know that we would need to draw upon all these newfound skills in the next two months.

CHRISTOPHER'S COMMENTS

When we were in Peru, we went to see some ruins. I thought it was really boring. Kids don't like ruins! I knew they were old but I didn't care. There were lots of different kinds of ruins, and it took us a long time to see them all. We walked around a lot and I got really tired. Now when I look back at pictures of the ruins, they look really cool and kind of scary, especially the city of Chan Chan.

Even though there were some parts that were boring in Peru, there were also lots of fun parts too. The catacombs in Lima were very scary. In one there was a pile of skulls in the middle, then a circle of long bones around it, then a circle of skulls, then a circle of long bones, and then a circle of skulls again. There were a lot of bones!

In the town of Pisco, I got to pet a penguin, but I think it was mean to keep the penguin as a pet. Then we took a boat to an island near Pisco with sea lions and sea gulls. There were lots of sea gulls on the rocks because the sea lions couldn't get that high. The sea lions stayed on the beach. It was much nicer to see all of the animals going free.

Typical Peruvian marketplace

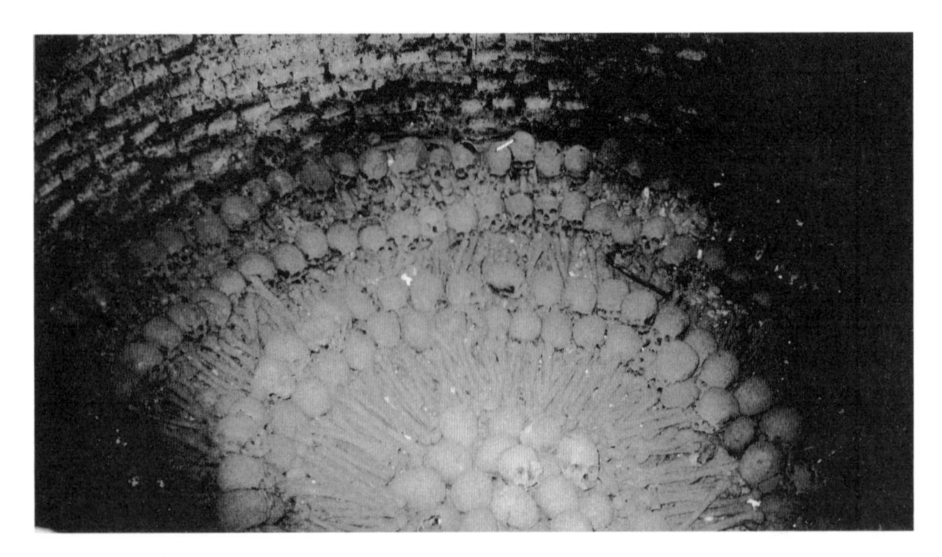

Grisly art in the catacombs of San Francisco Church, Lima

Next, we went on a little plane to see the Nazca lines. We had to take pills that made Mommy and me sleepy because we have motion sickness. I thought the lines looked really cool. My favorites were the spider, the hummingbird, and the monkey. I couldn't see the dog the first time so the pilot had to turn back around and Mom had to help me find it. I am glad we turned back! Near the lines there was a cemetery-type place with a lot of bones. Some of the bones were still mummies and in clothes from a long time ago. They were very scary. After that we went to a canyon where there were lots of condors. I really liked it because a condor flew right over our heads. There were also some plants that when you touched them, they closed up their leaves. There were lots of alpacas too.

The best part of the trip was Machu Picchu because it was so huge and also because it had llamas. It had things that looked like giant stairs in the mountains because they didn't want the water to roll down the sides. They needed it for their crops. Daddy climbed up Huayna Picchu. Mommy and I were too scared to do it because it was very dangerous. We were also scared about Daddy because he came back late. I liked being in the mountains and I really liked the llamas. Overall, I thought Peru was a little boring because of all the ruins but it was fun too.

TRAVELER'S TIPS

1. Use at least two current guidebooks. Cut out and staple together the sections you will need to carry around town.

2. Obtain hotel and tour recommendations from other travelers and trusted hotel owners and agency representatives whenever possible.

3. Always compare any information you receive with several other credible sources.

4. Be friendly and conversational with vendors. You never know when an interesting opportunity might come up.

5. Welcome time spent in large cities as a way to complete necessary errands. You may need to visit a main city for this purpose.

6. Whenever ill, begin a medical diary. Note times, temperatures, and medicines taken. Know how to convert Fahrenheit to Celsius. Make sure your thermometer is accurate!

7. Place valuables in a sealed and signed envelope before turning them over to the hotel safe. Ask for some kind of receipt. Lock all luggage and chain it together. Never leave your valuables (e.g., cameras or computer) behind.

8. Carry small local change for taxi rides and meals. Give exact change whenever possible.

9. Clarify fees ahead of time and always ask exactly what is or is not included in the price.

10. If something doesn't work in your room, talk to the management. They are usually happy to help. Remember a smile is your best friend.

11. Bring along extra snacks and food on guided tours in case your child does not like the food available. We always carried a plastic bag filled with bread and chips along with a large water bottle.

PIURA

Hospedaje California

Junin 835
Tel: 328789

Clean, friendly, inviting family hotel for US$8 a night.

HUANCHACO/TRUJILLO

La Casa Suiza

Los Pinos 451
Tel: 0051 (44) 46-1285
http://www.casasuiza.com
casasuiza@casasuiza.com

Comfortable, very clean, family-run hotel; double room with breakfast for US$12 a night. Backpackers' favorite, great place to get information. Will arrange day tours of recommended ruins.

Trujillo must-see sights include the extensive intricately carved ruins of **Chan Chan** and the huge temples of **Huacas del Sol y de la Luna**. Don't forget to ask at the snack shop about their video describing the sacrifices that took place there.

MIRAFLORES/LIMA

Olimpus Hostel & Lodging

Diego Ferré 365 (12th block of Av. Larco), Miraflores
Tel: (51 1) 241-5875 or 2426077
www.olimpusperu.com
olimpusperu@terra.com.pe

Great location in trendy Miraflores district, about a block from the coast and within walking distance of SAE Clubhouse. One of our favorite hotels to date. Very clean, nicely decorated with carpeting, family-run establishment with very comfortable beds, hot water in the shower and the sink, for US$20 a night, including continental breakfast.

South American Explorers Clubhouse

Calle Piura 135, Miraflores
T/F: (51-1) 445 3306

Great resources for members, including book exchange. See Chapter 1 Resources section for more details.

Recommended sights in Lima include:

Changing of the guards at the **Palacio de Gobierno** (Government Palace) in the Plaza Mayor, a UNESCO World Heritage site.

Museo de la Nación (National Museum on Javier Prado Este, San Borja) for a historical perspective of the fascinating cultural history of Peru.

Museo Rafael Larco Herrera (Av Bolívar 1515, Pueblo Libre) for its extensive handicrafts.

Museo de la Inquisición (Spanish Inquisition Museum, Junín 548) is great for kids who love gore but may be a little scary for younger children.

Catacombs containing thousands of bones in elaborate displays beneath the **Museo del Convento de San Francisco** (San Francisco Church on Jr Lampa).

Parque de las Leyendas (Block 24 on Av La Marina, San Miguel), a large zoo with animals from three Peruvian regions and other recreational activities for kids.

PISCO

Hostal La Portada

Av. Alipio Ponce No. 250
Tel: 034-532098
hostallaportada@terra.com

Clean hostel for US$13/night.

Take a tour of the **Paracas National Park**, including a boat trip to **Isla Ballesta**, with the many sea birds, penguins, and sea lions, and a stop at the **Paracas Museum** to check out the deformed skulls. Make sure to sample the local drink, a **Pisco sour**, before you leave!

ICA/HUACACHINA

While it is better to stay outside of Ica in Huacachina, we found the management quite shady at Casa de Arena. Still, the hotel had a little pool and bar on the premises, with basic rooms and clean shared bathrooms for US$10 a night. Do not allow them to arrange a wine tour or a flight over the Nazca lines for you. Try the free sand boarding at your own risk!

Arrange your own visit by taking a taxi to the **wineries**:

El Carmen is a traditional winery with an ancient grape press made out of a huge tree trunk.

El Catador (The Taster) has a wide variety of reds, whites, and the traditional pisco to fit any palate.

Bodega Vista Alegre, also with several wines and pisco, has a restaurant on the premises.

NAZCA

Aeroparacas Airlines

Ask for Pedro Alarcón Guerra by name.
Jr. Lima No. 185
Tel: 034-521027 034-699507
airnascatravel@hotmail.com

We met Pedro on the bus from Ica to Nazca and arranged an all-inclusive tour directly through him with the airlines to fly over the famous Nazca lines for US$100. The price included transportation, overnight accommodations, and a tour of other local sights as well.

Hostal Paramonga

Calle Juan Matta No 880

Acceptable triple with private bath and continental breakfast; this new hotel was included in our package arranged through Aeroparacas Airlines.

Must-see sights include a flight over the famous **Nazca lines** and the mummies in the **Cementerio de Chanchilla**, which is included in most tours. Make sure to clarify whether the entrance fee is included in your overall tour price.

AREQUIPA

Hostal Regis

Calle Ugarte No. 202
Tel: 226111
Regis@qnet.com.pe

Clean, beautiful colonial building with rooftop bar and courtyard in great downtown location close to two major sites of interest. Double with bath for US$17 a night, breakfast for another US$3 per person served by the courtyard. This hostel will also help arrange a two-day, one-night tour to the **Colca Canyon**, for reasonable prices (US$22 per adult, US$15 for children). This highly recommended tour to arguably the deepest canyon in the world includes a dip in hot springs, a visit to a small local Andean museum, dinner with a folkloric dance show, and if lucky, condor sightings.

Interesting sights include:

Monasterio de Santa Catalina (Santa Catalina No. 301), a gorgeous white colonial building full of picturesque archways and contrasting spots of colorful flowers.

Museo Santuario Andino (Santa Catalina No. 210), the resting place of Juanita, an Incan girl sacrificed on a nearby mountain.

Convento/Museo de La Recoleta (Recoleta Street 117), chock-full of interesting books, plants, trepanned skulls, mummies, and other Peruvian objects of interest.

CUSCO

Suecia II

Tecseccocha 465
Tel: 239757

Conveniently located near the central plaza, this clean, comfortable, family-run hostel serves breakfast in a sunny indoor courtyard and provides rooms with shared bath for US$18 a night. The establishment is also very secure and a good place to leave valuables if traveling on to Machu Picchu.

South American Explorers Clubhouse

Apartado 500, Cusco, Peru
Street Address: Coquechaca 188, Buzzer 4
T/F: (51-84) 245-484

Here's the place for members to pick up maps and current information about exploring Machu Picchu and the Sacred Valley. See the Chapter 1 Resources section for more details. Also try: www.andeantravelweb.com/peru

Frost, Peter (2000). *Exploring Cuzco.* Nuevas Imagenes S.A.

Provides maps and enough detailed information to enable travelers to take self-guided tours of the Incan ruins in the area. Can purchase from Cusco SAE Clubhouse.

Boleto Turístico Unificado, a single entry ticket that includes many attractions of cultural interest in Cusco and the surrounding area for US$20, is a good deal if you are intending to see several of the sites. Tickets can be purchased at any of the sites; our recommendations for families are listed below:

Convento de Santo Domingo (Convent of Santo Domingo) is a fascinating blend of Spanish architecture built on Incan stonework.

Unsaac Museo Inka (Cuesta del Almirante 103) houses Incan ceramics, gold, and other handicrafts.

Irq'l Yachay Museo de Arte de Niños Andinos (Ladrillos 491) has a wonderful display of an outreach project in which art therapy was brought to Andean children. Their artwork and a video of the program are available for viewing.

The Center for Traditional Textiles of Cusco (Avenida Sol 603A) has male and female weavers wearing traditional garments demonstrate the construction of various textiles.

La Tertulia (Procuradores 50) has such great "buffet" breakfasts (actually all-you-can-eat) that it is worth braving "The Gauntlet," the alleyway on which it is located, to get there.

Nearby Incan ruins of interest include **Pisac**, but be warned that parts of the trail may not be suitable for children, so you may wish to explore the Sunday morning market instead.

OLLANTAYTAMBO

Hostal Orquídeas

Tel: 204032.

Great view of the ruins, pretty courtyard with flowers, clean room with bath and breakfast for US$10 a night. Near the train to Aguas Calientes.

AGUAS CALIENTES/MACHU PICCHU

Hostal Pachakuteq

Up the hill on Avenue Pachacutec
Tel: 211061
pachakuteq@hotmail.com

Conveniently located, clean, very nice, double room with breakfast included for US$20 a night. Provides ample information about buses, etc. to Machu Picchu.

PUNO

Hostal Los Pinos Inn

Jr. Tarapacá 182
Tel: 054-367398
hostalpinos@hotmail.com

Clean, family-run, very comfortable hostel with private bath for US$13 a night. Will arrange very reasonable tours of islands in Lake Titicaca as well as bus tickets on to Bolivia.

La Hostería

Lima 501

Great ambience, large stone wood-burning pizza oven, friendly service, excellent food.

Visitors must take the two-day tour of **the floating islands of Uros**, **Taquile** with its textile history, and the serene island of **Amantaní** where locals provide lodging in their modest homes. A day tour of **Sillistani**, Incan ruins comprised of curved stone towers overlooking the lake, is also recommended.

Brazil
Peru
Rurrenabaque
Bolivia
Lago Titicaca
Sorata
Puno
Copacabana
La Paz
Villa Tunari
Cochabamba
Oruro
Sucre
Salar de
Uyuni
Potosí
Uyuni
Tupiza
Villazón
Paraguay
La Quiaca
Chile
Argentina

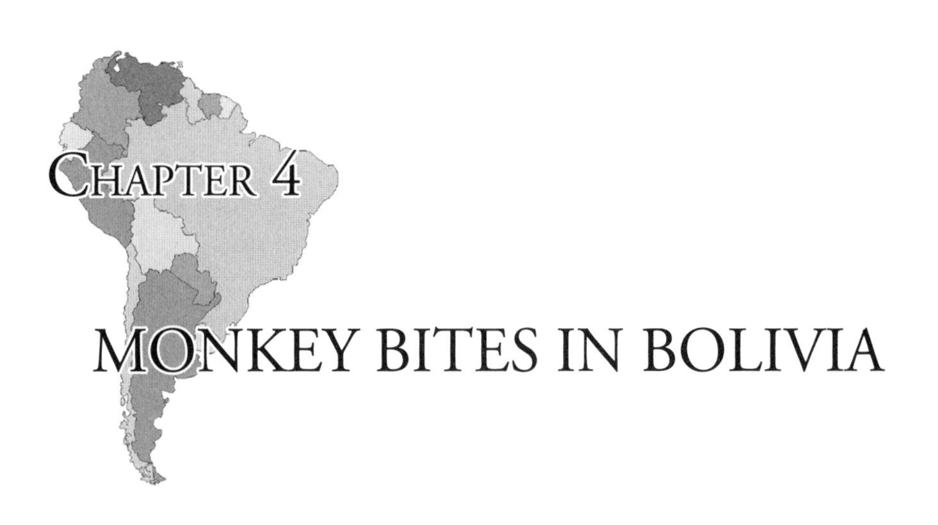

Chapter 4

Monkey Bites in Bolivia

Most travelers develop a love-hate relationship with Bolivia. The exotic sights and primitive lifestyle stimulate one's sense of adventure; however, the Bolivian culture can be quite at odds with a more capitalistic Western mentality. Yet for those seeking an authentic experience off the beaten path and full of exhilarating surprises, Bolivia is the South American country of choice.

Another Take on the Lake

We crossed the border on Día de los Muertos, the Day of the Dead commemorated on November 2, a fitting symbol of the end of our time in Peru and the birth of our Bolivian encounter. The journey circumnavigated Lake Titicaca and required a change of buses from the sleek Peruvian line to the not-so-gently used Bolivian machine. Several of us *viajeros* stepped in dog doo as we stumbled over chards of brick and rock in making the switch. As we groaned over the state of our shoes, Maximo (the Italian, London-based squatter) reassured us, "Don't worry! It's good luck!" This type of paradigm shift was the first of many mental overhauls brought on by this perplexing country. In the upcoming months we often found ourselves pondering unanswerable questions about why things were the way they were, and our mantra quickly became, "It's Bolivia."

Good luck *was* with us, as the spectacular Andean day remained bright, crisp, and clear. The cool blue of Lake Titicaca melded with the sapphire blue of the sky, broken by the uneven line of the rugged mountains. Christopher had been learning about South American cultures in his Social Studies workbook. As we gazed out of the bus windows, Fran and I administered a pop quiz, firing off questions such as, "What is this type of geological formation called?" "The altiplano." "What kind of farming are those people doing?" "Subsistence farming." "What does that mean?" "They grow only their own food." Christopher passed with flying colors. En route we sped by several graveyards and watched families celebrating their ancestors with elaborate picnic spreads amongst the headstones. Children ran around, flying colorful kites high overhead in the strong Andean wind. Despite the many hours spent wedged into our uncomfortable bus seats, these scenes made us feel as if we had spent the holiday in local style by the time we reached our first destination.

Our arrival in Copacabana contrasted sharply with prior Peruvian experiences. No crowds vied for our attention as we descended from the bus. No crooked taxi drivers lurked, hoping to overcharge us as they whisked us off to their hotel of choice. We enjoyed the calm welcome as we unloaded and began walking uphill to a recently opened hotel, Hotel Utama, recommended by other travelers for its large, healthy breakfasts. The new owner appeared eager to please, and we quickly agreed on a large room with a sliver of the lake visible through the window. Upon request he also arranged a guided boat trip for us to Isla del Sol (Island of the Sun), known as the birthplace of the Incan empire.

The next day we discovered that the voyage to Isla del Sol was much less organized than our earlier two-day island tour in Peru. Lacking the promised guide, we also did not receive even basic information about how long we would be at each site nor the lunch and bathroom options available. When we tried unsuccessfully to extract any helpful hints in Spanish from the crew, they just shrugged and looked off into the distance. In hindsight, we should have asked other travelers beforehand about the different tour operators and joined a more reputable company. Confused and worried about literally missing the boat, we disembarked when we first docked and set off at a brisk pace to see the Roca Sagrada (Sacred Rock) where Manco Copac and his sister-wife Mama

Huaca reputedly rose out of the water to give birth to the entire Incan civilization. Christopher fought to keep up with us despite the altitude. By this time we had all acclimated well with the virtual elimination of symptoms, but it was still difficult for his little legs to maintain our speed. We climbed the rock, snapped a few photos, and then enjoyed a more leisurely stroll back. The sun shone warmly as we gazed across the crystal blue waters from several vantage points high on the island. Within sight of the boat, Fran and I stopped to dip our feet in a clean, albeit chilly, section of the lake. Christopher hooked up with two native children to fly a kite left over from the Día de los Muertos festivities. We embarked without incident and, at the next stop further south on the island, we located some food options. Joining several other groups for lunch, we unexpectedly reunited with our Italian friend, Maximo. While chatting with him, we learned that the island did not have any public restrooms. The situation became urgent for Christopher, and Fran ended up holding him in a squatting position as he did his business in the corner of a field. Now that's going native!

Braving the Bolivian Bus System

As we set off through our third South American country, we quickly learned that the Bolivian bus system possesses a unique set of challenges. The buses were typically run-down and filthy, often with immovable seats and inadequate foot room or storage space. Fellow passengers pressed their belongings into the openings around our legs. Reclining backs proved to be a mixed blessing; invariably, the gentleman in front of us would lean into our laps, severely limiting any kind of activity but affording us an excellent view of his infrequently washed head. Even on the better buses, specially advertised "extras" such as movies or music often resulted in ear-splitting mariachi noise for miles or intensely violent, poor quality American movies dubbed in Spanish. We were repeatedly subjected to the same Bridget Fonda flick about a heroin-addicted prostitute teaming up with a martial arts master to exterminate a pimping drug lord. Not great subject matter for a seven-year-old! Added to the hubbub, vendors often boarded the buses and spent twenty minutes loudly peddling their wares. We actually enjoyed this diversion and treated the show like a free Spanish lesson. On the worst buses, the smells and sounds of livestock and *campesinos* crowded into close quarters tended to overshadow the benefits of the genuine cultural experience. Desperate for fresh air, I once opened a window. However, due to a baffling law of physics, the configuration of the bus did not allow for even a slight breeze. Regardless, another passenger asked me twice to close the window for reasons I could not fathom.

Furthermore, most of the buses lacked bathrooms, or if they did contain this highly advertised service, the doors remained locked despite multiple desperate pleas to the driver. Instead, at every stop the men lined up right next to each other on one side of the bus and urinated in unison. The women sought out a spot further from the group, doing their business on the ground under the cover of their skirts. To aggravate the situation, the bus companies typically scheduled a break only about an hour into a trip lasting eight hours or longer, and then drove continuously for the rest of the ride. "Why are we stopping now?" even Christopher would ask. "It's Bolivia," Fran and I always responded in unison.

Further complicating the picture, the Bolivian roads were as taxing as the buses. When we started strategizing how to explore this complex country, we realized that no obvious route connects the major sites, unlike in Peru or even Ecuador. In fact, many areas remain completely inaccessible during the rainy season. "Inaccessible?" I scoffed. "Where there is a will there is a way!" My naïve American optimism was absolutely wrong. Bolivian roads proved to be undeveloped and, at times, nonexistent. On one trip the bus took a sharp right down a river embankment just prior to a bridge. The bridge was under construction, so I assumed we were simply circumventing it by crossing the riverbed and going up the opposite bank to continue along the road on the other side. Wrong! The bus followed the dry riverbed for about fifteen miles before lurching back up, where it wove through trees and rocks for several more miles along a steep incline, and finally joined a relatively level stretch of land. The intermittent tire marks in the dust were the only indication of the route. Clearly, during the rainy season, this path would become absolutely impassable, as the gully flooded with several feet of water and the sides ran with slippery streams of mud.

While the transportation system can be quite frustrating, by its very nature it ensures that many parts of landlocked Bolivia remain less reachable than other areas of South America and, therefore, less contaminated by outside influences. We found that it was easily worth putting up with these inconveniences in exchange for some of the most incredible experiences of our entire trip. We were able to immerse ourselves in unspoiled natural surroundings and get close to the exotic wildlife in a way that is not possible in most parts of the world. The difficulty trekking to these remote locations adds to the excitement and strengthens the connections between people, both native and foreign, who find their paths crossing in such isolated places. Bolivia is not for tourists wanting a relaxing vacation spot but, rather, for seasoned travelers looking for a highly rewarding challenge. We traveled in this captivating country for two months and just barely scratched the surface of its many intriguing possibilities.

Caimans and Howlers and Frogs. Oh My!

Finding ourselves in Bolivia at the beginning of the rainy season, we raced to stay ahead of the weather as the torrents pushed at our backs. In La Paz we settled into a very cheap but friendly backpacker's hotel called the Posada El Carretero. The innkeepers proved to be extremely helpful in a variety of ways, and we felt totally comfortable leaving the bulk of our luggage there to travel to Rurrenabaque at the heart of the Bolivian wilderness. The tiny settlement of Rurrenabaque, affectionately nicknamed "Rurre," serves as the starting point for highly recommended tours into the surrounding rainforest and wetlands, or pampas. We were particularly interested in visiting the nearby Madidi National Park, a pristine jungle featured in a *National Geographic* magazine article, as well as the pampas, home to many exotic animals.

Deemed the "most dangerous road in the world," the route to Rurre via Coroico has been described by fellow travelers as 28 hours of sheer hell, scrunched in a small rickety deathtrap, clinging precariously to the side of some of the highest mountains in the world. On one side of the bus, the views of the spectacular scenery also reveal the skeletons of buses whose former passengers never completed the trip. Even more disturbing, some people brave the one-lane road on bicycle, rendering it that much more treacherous for the vehicles that swerve to avoid them. At the South American Explorers Club in Cusco, Peru, we read a very troubling account of an Israeli bicyclist who died on such a "tour." The writer emphasized that the road's reputation should be treated as a very real warning, not as an invitation for adventure. Another independent traveler we met at Machu Picchu's Sun Gate said that he rode the bus there, but after seeing the carnage where another vehicle had tipped over just days beforehand, he purchased a plane ticket back to La Paz immediately upon arrival. We agreed, as a family, to forgo the overland ride and invest in the US$100 per person roundtrip flight; it certainly seemed like money wisely spent.

Purchasing plane tickets to Rurre turned out to be an adventure in itself. We traipsed all over La Paz looking for the airline offices, hoping to save a bit of cash by buying tickets directly from the airlines. Following a recommendation in our guidebook, we also met with a travel agent offering a very pricey tour out to the Chalalán Lodge in the Madidi National Park, with airfare included in the package. In a stroke of brilliance, Fran thought of calling the Chalalán Lodge office in Rurre to inquire about available flights and to see if we could arrange the tour directly through them. Using a pay phone on a crowded street corner, an apparently disabled beggar began harassing us, insistently shoving his hat directly into our faces and babbling incoherently. We shouted at him to leave us alone, but he persisted until Fran finally pushed him away, not once but twice. Meanwhile, poor Fran was trying to communicate in Spanish over a faint, staticky, long-distance phone line. Miraculously, he got the information that we needed. They advised us to buy the plane tickets from a travel agency in La Paz and then organize trips to Madidi National Park and other points of interest through the companies based in Rurre.

The flight out was breath-taking, as the brown jagged edges of the Andes gave way to lush green tropical rainforest threaded with wide ribbons of deep blue water. The plane landed on a stretch of grass, little more than a football field, and the airlines transported us by jeep from the one-room "airport" to their office in town. A cute, comfortable, laid-back, pioneering settlement, Rurre consists of an overgrown square and a few dirt roads sprinkled with a handful of restaurants, bars, and tour agencies catering to the dozens of *viajeros* there. Considering the isolated location, the restaurants, such as the Moskkito Jungle Bar with its bamboo walls and thatched roof, serve a surprising array of food, including hamburgers, fries, and pizza. We noticed large groups of Israelis eating, smoking, and occasionally breaking into song around tables outside of the restaurants. After their mandatory military service, young Israelis are expected to see the world before entering institutions of higher education. Some admitted to us that they didn't even enjoy traveling but felt pressured to do so because "everyone else was doing it." As we talked to three delightful young men, they complimented us, impressed at our willingness to travel with Christopher. We reassured them that life doesn't have to stop after childbirth! Furthermore, our journey together was a piece of cake compared to the courage they mustered every day to defend their homeland.

Our first order of business involved locating the office for the Chalalán Lodge, a community-based resort supported by international funding. Together with the indigenous people, Israeli-born Yossi Ginsberg wrote the grants for this venture after his terrifying experience lost in the rainforest (as documented in his page-turning novel titled *Escape from Tuichi*). The project provides funds to construct the lodge and train local residents in managing it with the goal to become self-sustaining after six years. In this way, they hope to maintain their rainforest and way of life through tourism and education rather than pillaging it for lumber and other limited natural resources. Our stay at the lodge was expensive, but half of the money supports its upkeep while the other half goes back into the community to build schools and other social programs. We considered it an excellent investment.

Our hosts picked us up in Rurre and transported us by motorized canoe for five hours up the Beni and Tuichi rivers. I felt a thrill of excitement to be traveling upon the same waters that Yossi had described so harrowingly in his book. We then walked for 30 minutes to the lodge, richly crafted out of native wood and other natural materials. Nestled deep in the Madidi National Park, the luxurious accommodations contain one main dining and recreation room in which the delicious meals are occasionally accompanied by impromptu musical performances given by the staff. Guests sleep in private bungalows with huge, soft beds draped with mosquito netting. Hammocks are slung across small porches out front, and a short trail leads through the foliage to the clean, tiled outhouse with excellent hot showers. We immediately felt at ease in our new surroundings and were soon joined by an incredibly knowledgeable native guide named Sondro. At our request, he patiently explained everything in simple Spanish so that we could practice the language. Sondro reminisced about growing up in the rainforest, where his childhood pets included a baby armadillo and an ocelot. When he released them, he noticed that the animals had difficulty fending for themselves. For example, his armadillo could not dig a proper hole to cover itself in order to hide from its natural predators. As a result, Sondro learned not to feed or touch the animals in the forest. We really appreciated his respect towards the wildlife and tried to disturb them as little as possible.

For three days and nights, Sondro escorted us on several hikes and canoe rides in the park and around the nearby lake. On one trail, Sondro poked a nondescript pile of dirt that he recognized as jaguar dung. He pointed out the bits of bone and fur in the scat that indicated it had eaten a deer about a week ago. Another time, I asked him about a high-pitched squeaking sound, and Sondro informed me that it was a special type of poison dart frog. He left the path and searched in the jungle for a few moments, then showed us a tiny brown frog he had uncovered in the middle of some leaves. I absolutely could not believe that he had followed the sound to that tiny frog camouflaged so well in the middle of the rainforest.

Frogs seemed to pervade our time at the Chalalán; we saw five different types in total. Sondro found several rare Suriname toads, which are visible only at night and look like squashed brown leaves when floating in murky water. He poked one to demonstrate how they act dead as a form of protection. Apparently, a visiting researcher claimed that none of these frogs existed in the area. It turned out that he had come in the wrong season because Sondro had subsequently discovered them in the shallow stream several months later. On the way to our cabin that night, the beam of my flashlight illuminated a brilliant green frog with its long sticky toes curled around a thin vertical branch, peering right at me. The scene was straight out of those ubiquitous posters encouraging conservation of the rainforest. But perhaps my most dramatic amphibian encounter was with a brown, lumpy tree frog in the shower! After watching it hop up the wall, I quickly wrapped myself up and dragged poor Sondro into the bathroom for consultation. He assured me that the species was not poisonous, so I just went ahead and took showers with the frog and his friends every morning. They seemed to enjoy it!

In addition to frogs, we saw many other interesting wildlife, including a variety of birds (toucans, macaws, miniparrots, and the rare great patoo), snakes, scorpions, and monkeys (yellow monkeys, capuchin monkeys, and the rare dusky titi monkey). Sondro said that he had heard the great patoo for weeks before he finally located it high in the forest canopy. During night tours of the lake, we spotted the flickering red glow of caiman eyes and cautiously tiptoed by hairy spiders as big as my fist. Contrary to the Indiana Jones movies, tarantulas do not weave large webs but, rather, inhabit holes in the ground and come up at night to catch small insects. This piece of information would prove to be very important later on.

We all came away from the experience with a heightened appreciation of the rainforest as well as new skills. Sondro had several books in which he showed us the different types of jungle creatures and how they lived. Christopher, who has always had an intense interest in books, borrowed them whenever he could to read up on the animals and insects we had observed. Talk about the ultimate home-schooling field trip! Fran and I both have a background in biology, and we loved sharing our enthusiasm for nature with Christopher, proudly nurturing his growing passion for animals. To avoid scaring off the wildlife, we all practiced treading quietly and carefully, which was sometimes a challenge for a seven-year-old. We also learned to utilize all of our senses. Typically a very visual learner, I noticed myself developing better auditory skills as I became increasingly able to pick out such sounds as that high-pitched squeak of the poison dart frog, the soft repetitive whisper of the great patoo, and the distinctive melody of the oropendola, a weaver bird whose lyrical song spans more octaves than an opera singer. We all became increasingly comfortable with life in the rainforest and were disappointed to see our short time at the lodge come to an end.

Back in Rurre we stayed at the basic but very accommodating Hotel Tuichi while we geared up for our next adventure. The hotel hung hammocks in the central courtyard, and we spent hours chatting with the extremely friendly, hard-working young manager, getting tips and advice on arranging our tour into the pampas. Several different agencies provide a tour to these wetlands. Folks who negotiated the cheapest tours (US$11 a day per person) complained that they had to sleep on the ground. For that price, I'm not sure what else they expected. Tourists chartering the most expensive tours (US$40 a day per person) had private beds and showers but did not have much to say about the star attraction, the wildlife. We planned to spend somewhere in the middle of the range (about US$20 a day per person), and the manager directed us to Agencia Fluvial next door. Coincidentally, the owner, Tico, was the very same person who rescued Yossi Ginsberg from the jungle years ago. It was comforting to know that such a knowledgeable person would be around if anything went awry.

As we readied the jeep for our tour, we quickly bonded with other members of our group, a lively collection of ten travelers from Great Britain, Australia, Germany, the Netherlands, and the United States. We rode for three hours past the tiny town of Reyes and then canoed on the Yacuma River through the pampas for several more hours to enjoy the flora and fauna. The pampas consist of natural grasses that stretch for many acres and fill with water during the rainy season. In the dry season, the river lowers to reveal the plants and wildlife hidden below the surface. Some rivers almost dry up completely so that visitors can see fish splashing around in them, just like an episode of *National Geographic Explorer*. Animals congregate at the dwindling water sources to feed and drink, rendering them highly visible to passersby such as ourselves in canoes. Within a few feet of our boat, we saw dozens of caimans, some over six feet long, resting with their enormous mouths wide open to reveal rows of shiny, formidable teeth. Large families of capybaras munched on reeds at the water's edge. The biggest rodents in the world, capybaras can grow up to 100 pounds, rivaling an average size dog. We counted dozens of types of birds, including toucans, storks, ibises, eagles, and kingfishers. Our group was even lucky enough to witness a heroic battle between a heron and a poisonous green snake. Our guide told us that the bird would have to bite off and discard the snake's head to avoid ingesting its poison. Ultimately, the heron won, and we cheered her on as she flew away with her prize.

In contrast to Sondro's deep-seated respect for the environment, the pampas guides tended to manhandle the animals. Catching an anaconda seemed to be some type of macho competition among them. While one guide wrestled with a massive snake twisted around the roots of a tree, our guide, Oscar, stopped the boat and encouraged everyone to touch it. Oscar really wanted to pick one up and drape it over us, but our ecologically-minded group actively discouraged him from doing so. Another traveler told us about a guide who tied up a caiman for photo opportunities and then caught baby ones and let them run around the bottom of the canoe for the benefit of the tourists. Christopher, Fran, and I were alarmed at their mistreatment of the animals, and we worried about its impact on the delicate ecosystem in years to come. Like the ill-fated flamingos in the Galápagos Islands, present tourist demand for these types of experiences pressures the locals into providing them but may cause the long-term disappearance of the very same animals that visitors are coming to see.

Case in point, we made another stop to feed some bananas to a group of adorable little yellow monkeys. After watching the other travelers have such a good time, we couldn't resist allowing Christopher to participate in the fun despite our reluctance to encourage the monkey's reliance on people for food. Later, at our campsite, we were greeted by Pedro, a huge caiman who routinely ate the rubbish from our meals. Once I washed my hands at the water's edge and was startled by a greeting from our resident pet, rising up from the water looking for a handout (literally). Before we left the site I took a picture of Christopher near Pedro. That picture still scares me to death. Within the viewfinder Christopher appeared to be at a safe distance from Pedro, but once developed the photo shows little space between the two. I call it my "bad parent" picture and even took it out of the photo album until Fran teased me so much I felt obliged to include it again. Given their increasing dependence on humans, it is easy to forget that these animals are still wild and dangerous.

My "bad parent" picture; Christopher posing with "Pedro"

For two nights we slept in a communal structure consisting of a tarp stretched over us and the sides staked into the dirt ground. Mosquito nets protected our individual cots. At first I was concerned about the thinness of the mattresses, as my back is quite unforgiving in these types of circumstances. For fear of evoking the "spoiled American" image, I didn't say anything to my tent mates. As I reluctantly retired to bed that night, I was thrilled to discover that Christopher and Fran had secretly saved the day. By adding Christopher's mattress to my own, they provided me with double-padded luxury. Despite my weak protests, they insisted on sleeping together in Fran's small cot. What a wonderful family I have! I slept in comfort until awakened by yet another surprise, not nearly as pleasant as the first. Horrific guttural noises rang out through the forest, coming from right above our makeshift shelter. The deep, sputtering snorts and hoots sounded like a supernatural choir of the damned. I lay there, eyes scrunched shut, trying not to breathe or make a sound. Thankful that I was in the middle of the group, I hoped that the scary beasts would first devour those unfortunate tent mates closest to the flimsy walls, thus allowing me a quick get-away if necessary. After about five terrifying minutes of silently planning my escape route, the alarming sound slowly drifted away. When it appeared safe to come out, we all tentatively emerged from beneath our mosquito nets and sleeping bags. Timidly asking each other what could possibly have made such a racket, Oscar informed us that we had just been serenaded by a large group of howler monkeys, who promptly raided our supply of bananas as compensation for this performance. I added the sound to my growing list of recognizable jungle noises, and it soon became one of my favorites.

Our day featured a long hike through the pampas. The sharp, shoulder-high grasses sliced into any exposed flesh like a giant paper cut. Besieged by reeds towering over his head, poor Christopher got the brunt of them. After his third or fourth wound, Fran hitched him up on his shoulders and they carried on, unscathed. At the pampas' edge, we passed by another tour group languishing in the shade of a tree near the depleted river. Unmotivated to continue, they smugly declared that they had sent their guide off to bring them an anaconda. We promptly dubbed them the "Lazy Group" and giggled at their lack of initiative.

Catching piranha in the Bolivian pampas

Intrepid travelers ourselves, we gallantly followed Oscar along the riverbank, despite intense humidity and fierce mosquitoes, in quest of the elusive anaconda. Thanks to Fran's keen eyes, we were rewarded with four glimpses of the huge reptiles in various colors, one reaching up to 15 feet. At the end of our trek, we relaxed by a shallow pool where a nest of over 30 caimans had just hatched. The little lizard-like babies appeared a bit shell-shocked as they slowly advanced into the cool water. On the return trip we ran into the browbeaten guide of the Lazy Group, still searching half-heartedly for an anaconda. He happily joined our energetic troop for a while until the time came to return to his lethargic flock. As we braved the biting grasses for a second time, Fran emerged as the hero of the day. While the rest of us had enough trouble just dragging our own bodies back to the starting point, he managed to carry a 50-pound, squirmy child on his shoulders as well.

Piranha fishing was next on the itinerary. Oscar handed out simple hooks tied onto fishing line, and we baited these with bits of meat. After throwing the line in the water, the trick was to quickly jerk the fish up into the boat before it stole the bait. Some folks soon got the hang of it and caught several fish, while others of us did not have much luck. Fran caught about six, I barely managed to catch one, and poor Christopher became increasingly frustrated as the piranhas kept swiping his bait. Later, our cook breaded and fried them whole, and they turned out to be a delicious treat. Being polite, Fran and I left the last one in the serving pan. We both still regret that decision, but the image of that delightful candlelit evening spent socializing with our new friends, deep in the wilderness, with the unique sounds of the pampas all around us, lingers on.

To beat the sticky heat, I welcomed a swim in the river alongside the caimans and piranhas. Oscar reassured us that one area was safe, but we believed him only after he tested the waters first. Without proper showers, I even brought my shampoo and soap in with me although a rugged East German named Sven pointed out that the chemicals in the shampoo were not very environmentally friendly. I was torn between being ecologically conscious and having clean hair. When the cook asked to borrow some and began to lather up, I broke down and guiltily used a dab. After a few minutes, the Lazy Group paddled by. We

Capybaras, the biggest rodents on earth

cheerfully greeted their guide and invited him to join us. "Swim?" He looked hopefully at his group. They remained sprawled out on the boat, barely making the effort to shake their heads no. Disappointed, he sadly paddled away. Instead, pink river dolphins swam with us, their salmon-colored backs appearing oddly out of place in the muddy, opaque river. Some small fish began nibbling at Fran and Sven, and after hearing them yelp, it didn't take much to get me out of the water.

A serene moment during our last morning in the pampas created one of my nicest memories of the trip. I poured myself some coffee and walked to a quiet spot on the river. On the way I came face-to-face with a band of little yellow monkeys, no doubt searching for food. They surrounded me, chattering in a friendly but somewhat insistent way. Once they realized I had nothing to offer, they loudly expressed their irritation and moved on. When I sat down at the water's edge, I was delighted to see two dolphins, a fully grown grey female and an adolescent male, its developing back a mottled gray and pink. Lifting their bodies in graceful curves, they circled the area for a few moments before swimming away. I finished my coffee and headed back to camp, paying silent tribute to a truly special place in the world.

The return trip to Rurre and on to La Paz presented a new set of obstacles. Finding ourselves in a dusty, make-shift "bar" in Reyes while reloading the jeep, we took advantage of our reentry into civilization and treated ourselves to a cold one. Before I knew it, Sven had convinced me to sing karaoke with him to the tune of "Born to Be Wild." I must admit that my pitch was definitely a bit wild! Barely making it out of there before the rotten vegetables started flying, we continued intact to Rurre and prepared to fly back to La Paz. Easier said than done! We checked into the tiny airline office and waited for hours, only eventually to be told that the plane had never even left the city due to bad weather conditions. Hotel Tuichi was full, so we spent the rest of our day hunting around for another hotel. Over the next two days, we became permanent fixtures of the cramped, hot, dusty airline office. Our sanity was preserved only by the discovery of a huge, clean, refreshing swimming pool right up the street from our temporary residence. The kindly owner served food and drinks pool-side, and colorful birds and animals joined the guests lounging

Rainy season in La Paz

on the well-manicured ground. Due to our numerous false starts with the airlines, we left and returned so frequently that we soon became a running joke with the owner, and he graciously waived our entrance fee after a while. Thank God for that pool.

A Close Encounter with the False Police

We finally made it to La Paz, and the staff at Posada El Carretero warmly greeted us, handing over a document indicating that our long-awaited supplies from the U.S. were being held at the Customs office. Two weeks beforehand, we had mailed home some souvenirs and completed workbooks, sewn up in a muslin cover by a blind woman stationed near the post office door. While there, we introduced ourselves to the gentleman at the Customs office and inquired about the procedure for receiving a parcel from abroad. We figured that by getting to know someone in Customs, we were less likely to have incoming items "lost" or stolen. The official treated us with the utmost respect and our package subsequently arrived without incident. However, my father had insured the package for US$200, written clearly on the mailing label. The man pointed to a posted sign indicating that we were only allowed to import items worth up to US$100 from a foreign country. Beyond that we were required to pay a 30 percent tax on the total amount so that we owed US$60 for our package. Yikes! Extremely apologetic, he awkwardly admitted that it was a lot of money for such a small box, but he had no choice. How frustrating that we had not noticed the sign earlier so that we could have alerted my father and avoided the fee. Still anxious to retrieve the package, we grudgingly proceeded to take the invoice to a local bank, paid the tax, obtained a receipt, and then brought it back to the post office in exchange for the parcel.

The whole process ate up the better part of a day, but when we opened the package back at our hotel, it seemed as if Christmas had come two weeks early. Unable to find tampons for the last five months, I had written a desperate email asking my mother to send them. I reasoned that if a box was already coming from home, the remaining space could be filled with certain types of shampoo, conditioner, facial cleaner, toothpaste, dental floss, deodorant, and camera batteries that were not otherwise available in South America. My itchy scalp, sore teeth, and distressed skin cried out for relief from my favorite brands. My parents even tossed in some extra Harry Potter cards for Christopher, thus breathing new life into our overplayed card game, and a little friend called Scabbers, the mouse turned villain in the third *Harry Potter* novel. Despite the high price tag, we felt unimaginably grateful to my parents for these small luxuries that made such a big difference.

We set out for the Internet to email our thanks. With Fran checking work-related messages and Christopher deep in the throws of *juegos en red* (computer games networked so that several children can play them together in the same café), I decided to return to our hotel on my own. Lost in thought, I was suddenly jolted back to reality by a false policeman. The man claimed to be working undercover tracking down tourists with cocaine, and he asked to see my identification and to search my backpack. Another man, his accomplice, walked by, and the alleged policeman asked to look in his bag. The accomplice opened his pack and then motioned for me to do the same. Fortunately, I was prepared for them, having been well informed about this type of scam. In addition to warning posters donning our hostel walls, many *viajeros* in Bolivia had related personal stories about being robbed by people who pose as policemen searching for drugs. Often working in pairs, one acts as a plain-clothed policeman while the other pretends to be just a businessman passing by. The businessman goes along with the "policeman's" requests in an effort to normalize the situation and trick the traveler into complying with him. The "policeman" asks for ID and then, through sleight of hand, he steals the person's money. Sometimes, they coerce the travelers into boarding a passing taxi, telling the driver (who is also in on the scam) to go to the "police station." The cab pulls into a deserted side street where they rob them. The crooks may also check the person's bag and remove a camera or other valuables so quickly that the victim does not even realize his belongings are missing until much later.

Luckily I knew not to give them anything, but being a woman alone on an empty street with two dishonest men created a very uncomfortable predicament. They blocked my path towards the hotel, and when I tried to get around them, the "policeman" put out his hand to stop me. I insisted that I did not have anything on me while considering my options. I was wearing bulky clothing that hid my neck pouch with our passports, some credit cards, and money tucked inside. I also carried a daypack with our guidebook, camera, and a few other items. The "policeman" continued demanding to search my bag, and I stalled for time, alternating between pretending not to understand him and indicating that my husband had our valuables. After a few moments, one of the hotel staff appeared at the end of the street. I immediately pushed my way around the two thieves, striding quickly up the hill towards her. I thought that if they followed me and I needed to run away, at least there would be two of us handling the situation. At that point, the "policeman" smiled, politely said "goodbye," and let me go without any trouble. I joined the woman and recounted the scenario; she continued to watch the crooks go down the street as I sped to the hotel and updated our trusted innkeeper. He raced out of the building in pursuit of the men but was unsuccessful in catching them. After that incident I avoided walking almost anywhere by myself. I considered myself very lucky that nothing worse had occurred, particularly after receiving notice over the Internet two years later that organized criminals had begun posing as taxi drivers and then kidnapping tourists to obtain their bank codes and subsequently drain their bank accounts. In 2005, one German couple died as a result. It is therefore very important for anyone considering a trip to Bolivia to research the current safety concerns of the country and take appropriate precautions.

Keeping a careful watch on our belongings at all times was also essential, especially when loading and unloading the buses. In addition to locks on the zippers, we strapped or locked our bags together whenever possible. Furthermore, we developed a routine for taxi rides. We had heard of another scam where two women secured their backpacks on the top of a taxi, and when they tried to get into the vehicle, the driver drove away with almost everything they owned. To avoid this problem, we always opened at least one door before putting anything in or on the taxi. Christopher and I would typically slide in with our most important bags (a daypack and a bathroom pack), and Fran would hassle with loading the rest of the luggage (two backpacks and Christopher's book bag). Similarly, once we stopped at our destination, Fran would get out and deal with the luggage while I would have the change ready

The Witches' Market off Calle Sagárnaga

and wait until everything else was unloaded before leaving the taxi. Of course, rip-offs vary by country so that travelers should become familiar with the dangers unique to that area. For example, Daveed pointed out that in certain countries, taxi drivers may try to kidnap the woman or child if they used this method. To maximize safety, it is important to check the guidebook and/or websites and talk to locals and other travelers about these concerns. Once we developed our system, Christopher was very good at opening the door and hopping in quickly with me. He was really getting to be quite the little traveler!

Despite the run-in with the false police, La Paz began to grow on us. We found Bolivians to be very friendly and helpful, and their attitude towards foreigners was much more laid-back than the constant hustle we had received earlier throughout its neighbor, Peru. We understood Bolivian Spanish very clearly, perhaps due to our increasing familiarity with the language, but also because the people were patient and tolerant of our efforts. As an added bonus, prices in Bolivia were very low, and we were able to indulge in such luxuries as a fancy Sunday buffet brunch at the Hotel Paris, one of the nicest establishments in town. Finally, the city itself contained some interesting nooks and crannies. Along Calle Sagárnaga, we stocked up on hand-made alpaca sweaters, hats, and gloves to protect ourselves against the fast-approaching rainy season. Turning a corner, we found the Mercado de Hechicería (Witches' Market), sporting stalls stuffed with unusual natural remedies, including llama fetuses. Although the museums kept erratic hours, we managed to see some interesting cultural and handicraft exhibits at the Museo Nacional de Etnografía y Folklore (National Museum of Ethnography and Folklore) and the Museo Nacional de Arqueología (National Museum of Archaeology), housed in a grand building adorned with stone carvings reflecting native motifs.

We purchased warm clothing in the nick of time, as torrential downpours soon dumped masses of water on the city every afternoon. Already difficult to navigate due to the tiny sidewalks, steep hills, and crazy traffic patterns, the streets of La Paz became virtual rivers running over three inches deep. Several times we saw locals slip and fall on the treacherous walkways, and not to be left out, we took a few tumbles ourselves. The tarp overhanging the courtyard at our hotel became sodden with hail and rain and eventually collapsed. With everything dripping and disintegrating all around us, it was time to head for higher ground.

Only two hours away by bus, the tiny colonial town of Sorata snuggles high in the Andean hilltops. We chose a hotel with the best view, appropriately named Hostal El Mirador (The View Hotel). The windows on both walls of our large corner room exposed a breathtaking panorama of the mountains. Breakfast on the terrace overlooked a deep gorge that stretched on for miles, although Christopher was much more interested in the antics of the family's pets. While meandering along the dusty streets, we scrutinized a menu posted beside the door of one of the restaurants clustered around the central square. After five months of *pollo, papas, y pan* (chicken, potatoes, and bread), we were delighted to find a few Italian dishes instead of the typical Bolivian fare. We eagerly investigated the offerings of the other restaurants, and curiously, all four of them displayed an identical Italian menu. Why did all the restaurants in town offer the exact same meals, and such an unlikely cuisine at that? Lacking any other explanation, we just shrugged and said our mantra. "It's Bolivia." We ended up eating pasta in the main square for the entire length of our stay.

The local children provided a welcome diversion from the monotony of our Italian meals. Enthralled by Christopher's Game Boy, some fights broke out as they vied for a turn at the electronic toy. Amidst refereeing the disagreements, we also discovered that the Bolivian Duvacell batteries did not last nearly as long as the original American Duracell brand, although the packaging looked remarkably similar to the untrained eye. Children were not the only ones interested in our U.S. products; South Americans of all ages frequently asked us about the prices and quality of U.S. brands. After watching many of our Bolivian purchases instantaneously break, quit, or fall apart, it was easy to understand why. However, even after acknowledging that U.S. products could be a worthwhile investment, it still struck us as odd to see a woman wearing a traditional skirt, bowler hat, and hand-woven alpaca sweater with a Tommy Hilfiger T-shirt stretched over the top.

"Only to Give, Not to Take"

Following the call of the jungle, we traveled southwest towards our next volunteer opportunity at an organization known as Comunidad Inti Wara Yassi (CIWY). We had planned to pass quickly through Cochabamba, stopping only to change buses and pick up needed supplies for CIWY. However, the large, modern city soon sidetracked us with its many diverse restaurants and exciting nightlife. On a busy street lined with enticing eateries, the trendy, art-inspired Picasso restaurant served excellent Mexican food and *trencitos*, little trains of six different specialty drinks for under US$4. The next day we discovered a vegetarian buffet restaurant named Gopal, and as we struggled to comprehend the process of obtaining and paying for the delicious-smelling food, a local woman approached us to explain the procedure. Not only did she join us for lunch, but she also proceeded to show us around the city, introducing us to some beautiful parks and landmarks. Reminiscent of our lady friend in Quito, we were again astounded at the friendliness of the Latino people and relished our time spent with her.

Even our hotel, the family-run Hotel Oruro, turned out to be a wonderful surprise. While we had originally chosen it due to its proximity to the bus station, our nicely decorated room came with a functioning cable TV and a sparkling clean bathroom spouting lots of hot water. We hadn't encountered such luxury in over a month, not since Arequipa, Peru. In the days ahead, while covered in animal filth and sweat at CIWY, we often longingly recalled the seemingly palatial Hotel Oruro.

We bid the friendly family a fond farewell and boarded the rickety bus to the tiny jungle town of Villa Tunari. There we eagerly anticipated meeting up with our old friend Daveed, who was already volunteering at CIWY, the only wildlife refuge in Bolivia. A unique organization run almost entirely by volunteers, CIWY originated as a project to help Bolivian street children. At their initiative, the budding agency evolved into its present-day mission, to rescue and rehabilitate exotic animals of the rainforest kept illegally in captivity. CIWY requires a 15-day commitment from its volunteers, so we planned to stay for at least that length of time. While we were looking forward to the experience, I was wary of how well Christopher would be able to remain committed to the project. Fran and I stressed to Christopher the potential difficulties of the assignment, but he really wanted to work with the animals, so we all agreed to do so as a family.

In the middle of an afternoon rainstorm, the bus dropped us off on the side of the main road in Villa Tunari. Ducking under the sagging canopy of a roadside restaurant in an effort to avoid the deluge, we ate a very large lunch of local fish cooked whole. When the rain lightened up, we dragged our stuff around the small tropical settlement in search of a place to stay. The humidity engulfed us, covering us in sweat. Struggling with the bulk of our luggage, Fran's dripping shirt looked like he had been out in the earlier downpour. We headed for the town plaza, assuming that there would be some sleeping options there, but the only affordable, albeit overpriced, room available had a trail of ants crossing the width of one wall. Unwilling to continue our sticky quest, we unenthusiastically agreed to bunk with the unwanted intruders and set off for CIWY. While CIWY encourages volunteers to use their facilities, the rooms and showers there were so moldy and disgusting that I insisted on investigating cleaner options. (Fortunately, the volunteers have improved the CIWY residences dramatically since then.) After a joyful reunion with Daveed, he shared his carefully garnered information regarding the other sleeping arrangements throughout the tiny town, with particular emphasis on the time and intensity of any resident rooster crowing. The next day we moved into a clean, modern set of rooms, without any roosters, above a small shop on the main street. We opted for a cramped room with three beds in order to take advantage of the private bathroom.

We sure came to appreciate that shower. The work at CIWY was hard, hot, and dirty, but the rewards in getting to know the animals and people there far outweighed the difficulties. On our first introduction to the park, we walked into the capuchin monkey area around feeding time. Quick as a wink, two monkeys ran down my back and into my pants. When they began rummaging around in my underwear, I broke down and started squealing for help. Meanwhile, Fran sported a matching set draped around his neck. Connected by their tails, the little devils seesawed back and forth as they pushed and pulled at each other, jockeying for space. Christopher wisely stood a few steps back down the path, and when some monkeys began to approach him, the volunteers became alarmed and told us all to leave. Many of the monkeys had been abused by children while in captivity and could be very hostile towards them. Ironically, in exchange for the use of the land, the government requires the park to remain open to the public. The unruly children of the large, extended Bolivian families often taunted the animals and strayed from the trail. Volunteers working with the monkeys tried to ensure the safety of the park's guests; however, despite their best efforts, these children often got bit during their visits.

As a precaution, the volunteer coordinator warned us at the outset that our son was not to work in the monkey park. Instead, Christopher and I were assigned to take care of the six bird cages and three turtle pens near the main building. After seeing the monkey and coati bites sustained by the other volunteers, we were both quite happy to oblige. Coatis, deceptively cute little animals that look like raccoons, have ringed tails and long snouts full of sharp teeth. Also wary of the monkeys and coatis, Fran quickly busied himself constructing cages and doing general maintenance. He particularly loved lugging heavy loads of supplies through the rainforest to the top of a mountain where the volunteers were building a cage for a puma. Even the unflappable Daveed suffered through an incident in which two monkeys climbed on each of his shoulders and severely bit his ears. After that he stopped working with the monkeys and put his efforts into supervising a rambunctious baby puma instead. Since his email address was originally Monkey Face, we began calling him Monkey Ears in memory of the event, and the affectionate nickname remains to this day.

Although malaria reportedly does not exist at CIWY, many of us took malarial prophylactics as a precaution anyway. Lariam was our drug of choice, and it yielded some interesting psychotropic side effects. Fran and I found that our dreams intensified, lasted longer, and became much more realistic. In that hazy state between sleep and relative alertness, I believed each dream so intently that much time would pass in my day before I could be convinced otherwise. One of my favorite volunteers, a pretty British girl named Kate, said that she frequently woke up her boyfriend, James, in the middle of the night, stressed out about the monkeys escaping again. "Look, there's another one!" she would shout, pointing around the room. Disturbingly, Daveed suffered from a lack of motor skills after taking his tablets, to the point where he could not even put on his backpack without assistance. Fortunately, beyond the dreams, which really could be quite enjoyable, Fran, Christopher, and I did not experience any difficulties.

Taking care of the birds and turtles started out as a fairly easy task, but after about four days we received many new birds and it developed into a real challenge. The numbers increased from six cages to sixteen. I became very overwhelmed and, unfortunately, directed some of my frustration at Christopher. Despite his initial enthusiasm, he spent much of his time hanging out in the hammock talking Harry Potter with the other volunteers who passed by or playing with the six kids that lived in the room next door. I felt resentful of his ability to relax and enjoy himself while I was stuck cleaning out bird poop and trying frantically to feed all the birds on time. The responsibilities had grown too large for me and a seven-year-old to handle, so thankfully, other volunteers soon pitched in to help us. I was especially touched by how many of the people at the reserve offered their support with the staggering amount of birds, despite having so much of their own work to do.

While I don't really consider myself to be an animal lover, I adored our little charges. I loved watching a group of eleven white-headed parakeets snuggle together, kissing and grooming each other. One boisterous parrot showed up at mealtimes and landed on my shoulder, squawking loudly as he waited for a handout. I found this very endearing until a fellow volunteer told me that the bird had become impatient with him and tweaked his earlobe. "It hurt! A lot!" he insisted. That news, in combination with Daveed's ear-damaging incident, rendered me much less enamored with the shoulder routine. I subsequently spent a lot of time removing the parrot from his perch near my ears. Another notable bird was a feisty toucan that Christopher named Draco Malfoy, after an evil character from the *Harry Potter* series. Draco apparently had been kept in a cage so small that the poor thing had been unable to turn around completely for ten years. Whenever I tried to feed him or clean his cage, he made a warning sound by rapidly clicking his long tongue against the length of his bill and then snapped at me. I frequently overturned food trays and water bowls in an effort to avoid his sharp beak. Eventually

Draco was moved to a much larger cage, where he could hide in the back at feeding time. He didn't give me any more problems after that and became quite a likable bird. One brave volunteer even fed him by hand, but I was never that courageous. We also took care of a very sick parrot named George. He arrived with a beak so damaged that he initially needed to be fed with a syringe, but he kept improving and eating more foods every day. Very friendly and docile, he took bananas gently from our outstretched hands. By the end of our stay, he was eating seeds and grains again. We were so proud!

As in the Madidi National Park, my hearing became increasingly tuned in to various bird calls. Soon I was able to recognize the very soft cry of a hawk, which sounded strangely vulnerable compared with its powerful beak and claws. Whenever I heard it, I ran inside to find some raw meat. The hawk swooped within a foot of my head and took the meat right out of my hand. His gracefulness and freedom of flight lifted my spirits whenever I saw him.

The stinkiest job assigned to Christopher and me involved cleaning out the turtle "tanks." Luckily, I don't have a very good sense of smell, and this shortcoming turned out to be a benefit in completing this nasty task. We did not have decent plugs for the makeshift tanks, and after just a day or two, maggots would eat the bits of meat caught in the cloth we were using to stop up the drains. Although that part of the job was incredibly gross, I found it very relaxing to watch the turtles swimming around while the water filled the tubs. Interestingly, Fran and I noticed that one smaller turtle, most likely a male, kept harassing another larger turtle, probably a female. The smaller turtle rushed up to the larger one, head-on, and then repeatedly fluttered its front flippers close to the other's face. Laughing about how irritated the larger turtle must feel, we guessed that the behavior must be some kind of mating ritual. Sure enough, when Christopher and I were cleaning the tank a few days later, we saw a strange shiny object on the cement floor. I bent over to examine it but unfortunately, another turtle beat me to it. One bite and yolk began oozing out of the egg. Christopher, who is quite sensitive to any type of trauma to animals, became very upset and needed the better part of the morning to get over it. Also distressed, I questioned the veterinarian about the exposed egg, trying to get some ideas about

Daveed poses with rascally Roy

what to do if another egg materialized in the future. He informed me that unfortunately, the pens do not have sand for the turtles to bury their eggs as they normally would in the wild. Sadly, CIWY could not help the turtles breed.

Occasionally we managed to squeeze in a much-needed break to visit the different areas of the park, and we all became attached to some of the other animals at CIWY in addition to our own charges. A lovely British couple, Suzanna and Dan, made a special effort to introduce Christopher and me to a large puma named Gato during an intense afternoon shower. We also were invited to accompany an ocelot as it was released back into the jungle. My favorite creatures were an enchanting group of baby armadillos, whose rubbery texture reminded me of squeaky toys. Constantly moving, the little beggars would insistently root around in my lap, searching for food. Fran enjoyed visiting a cluster of tiny brown bats that hung from the ceiling of a supply closet. Roy, the playful spotted puma in Daveed's care, quickly endeared himself to our son. Whenever Christopher walked by, Roy loved to spring out of his hiding place and tackle him around the ankles. Daveed tried to minimize human contact with the puma by using a feathery toy instead of his hands to interact with him. Always thinking creatively, Daveed put this toy to good use; every time a rooster crowed, he would dangle it annoyingly in front of Roy, encouraging him to pounce. We all hoped that one day Roy would help eradicate the crowing rooster population.

Hadar, one of the long-term Israeli volunteers, took a particular liking to Christopher. He knew that Christopher really wanted to spend some time with the monkeys, and Hadar had extensive experience with them. He coached our son on proper primate etiquette and then carefully supervised a trip to visit the spider monkeys in a different part of the park. Christopher absolutely loved grooming one of the gangly black monkeys and couldn't wait to tell everyone about it. He was so excited to see the capuchin monkeys later that day that I decided to accompany them to the park. Christopher sat down on a bench, and one of the small brown monkeys immediately jumped on his lap. She hugged him and babbled in his ear just as any human mother would do with her doting child. Apparently she couldn't have children of her own so she seemed to have "adopted" Christopher as a substitute. Unfortunately

CIWY staff member shows off her babies, including my favorite baby armadillos

another monkey barged onto the scene, possibly jealous of all the maternal attention being showered on Christopher. The two started fighting, and despite Hadar's best efforts, Christopher got a shallow bite on his arm. He behaved so calmly that I didn't even know he had been bit until Hadar pointed it out. I took him to the first aid station and the park director, Nena, cleaned him up. About an hour later Christopher was begging for permission to return to the park. Despite my understandable hesitation, I just couldn't deny his enthusiasm for the monkeys, and the second visit went off without a hitch (or a bite).

As an added bonus, we forged several relationships with like-minded travelers volunteering at CIWY, and we valued these friendships at least as much as our experience with the animals. In addition to Daveed, we enjoyed swapping tales from the road with fellow travel addicts Kate and James, as well as a high-spirited American named Murray. While originally planning to travel throughout South America for a year, Murray made the mistake of landing first in Buenos Aires, and after nine months he had tremendous difficulty tearing himself away from that fabulous country. Another delightful couple, Frank and Alma, with a biting Irish wit took up residence in a room across the hall. Alma gave me a hard time whenever she overheard us playing the card game, Harry Potter. "You need to let him win a couple of games. You are too hard on him!" she insisted. "Life is hard!" I responded. "It's not that hard!" she shot back at me, but I still never managed to throw a game. At lunchtime we all frequented a local "restaurant" comprised of a cement patio with some plastic tables and a grill. The friendly owner willingly tolerated sweaty, stinky volunteers, serving us tasty sandwiches and cold peach juice that just hit the spot. We often gathered together after work as well, eating hot *empañadas* prepared by the mother of Christopher's six playmates living at the CIWY office building or sharing inexpensive communal meals before dropping from exhaustion into our beds.

Our eclectic group of volunteers made for some very interesting and festive intercultural celebrations. One evening, the Israeli contingency treated us to a traditional Hanukah feast. They fried several types of donuts, lit the Menorah, sang some Hebrew songs, and shared the story behind the holiday. A few days later, one of them made a very touching speech on his last day at the reserve. With tears in his eyes, he commented that it was amazing for him to see so many different people come together and work towards a common goal, "only to give, not to take." Considering the turmoil that he and the rest of his countrymen go through every day, his words were particularly poignant to us all. A few days later, on my 37th birthday, Daveed and Fran cooked up an elaborate dinner over the primitive gas cook stoves. Because other volunteers had made spaghetti the night before, they had to change their original dinner menu but the resulting frittata was a big success. Every single person connected with the park was in attendance, making the night particularly special. Christopher even got many of the guests excited about playing his Harry Potter card game, and he organized the large group into three competing teams. The heady mix of delicious food, cheap drinks, and Harry Potter made for a fabulous evening. What a memorable way to spend my birthday!

Keen on giving something back to our new friends and perhaps raising some money for CIWY, I agreed to make lunch with Kate for the volunteers. The irony is that, while I never use my beautiful kitchen at home with all the latest conveniences, I chose instead to cook a meal for 30 people on essentially camping equipment in the middle of the Bolivian rainforest. Arriving at the reserve somewhat distracted by this upcoming challenge and in a hurry to serve breakfast to the loudly squawking birds, I began to pull on one of the Wellington boots I had left there overnight. I immediately felt a very substantial movement in the toe of the boot! Utter terror began to set in as I realized what might be lurking there. I quickly pulled it off to see a gigantic spider on my right foot. The thing was brownish black, at least three inches across, and had a body about the size of my thumb. Being the calm, rational person that I am, I shrieked bloody murder and began hopping around the patio, flailing my foot wildly in an attempt to kick it off. Luckily the very frightened spider jumped off on its own and scuttled away. It took me almost five minutes to put on my boot after that. Daveed, cranky after a long night of trying to keep the baby puma out of his bed, started chewing me out for waking him up with my screaming. I was not apologetic. Later I found out I was lucky on two accounts. First of all, I saw the same spider in the Orquidarium (a museum devoted to orchids and related insects) down the street and was reassured by the owner that it was not poisonous. Second, I heard about another volunteer that experienced a similar situation at CIWY, but he was bit by a tarantula and ended up going to the hospital. So I suppose things could have been much worse, but it was months before I was able to put my shoes on without using some relaxation techniques first. Fortunately, our lunch fared much better and received rave reviews. Murray said our potato salad made him feel as if he was back home celebrating the 4th of July.

During our work at CIWY, our Western mentality occasionally clashed with the Bolivian way of thinking, and some decisions struck us as odd. For example, two birds remained together in the same cage even though one of them was clearly very ill. When I asked about it, I was told, "Because they are friends." One day I was quite frustrated to find the end of our perfectly functioning hose sliced off for use as a "splash guard" for the sink. While to me, a little water sprayed on filthy clothing in the rainforest did not seem to be a significant problem, the hose was rendered useless for many of its former purposes that I conducted several times a day. After Fran and Daveed produced several well-made, secure cages, a staff member wasted valuable time and materials in fashioning a poorly constructed cage that was easily escapable by our sneaky little charges. The dome-shaped top was supposed to "give it more air," but in reality made it nearly impossible to keep the birds contained and failed to keep the lightweight plastic secured on the cage to protect the birds from the rain. Of particular concern, a bird that was ready to be released back into the wild stayed at the refuge. The only reason I was given for this was that the organization would be accused of selling it if it disappeared. While I felt that we were providing a suitable environment for all of the animals, these types of scenarios left me feeling unclear regarding our mission and goals for them. Instead, I simply resigned myself to our usual explanation, "It's Bolivia."

The encroaching rain rendered transportation to CIWY increasingly difficult. Our Canadian friends, Rich and Cyndi, valiantly attempted to visit us at the reserve but were unsuccessful due to a massive mudslide that held up all traffic in either direction. After sitting for about 12 hours, they followed the locals' lead and took alternate transportation back to Cochabamba. Another volunteer on that same bus braved a more adventurous route. She had sought treatment at the hospital in

Robin and fine feathered friends

Cochabamba for an infected coati bite on her ankle. Tired of waiting, she took matters into her own hands and waded through the mud on her swollen, bandaged leg to the other side. She managed to catch a ride to Villa Tunari and showed up late that night at the reserve. Talk about going above and beyond the call of duty!

With the weather worsening, we decided to leave after our 15-day stint at CIWY. I choked up during my farewell speech as I expressed my gratitude to our newfound friends. Nena, the director, gave us special certificates to commemorate our experience as the park's first family of volunteers, and one of the staff made us each a beautiful hand-painted T-shirt. She appropriately drew a bird resembling our beloved George on my shirt, a spider monkey for Fran, and a delightful picture of the baby puma, Roy, for Christopher. As we admired the gifts, I thought about how we had come "only to give, not to take." In reality, we left carrying with us incredible memories and friendships to last our lifetime. Christopher also had the opportunity to indulge in his passion for animals and work alongside a veterinarian, an experience that will influence him and potentially his career path for the rest of his life.

We tried to cheer ourselves up by scoring the front seats of the bus back to Cochabamba. But bad Bolivian bus karma interceded again. No floor space or metal wall divided our seats from the doorway so that our feet dangled right over the front steps. Locals crammed into the scarce remaining space all around us during the many stops. Fran had one very large woman sitting right on his feet, with no possibility of moving his knees, for the entire trip. A young man thrust himself between my legs. While I tried to tolerate this for a few minutes, I finally gave in to my Western sense of propriety and pushed my legs closed in a slightly more demure and comfortable manner. Meanwhile, a boy played with a baby coati which began climbing on us. Vividly remembering the wounds resulting from nasty coati bites at the reserve, we drew the line and forced the young owner to retrieve the animal. This trip approached the hellish night ride to Arequipa as one of our worst bus experiences. But when we arrived at Cochabamba, we shook it off as soon as we saw several stalls full of shiny tinsel and natural materials to create nativity scenes. The extravagant Christmas decorations seemed out of place in the hot, dusty Bolivian streets but set a festive mood for the unique celebrations that lay ahead.

Christmas in Bolivia

Full of holiday cheer, we headed on to Sucre. True to our other incomprehensible Bolivian experiences, confusion even surrounds the nation's capital; La Paz is the seat of the government and therefore often referred to as the capital city, yet Sucre is the legal capital. We had heard wonderful things about this large colonial city in the center of Bolivia and were looking forward to spending Christmas and New Year's Eve there, reconnecting with fellow travelers Daveed, Canadians Rich and Cyndi, and Irish CIWY volunteers Frank and Alma. Surrounded by the beautiful Andes Mountains, Sucre lived up to its excellent reputation. The weather was warm and dry, allowing us to air out after the humidity of the rainforest. Easily navigable on foot or by local bus, the city attracts many travelers and "expats" (foreigners who relocate there from all over the world), with a resulting array of great restaurants (including French, German, Swiss, and Dutch foods), museums, tourist services, and attractions.

Relying again on recommendations from Rich and Cyndi, we stayed in a family home near the bus station. The Hernaiz family, led by their effervescent matriarch Mama Vicky, proved to be very welcoming and invited us to join them for their holiday celebrations. Their father grew grapes in the countryside, and he allowed us to sample some of his delicious red wine for the Christmas season. Extremely patient with our Spanish, they provided us with some much-needed insight into the local customs. Vincente Hernaiz explained his desire to buy elaborate presents for his nieces and nephews, but other family members discouraged him from doing so. "We don't want it to be like it is in the United States," he said. We couldn't agree more. Instead of focusing on presents, the most important themes were quality family time and spirituality. Together with Rich and Cyndi, we purchased a game for the children, and everyone had a great time playing together in the spirit of the holiday.

At our request, Mama Vicky also arranged Spanish lessons for us. While the language schools were closed for the holidays, she found teachers willing to tutor Fran and me at the house for about US$3 an hour. The individualized Spanish instruction not only enabled me to practice the language but also provided an opportunity for more in-depth cultural discussions. My teacher was *mestizo*, meaning that one of her parents was a *campesino* and the other was a city dweller of Spanish heritage. She informed me about life in the *campo*, the country, indicating that it was not nearly as difficult and unpleasant as it was often portrayed. Until recently, very few people begged in the city. Because people gave them money for their efforts, however, an alarming number of *campesinos* have flocked to the streets in the last few years. They recruit large groups of children by promising compensation to their parents, and consequently, initiate youth into the system of panhandling in the hopes of getting a few more pennies from sympathetic strangers. My teacher emphasized not to give them any money because this practice just encourages further dependency and poverty as the *campesinos* turn away from their traditional ways of making a living. The beggars were particularly prolific and forceful around the holidays, which, in turn, discouraged tourism and further impacted the local economy. As we walked down certain streets, the destitute children became angry and provocative when we did not respond to their demands. Daveed ventured out to capture some photographic images of "Christmas in Bolivia" and returned somewhat disheartened. I teased him, saying that I could show him a picture of Christmas in Bolivia. I held out my hand and said, "It's Bolivia." He wasn't impressed.

My Spanish instructor also expressed concern at how the U.S. was considering spreading herbicides or insects to kill all the coca plants. It reminded me of a prior conversation I had with a drug enforcement agent in Villa Tunari. He, too, was angry that the U.S. was trying to eliminate the use of coca leaves, a tradition that has endured in Bolivia and most other parts of South America for generations. He asked me, "Do you see anyone here in Bolivia with a cocaine problem? The problem is only in your country." I had to agree. When I asked why they bothered to follow U.S. policies, he grew sad and responded, "We need the money." In turn, I could understand the political ramifications of providing money to a government accused of drug trafficking. What a difficult decision for the Bolivian people, choosing between a centuries-old

Longest dinosaur tracks in the world preserved outside of Sucre

tradition and international aid. The high cultural price tag for foreign support weighed heavily on my mind.

In addition to enjoying our Spanish lessons, we relished every free moment spent in Sucre. Not only did we bond with the easy-going Hernaiz family, but we were also thrilled to spend time with Daveed again. He joined us in the "Dinotruck" to a site on the outskirts of town boasting the world's longest dinosaur tracks. Incredulously, we gazed up at the tracks of a carnivore overtaking its prey, a fatal struggle preserved in clay for millions of years. Daveed noted that the guide asked a question regarding dinosaurs to the group, and Christopher was the only one who supplied the correct answer. The home-schooling lessons seemed to be working splendidly. Daveed stayed with us through New Year's Eve, or as the Dutch call it, "Old and New." At his suggestion, we kicked off the festivities at a party in an authentic Dutch pub downtown and then headed back home to our host family for a huge midnight feast. As the night wore on we learned that Bolivians don red undergarments on New Year's Eve to bring them good luck in the upcoming year. We got a big kick out of watching Mama Vicky and the other women winking and flashing us a bit of red to demonstrate their adherence to the tradition. That certainly explained the preponderance of bright red underwear we saw hanging in the store windows around town. The next day Daveed whiled away the traditional New Year's Day hangover playing many rounds of Harry Potter and other games with Christopher. After that day he refused to hear anything about that lovable wizard again.

Our Irish friends, Frank and Alma, also joined us for some sightseeing around Sucre. On our first outing, I mistakenly told the bus driver that we wanted to go to the Recoleta instead of our actual destination, the Glorieta. We then spent over two hours on the bus trying to rectify the situation. The next day we fared much better, as we chanced upon a fabulous textile museum called Asur Museo de Arte Indigena. We listened to music from traditional instruments as we watched artisans weave extraordinarily complex tapestries. The regimented, symmetrical designs produced by the people of Tarabuco contrasted sharply with the disorganized, fantastical creatures in textiles created by the Jalq'a people. The tapestries provided a fascinating insight into the mentality of these two very different cultures.

Young miner deep in the bowels of Cerro Rico, Potosí

We enjoyed the weavings so much that we decided to make the pilgrimage out to the small village of Tarabuco. We boarded a bus with Rich and Cyndi one unforgettable Sunday. About a third of the way there, the bus broke down and we all got off. As we soaked up some sun by the side of the road, a truck stopped and offered us a ride. Typically used by the farm workers for transportation, the back of the truck was partially covered by a tarp, and had some wooden benches and metal posts for support. We quickly abandoned the bus and scrambled into the truck, thankful for the unique travel opportunity. The unobstructed panoramic view from our new vantage point was fantastic. Halfway through the ride, some local women got on. Other passengers began questioning them about the contents of their baskets, and before we knew it, lunch was served. The Tarabuco market proved to be *vale la pena*, or "worth the effort," to get there. We marveled at the villagers dressed in a rainbow of textiles and purchased some samples of their workmanship that hang on our wall today.

Losing the Plot

We had grown quite spoiled by Mama Vicky and her wonderful family, but it was time to press on. We were eager to see two of the greatest attractions in Bolivia, the silver mines of Potosí and the Salar, the great salt flat of Uyuni, before the rains rendered the roads impassible. After getting soaked upon arrival at Potosí, we visited the historical mint housed in an ornate, colonial building. We were most impressed by an old wooden coin press, designed to be drawn by six horses, which filled a large room. Through an agency based at our hotel, we joined a tour of the silver mines of Cerro Rico (Rich Hill) on the outskirts of Potosí. While our guide gave us some basic instructions, we marveled at the brightly colored pools of water mixed with minerals glowing red, blue, and green. A 67-year-old woman, having never taken a day off work in her life, sorted through the rubble at the entrance to the mine, hoping to spot something valuable. Chewing coca leaves and carrying gas lamps for light, we entered the mine and paid homage to El Tío (The Uncle), a spooky figure that guarantees safe passage to those who give him offerings. With El Tío on our side, we squeezed through tunnels,

Resting on the Island of the Fishermen in the Salar

some with asbestos crystallizing on the walls, and slid down thin chutes into the pitch dark. We gave all of our coca leaves away to the first miners we met, as we had trouble keeping track of the plastic bags and didn't want them to come into contact with the flames of our lamps. Deep in the bowels of the mountain, we encountered a 13-year-old boy and his father. They gave Christopher a small rock laced with minerals, and let Fran try his hand at mining with their pick in that cramped, dark space. I regretted giving all our coca leaves away instead of saving some to give to those two. Luckily, I had brought a few chocolates with me, just in case, and the boy seemed excited to have the treat. After we emerged from the ground, the guide demonstrated how to set off some dynamite, much to Christopher and Fran's delight. Unfortunately, with the exception of a friendly German named Manuel, the other members of our group whined about the dirty, claustrophobic conditions. I'm not sure what else they had expected from a mine, but despite their annoying complaints, we thought the tour was fascinating. We felt very appreciative of our lives in comparison with the hardships those people live with every day, especially the boy not much older than Christopher.

In Uyuni, we debated about how best to experience the Salar, the world's largest salt flat, covering over 4,800 square miles. Long ago, the lake was forced up from the ocean and most of the water evaporated, leaving miles and miles of flat, blindingly white salt with small, cactus-covered hills such as the Isla de los Pescadores (Island of the Fishermen) jutting out of its smooth landscape. We investigated our options for a day tour instead of the popular four-day jeep trip through the Salar to the Atacama Desert in Chile. Reputedly, the longer rides were often fraught with delays due to break-downs, horrible hostels, and unappetizing food. We had also heard mixed reviews about the sights along the way, and were concerned about how well Christopher would hold up for four days confined to a jeep. We eventually chose to spend a day in the Salar and then continue south from Uyuni into northern Argentina.

Our small tour group set out from the tiny settlement of Uyuni, and within a few minutes, we arrived at the Salar. After learning about how the locals collect and process the salt, we watched two little girls carefully bagging the end product, using a blow torch to seal the plastic.

Christopher standing on a pile of salt

Working steadily, they appeared to be about the same age as Christopher. We gladly paid them a few bolivianos in exchange for a photo. Outside, Christopher enjoyed climbing on the salt piles, shouting "Look Mom, I'm standing on our food!" We then snacked at an amazing hotel made entirely of salt, including the chairs, tables, and beds. Crumbly salt was everywhere. We wondered what it would be like to spend the night there, likening it to sleeping in a sand castle. We drove further over the unbelievably flat expanse of white to the Isla de los Pescadores, and hiked on the "island" amongst the cactus and birds to a lovely viewpoint overlooking the Salar. Fran spotted a viscacha (those cute little rabbits with tails) zipping down the trail as we returned to the jeep for a picnic lunch. While the others ate, I took a short walk by myself on the mind-boggling salt, even going so far as to sample a small slice to make sure it was real. All too soon our guide rounded us up and fought somewhat unsuccessfully to stay awake as he drove back towards town. Recapping our day, we all agreed that the short trip was perfect for us.

With the exception of our fabulous day on the Salar, we devoted all of our remaining energy to getting out of Uyuni. This experience was one of those cases in which the difference in our Western capitalistic thinking came head to head with the Bolivian transportation mentality, and the results got ugly. All travelers in Bolivia who are worth their salt (pun intended) go to the Salar, and there are many buses and trains to get there. However, the choices for getting out of Uyuni are drastically limited, and many visitors get stranded there for days due to the poorly scheduled departure options. The train leaves only two days a week at ungodly hours (e.g., 1:00 a.m. or 2:00 a.m.) and drops off passengers in strange cities at equally ungodly hours (e.g., 3:00 a.m. or 4:00 a.m.). The railway company just couldn't work any harder at making the schedule more unpalatable and less likely for anyone to use. Furthermore, while there are several bus companies in Uyuni, each and every one leaves for the same destination, at the same times, and typically on the same days as the trains. So all the buses depart Uyuni for Tupiza, near the Argentine border, at the same time on Wednesday and Sunday, which, coincidentally, is the same time as the train. Why? It's Bolivia. Apparently, if something works, everybody copies it. At least this is the response my Spanish teacher in Sucre gave me as I struggled to comprehend this ludicrous yet recurring state of affairs. This copycat mentality directly contrasts to that of the United States, where everyone strives to come up with an original and improved idea to attract consumers. Fortunately, Daveed had informed us of another option, a jeep (called a *rapidito*) that leaves Uyuni daily. Strangely, no one advertises these jeeps, very few people know about them, and even the company that offers this service does not acknowledge it unless repeatedly pressed for information.

Having been forewarned about these problems, we immediately headed to the train office upon arrival. Amazingly, they had a special train leaving Uyuni at 11:00 p.m. and getting to the Argentine border at around 6:00 a.m. Great! The next step was getting tickets. Here things got trickier, as the ticket counter does not have any regular hours, and no one knows exactly when it is open. Dozens of travel agencies abound which offer the exact same tours, but not one of them sells tickets out of Uyuni, with the exception of those for the four-day jeep trips to Chile. Being persistent, we trekked to the train station twice trying to buy tickets. The first time the window remained closed. The second time the window opened too late for us to purchase the tickets because we had to meet our tour to the salt flats. Rats! So the next day poor Fran arose very early, as three different people suggested three different times to get to the ticket window, and he patiently waited there for hours. The man at the counter sold tickets to the Bolivians before and after him in line, but after much fumbling with the computer, he told Fran that the train was sold out. He suggested that since they might add another car, Fran should come back at *mediodía*. It is common knowledge that at *mediodía*, or noon, everything shuts down for hours during lunch and *siesta* (their nap).

Determined to get there before *mediodía*, we ate an early lunch that set the tone for what was to come. I ordered a salad and while I was charged full price for it, the salad came with only half of the ingredients listed. When I questioned the waitress about the missing items, she simply shrugged. Even more distressing, I found an unadvertised addition, a big old bug at the bottom of my plate! I called over the rude waitress, who simply stared at it for a few moments before going back to her magazine. When it came time to pay, I refused to pay for the salad. The waitress brought out the owner, who tried to discredit my complaint by saying that I had eaten most of the salad. I told her that if I had known the insect was there, I would not have eaten it. That sentence was certainly a challenge to say in Spanish. The owner finally acquiesced, and we managed to get out of there with enough time to arrive at the train station at least 20 minutes before *mediodía*. While we stood in line, a Bolivian man told us that he had just bought a ticket so there should still be some seats left on the added car. Despite others pushing around us, vying for the salesman's attention, we patiently waited our turn and got up to the window right before *mediodía*. SLAM! The same guy that told Fran to come back at *mediodía* slammed the window shut in our faces. Well, I lost my temper, or as the Brits say, I "lost the plot." I smacked the counter, kicked the wall, and let out a string of obscenities that could be understood in pretty much any language. The window stayed shut. There was no way that man was going to sell us the tickets.

Meanwhile, the clock was ticking on the dwindling space in the *rapidito*. We couldn't let that opportunity slip away by wasting any more time trying to buy train tickets. We walked back to the company that told us they sold tickets to the *rapidito*, but of course, the company was closed because it was *mediodía*. I was so angry that I was pretty useless, so Fran pulled me off the case and decided to go it alone. At about 2:00 p.m., he returned to that company only to be told that it was actually a different company that really sold the *rapidito* tickets. He located the other company and had to wait a little longer, but he finally managed to reserve two seats on the *rapidito* for the next morning. Wahoo!

Of course, the adventure continued. Our *rapidito* departed a half hour late, drove two hours, and then let us off in a little town for an hour and a half, requiring us to change vehicles. In the second jeep, they squeezed two grown men, Fran, Christopher, myself, and three bags all into the backseat. Moving a limb required major adjustments from all of our fellow passengers. Before we took off, Fran pointed out that several tires were bald. The driver changed them, but despite the effort, three of the replacement tires blew out during the trip. The driver needed to switch back to the original tires and make frequent stops along the way to inflate one of them with an old bicycle pump. With all of the time spent dealing with the tires, we arrived in the town of Tupiza two hours later than expected.

But no matter how much the Bolivian transportation system challenged my limited patience, the spectacular countryside soothed my agitated soul in a matter of minutes. The drive from Uyuni to Tupiza was one of the most beautiful rides we experienced in all of South America. The mountainous desert landscape resembled the U.S. national parks of Bryce, Zion, Arches, and the Grand Canyon, all rolled into one. Brightly colored mud, eroded into bizarre formations, rose out of the ground, surrounded by painted layers of earth, arches carved into rock, and deep canyons. We saw a mountain made up entirely of shards of jagged red rock, reminding us of a sculpture we fondly referred to as the "Integrated Man" on the Esplanade in Boston. The jeep drove right along river beds and around these fantastical shapes. The problems with the tires actually gave us an opportunity to snap a few photos and stretch, a necessity with five of us squeezed into one back seat. We would have missed all of this scenery on the night train, so the whole ticket ordeal actually turned out to be a blessing in disguise, albeit a very heavily disguised blessing initially. Given the beauty of the land, Fran and I animatedly discussed how the government should preserve the area as a national park. Some entrepreneur could buy the train company, put a glass dome on top, and run it daily as a major tourist attraction. With so many visitors nearby, desperate to leave Uyuni, they could charge ten times as much, and make a small fortune. So why doesn't anyone even run tours to this totally undiscovered area? Say the mantra: "It's Bolivia."

We had intended to stay in the town of Tupiza for a couple of days to check out the old stomping grounds of Butch Cassidy and the Sundance Kid and explore this beautiful area some more. However, the only buses heading south departed at 4:00 p.m. and 4:00 a.m. on a couple days per week. The rains loomed right behind us, threatening to wash out the nearly nonexistent roads in a matter of moments. We saw a bus with available seats leaving for the border right then, and upon discovering that it was the last one of the day until 4:00 a.m. the next morning, we went ahead and jumped on. Within two hours we had crossed over into northern Argentina. And so our time came to an abrupt end in perhaps the most difficult and quite possibly the most rewarding of all South American countries. Why? It's Bolivia.

CHRISTOPHER'S COMMENTS

I saw a lot of animals in Bolivia. Once I saw this funny cat and dog in Sorata, and they were sort of fighting. By the way, it was not a catdog like in the cartoon. First the dog would pick up the cat and walk with him. Then he dropped the cat by accident, and the cat would scratch at him. Then the dog would pick up the cat again, and they would do it all over.

We saw the most animals at Inti Wara Yassi. I think it was our third day when a new toucan arrived. I nicknamed him Draco Malfoy because of the way he looked, but then we learned he really was like Draco. Mom and I had to feed him because we took care of the birds. Whenever we tried to feed him, he would always snap at us and try to bite us. We fed him once or twice a day. Then there were some more birds, and they were all the same type. There were 11 of them. They would all scrunch together and snuggle, snuggle, snuggle. Sometimes when I got bored I would take a couple of papaya seeds, after we cut them out of the fruit, and I would look for the closest snuggle bird. Sometimes I had to make one of them come over to me by wiggling the seed in the cage. One would hop over and then grab it right out

Roy

of my fingers. Sometimes it would eat the whole thing, but sometimes it would just peel off the little layer of squishy stuff around it. There were some other birds too. They weren't as nice. They were pretty small. About the second time that I helped Mom put the food in the cage, one of the birds was really hungry and got impatient. He climbed up on the bowl. I thought it was OK, that he was just going to sit there until I put it down. But actually, he was super duper impatient and he nipped me! I dropped the food, and I don't think he got any. But after that, I was afraid to feed those birds.

Our friend Monkey Face, who we talked about in the second chapter, got bit in the ears by monkeys so his name changed to Monkey Ears. He was taking care of this really cute puma named Roy. Monkey Ears was training him to attack roosters. He had a toy with red and green feathers on it, kind of like a duster. He would make a noise like a rooster and wiggle it around, and Roy would try to attack it. It was really funny. But instead of attacking roosters, Roy would attack my boots. He must have thought my boots were really chewy or something. Maybe they tasted good.

One day, Mom and I went down to the monkeys with Hadar. They were capuchins. One of the monkeys came over

A capuchin monkey adopts Christopher

to me and started grooming me. She was hugging me and talking to me, but then another monkey came over. At first it seemed oK, like nothing bad would happen. But then they started to get more and more angry. I think they were playing around. One played too hard and accidentally bit me. It didn't really hurt because it was sort of a sudden thing. I didn't really know until I looked down at my arm. Then we had to go get it cleaned and get a bandage. I still have a scar from it today. It wasn't that scary, and it didn't hurt that much, so I wanted to go back the next day. And I did!

If any kids are interested in volunteering, this is my advice: Don't tell your Mom that you are really going to do it and then decide not to do it. Moms don't like that! I liked volunteering with the animals more than working with the kids in the school in Baños because I really like to work with animals. I learned a lot of stuff about animals from volunteering, like the different behavior that animals can have. But mostly, I just did it because it was fun. So kids, VOLUNTEER!

TRAVELER'S TIPS

1. Connect home-schooling materials with real-life experiences whenever possible.

2. Try to get vital information about a scheduled tour and/or bus trip ahead of time. Ask about timelines, number of rest stops, eating options, and bathroom breaks. On buses, ask about the seats and where the luggage is stored.

3. Please support ecologically-friendly agencies and those that reinvest in the indigenous community. Do not engage in or request activities in which nature and wildlife are disturbed.

4. Never give out any information to someone claiming to be a policeman. Do not get into a taxi directed by someone else. Insist on walking to the nearest police station if an incident comes up.

5. Make sure the taxi doors are open before loading in your baggage.

6. When receiving items from home or mailing out packages, ask about any import fees or weight restrictions.

7. Before volunteering, get a sound commitment from all family members. Bear in mind that young children usually cannot comprehend the full implications of unfamiliar volunteer opportunities, and you may have to pick up the slack when they opt out.

8. Make sure the volunteer site is child-friendly and safe. Ask about how your child can contribute.

9. Talk to the people who work at the site, as well as volunteers. Clarify the expectations as much as possible. Stress your family's skills and limitations to ensure a good fit.

10. Do not give money to beggars. It just perpetuates the cycle by encouraging them to continue to panhandle instead of relying on more traditional methods of support.

11. Be patient and tolerant! I realize this is much easier said than done.

RESOURCES

Note: Since our trip, there have been a number of reports of tourists being kidnapped and even killed to obtain access to their bank accounts. Make sure to take adequate precautions to protect yourself against thieves posing as false policemen and taxi drivers.

COPACABANA

Hotel Utama

Calle Michel Pérez esq. San Antonio (intersection of Michel Pérez and San Antonio)
Tel: 0862-2013 (National)
Tel: 00591-862-2013 (International)

New hotel undergoing renovations while we were there. Our comfortable room contained a private bath and tiny view of the lake for US$10 a night, including a large, healthy breakfast.

The tour of **Islas del Sol y la Luna** (Islands of the Sun and the Moon), organized by the hotel owner through Copacabana Tours, provided only transportation without ample information about necessities such as food, restrooms, or duration of the various stops, despite being billed as a "guided" tour.

LA PAZ

Posada El Carretero

Calle Catacora 1056 entre (between) Yanacocha y Junín
Tel: 2285271

Very spartan and dingy room with tiny bath for US$8 a night, including full use of kitchen facilities. Incredibly friendly and helpful staff assisted us by watching over our luggage while we set off for the jungle, and they also signed for our package sent from the United States.

We highly recommend the delicious buffet brunch in the elegant **Paris Hotel**, Plaza Murillo esq. Bolivar, costing US$11 for the three of us.

Other must-sees include the **Mercado de Hechicería**, or **Mercado de los Brujos (Witches' Market)**, for unusual natural remedies including llama fetuses. Nearby, we stocked up on warm woven clothes at markets along the **Calle Sagárnaga**.

Although the **museums** tend to have erratic hours and are often closed, we enjoyed our visits to these two:

Museo Nacional de Etnografía y Folklore, C Ingavi 916, has interesting exhibits on the different indigenous groups.

Museo Nacional de Arqueología, in a grand building adorned with stone carvings reflecting the native cultures, contains a wide range of artifacts of archaeological and cultural interest.

RURRENABAQUE ("RURRE")

Hotel Tuichi

C Avaroa y Santa Cruz
Tel: 0892-2372

Basic room with fan and shared bath for US$10 a night. Friendly management will safely store luggage and can provide loads of information about tours in the surroundings.

Chalalán Albergue (Lodge)

Rurre office Tel: 08922419 at Calle Avaroa Central
La Paz Tel: 243-4058 at America Tours (www.america-ecotours.com)

We highly recommend a stay at the Chalalán as a way to support the local people in their efforts to preserve the spectacular Madidi National Park, featured in *National Geographic* magazine. Located in the heart of the rainforest, this beautiful lodge provides a range of amenities as well as guided walks and canoe trips into the surrounding nature. If you have some time, it is cheaper to arrange your stay with their office in Rurre; otherwise, you can arrange it through America Tours in La Paz.

Agencia Fluvial (0892-2372), next door to the Hotel Tuichi, is our top choice for pampas tours, an absolute must for nature lovers seeking close encounters with monkeys, caimans, anacondas, capybaras, pink river dolphins, birds, and other critters. The owner is featured in the page-turning novel, *Escape from Tuichi*, by Yossi Ginsberg, who later returned to the rainforest to found the Chalalán Lodge.

Other must-sees include the **Moskkito Jungle Bar** (Calle Comercio Central) which has pool tables, good food, and great mixed drinks, as well as the glorious, clean **swimming pool**, which also has food available and wildlife on the surrounding grounds.

SORATA

Hostal El Mirador

Calle Muñecas 400
Tel: 591-2-289-5008

Family-run hotel with the best view in town. Our very comfortable room with private bath had a spectacular view for US$12 a night, with breakfast for approximately US$2 per person on the lovely terrace overlooking the valley.

COCHABAMBA

Hostal Oruro

Calle Agustin López No 864 (entre Montes y Av. Aroma)
Tel: 224345-553322-04117687

Very clean and comfortable, family-run, nicely furnished rooms with TV and private bath for US$10 a night. Close to the bus station.

Hostal Elisa

Calle Agustin Lopez 0834
Tel: 4254406
Tel/fax: (591-4) 4235102
helisa@supernet.com.bo

Another nice alternative with pretty courtyard, clean and comfortable rooms with TV and private bath for US$15 a night.

Picasso's

España 327

Trendy, artistic bar/restaurant serving *trencitos*, little "trains" of six different specialty drinks. Located on a street lined with trendy eateries.

Gopal

España 250, Galería Olimpia

Vegetarian buffet, excellent bread, nice courtyard.

VILLA TUNARI

CIWY (Comunidad Inti Wara Yassi)

Villa Tunari (Parque Machia), Chapare, Cochabamba, Bolivia
Tel: (outside Bolivia) 00591 44134621
Tel: (Inside Bolivia) 044134621
contactos@intiwarayassi.org
www.intiwarayassi.org

Help the other volunteers take care of exotic animals in the rainforest. It requires a 15-day commitment and willingness to work hard. They need you! Volunteers are encouraged to stay at the hostels run by the organization to raise money for food, etc., for the animals. The hostels were pretty gross when we were there, but we have heard that they have been improved. We chose instead to stay at the family-run hostel above a small shop next to the general store on the main street. Very clean, comfortable beds, with private bath for US$13. Breakfast served downstairs for another US$1per person.

The **Orquidarium** (Orchid House) is also very interesting, which features a guided tour to look at these unique plants and their symbiotic relationship with certain bees, as well as exhibits of other insects unique to the area.

SUCRE

Vicky Hernaiz

Nataniel Aguirre 209
Cell: 70320339—71171573
vincentehernaiz@yahoo.es
josehernaiz@yahoo.com
drhernaiz@yahoo.com

Mama Vicky will take wonderful care of you. Spotless rooms with semi-private bath in a family home for only US$5per person, kitchen available. Will arrange Spanish lessons in home for excellent prices.

Asur Museo de Arte Indigena

San Alberto No. 413 (Casa Capellanica)
Tel: 6453841
Fax: 6462194 – cas. 662
asurmuse@cotes.net.bol

A fantastic textile museum where one can see artisans at work, as well as hear music played on traditional instruments.

Dinotruck

Leaves daily from the Cathedral at 9:30 a.m., 12:00 p.m., and 2:30 p.m. Reportedly the longest preserved dinosaur tracks in the world. Great fun for kids.

Museo Universitario

Bolivar 698

Great deformed and trepanned skulls, as well as other objects of cultural interest.

POTOSÍ

Casa de Huespedes "Maria Victoria"

Chuquisaca No. 148
Tel: (062) 22144-22132
Fax: (062) 22144-22132

Pretty courtyard surrounded by clean, tiled rooms with private bath for US$12 a night. Inexpensive breakfasts also available. On-site **Victoria Tours** (main office: Bustillos No. 1196-A) can organize good, reasonably priced tours to the silver mines.

Casa Nacional de Moneda

Calle Ayacucho

Large mint of historical interest.

UYUNI

Hostal Marith

Avenida Potosi No. 61, casi esq. (almost at the corner of) Ayacucho
Telefax: 591-0693-2174

Clean room with private bath around nice courtyard for US$10 per night. Will do laundry inexpensively.

Colque Tours

Ave. Potosi No. 54
Telefax: 2693-2199
www.colquetours.com
colque@ceibo.entelnet.bo
colquetours@terra.cl

Best known tour company to the Salar. Will do one-, two-, and three-day tours. One-day tour included visit to the Salt Hotel, observation of salt harvesting, and an "island" (Isla de los Pescadores), costing US$40 for all three of us. It is important to note that Rich and Cyndi did not recommend this company as the driver changed their itinerary en route; we did not have this problem.

Don't forget to arrange your transportation out of town as early as possible. If heading south, ask for a *rapidito*. These jeeps leave at 7:00 a.m. daily. Be persistent!

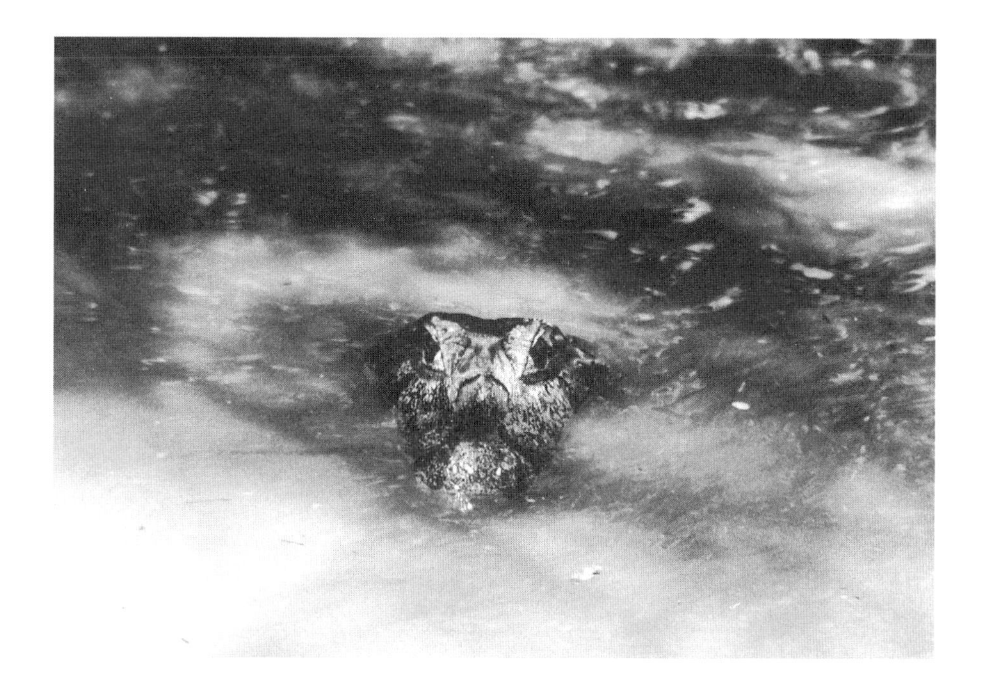

Bolivia
Villazón
Paraguay
La Quiaca
Chile
San Salvador
de Jujuy
Salta
Cafayate
Tucumán
Córdoba
Argentina
Uruguay
Buenos Aires

Chapter 5

Luxury in Argentina

Beware of the dangers lurking in Argentina. You might fall asleep in the hot tubs! You might get sunburned by the pool! You might gain weight from dining on rich steak and gourmet cheese! You might suffer a terrible hangover after drinking all that fabulous Argentine wine! Immediately after crossing the border into Argentina, the quality of everything—hotels, homes, food, wine, buses, and roads—increased tenfold while remaining almost unbelievably affordable to us fortunate Americans. We spent our first night at a nondescript town on the border between Argentina and Bolivia and then headed south to Jujuy. The trip overall was so comfortable that two forced stops by the police barely phased us. Searching for coca leaves and other illegal substances, they opened our bags and thoroughly investigated the contents. Christopher giggled when they inquisitively sniffed one of my tampons, a rarity in South America. However, the situation soon became less funny when one of the guards took Fran and our medication bag into a back room. Going through the containers one at a time, he questioned Fran about our vast quantity of prescription drugs. Fran himself could scarcely believe how many of our medications were for *el nariz* (the nose), as we all suffer from sinus allergies. The guard repeatedly asked if Fran was sick, and later I wondered if perhaps they were screening for anyone entering the country with a communicable disease such as AIDS. Finally,

Glorious rock formations in Jujuy province, northern Argentina

I offered the guards our stack of prescriptions for each and every one of the medications. Perhaps overwhelmed by the sheer volume of paperwork, they let us continue on our journey.

Similar to southern Bolivia, the desert scenery in northern Argentina continued to be spectacular, with unique rock formations and colorful painted hills jutting out of the arid landscape. Fran had heard that Jujuy was beautiful, and we were looking forward to spending some time there after traveling for two days nonstop (since Uyuni). We arrived in the eagerly anticipated town, but after one look around we were ready to leave again. Later we compared notes with other *viajeros* and discovered that we were not alone in our reaction; many shared the same first impression of this sweltering, dirty, nasty place. We decided that people must have been extolling the virtues of the province of Jujuy, not the city itself. To make matters worse, we realized that Christopher had left his beloved necklace with the stone turtle charm back at the hotel on the border.

We dug through our guidebooks, trying to figure out what we should do. "I remember there being some hot springs…." I commented, hoping to make the best of a bad situation. Sure enough, our book indicated that some thermal springs were indeed located about an hour outside of Jujuy, and apparently we could stay there as well. We hurried into a phone center at the bus station to call them. Typically run by one "operator," these wonderful phone centers allowed us simply to enter a private booth, make the call, and then pay the "operator" when finished. The process was infinitely easier than trying to figure out how to buy and use a phone card or, worse yet, fumbling around on a crowded street dispensing foreign change into a pay phone. So with the help of our guidebook and the phone "operator," we managed to contact the Termas de Reyes Hotel-Spa (translated literally, "Hot Springs of Kings"). The hotel representative informed us that they had a double available for US$60 a night, buffet breakfast included. Yikes! We thanked them and told them that we would consider it. After hanging up, we flipped over the price. We hadn't paid more than US$20 a night wherever we had gone, and Argentina had a reputation for being inexpensive due to its unfortunate financial crisis. But Jujuy proved to be so unpleasant that we didn't want to stay there, either. We finally decided to bite the bullet and try the hot springs for one night. If it was not worth the expense, we would continue on to Salta the next day.

The Argentine Equivalent of Heaven

Boarding a rickety, grimy bus, the route lifted us quickly out of the city squalor through green countryside to lush volcanic mountains. Our bus traversed a narrow road clinging to the side of a steep mountain high above a steaming river. We glimpsed the hotel, which appeared fairly nice from the outside, but we couldn't see much due to the slope of the hill. However, once inside the establishment our spirits soared. Termas de Reyes turned out to be a fabulous five-star resort situated on a natural hot spring. Our room contained the largest bed we had ever seen, a balcony with a gorgeous view, and a huge, newly tiled bathroom. With the turn of a faucet, we could fill our deep tub with water pumped in directly from the hot spring. In the elegant restaurant, we rejoiced over seeing something other than the omnipresent *pollo, papas, y pan* on the menu. Instead, we routinely savored the best fillet mignon in the world, followed by a broad selection of cheese and chocolate desserts, and washed it all down with bottles of rich Argentine wine. Furthermore, the facilities also included a giant, heated, outdoor, mineral water pool with air jets, a well-equipped gym, a big-screen TV, and a full service spa. At any time, hotel guests could access the spa and request that an attendant fill a tub with hot mineral water in a private room. The large tub easily accommodated all three of us, and a lounge chair by the window allowed us to take full advantage of the valley view. Perhaps best of all, the prices were so affordable (e.g., under US$30 for the delectable meal, and under US$20 for spa treatments), that our intended stay of one night stretched into an entire week. In all of that time, only Fran left the premises to pick up some extra cash and to retrieve Christopher's turtle necklace that the kind hotel staff had forwarded by bus to the Jujuy station.

After traveling for six months, we were poised to truly enjoy and appreciate the luxury. While I found life on the road to be very exciting, it also could be dirty, tiring, and at times, stressful. We had suffered through some nasty bus rides. Our belongings were becoming stretched, stained, and torn (especially my ill-fated jeans). To save money, we often stayed at places with a shared bath, which posed its own set of problems. Mid-night pit stops became a small adventure as I tried to quietly locate and put on my clothes and shoes in the dark, find the bathroom, and hope that it was not already occupied. I quickly learned to wear shorts and a T-shirt to bed for just such occasions. During the day, lugging our pack to the bathroom with all of our supplies and then trying to find a dry place to put it was also a challenge. Hot water was a rare commodity. At times, we slept on very thin, hard mattresses, and when available, the pillows came in a variety of forms, which sometimes included dismally flat, smelly, and rag-stuffed affairs. Our Canadian friend Cyndi even wrote a hilarious tribute to her pillow at home, in which she sang its praises while discussing the futility of trying to improve on a nasty pillow through such options as wrapping it in a towel or attempting to stuff it with various personal items. Only long-term budget travelers can truly sympathize with her yearning for a soft, clean, fluffy pillow.

Furthermore, daily tasks sometimes took on ridiculously magnified proportions. For example, trying to purchase some breakfast supplies could take literally all day. First, do we have someplace to store the food? Then, where do we buy it? Do we have transportation there? Do we have local money to buy it? Once at the market, do they have products that we know how to use? How do we ask for them in Spanish? Communication could be challenging and made every exchange at least a little more effort than that in English. How much of the item do we need (in whatever the local form of measurement is)? Once purchased, how do we get it home? Is there really place to store it? How do we cook or prepare it? An errand that would take only 20 minutes at home could stretch into a day-long adventure, and even then there was only a partial chance that we would emerge victorious in our quest.

In summary, we were tired. We were so ready for a break and a few of the comforts of home. Every single time we laid on our bed, we sent up a silent prayer of thanks for its softness. Each turn of the faucet spewing forth scalding hot water elicited a cheer. A fully prepared breakfast complete with sliced fresh fruit and steamy cups of coffee *sin la nata* (without milk scum) evoked moans of delight. Christopher played joyously in the enormous pool and watched videos for hours in English on the big-screen TV. We all relished spending quality family time in a safe and comfortable environment with activities that appealed to all of us. Now, hard-core adventurers may scoff at our weakness for material comforts, and folks back home may snarl at our complaints during a year-long "vacation." But truth be told, budget traveling for an extended period of time, especially with one or more children in tow, can be hard work. The actual act of getting on and off buses, finding places to stay, and dealing with the minutia of daily living is not always glamorous or relaxing. It is important to frequently take inventory of everyone's mental status to avoid burnout. We encountered our share of long-term travelers who became jaded and cynical, full of complaints at every turn. We refused to become them! We needed to recognize that we were experiencing "culture shock." In *The Practical Nomad*, Ed Hasbrouck offers a new definition of this familiar term. Instead of hitting the traveler immediately upon arrival, as the name implies, "culture shock" instead accumulates after four to six months on the road, when the novelty and excitement of travel wears off and the ongoing sensory overload becomes overwhelming. Bonnie Michaels and Michael Seef also emphasize in their book, *A Journey of Work-Life Renewal*, that "goofing off is okay—even on a sabbatical." Taking a vacation from our big adventure was therefore an important part of our self-care. Termas de Reyes was exactly what we needed to rejuvenate our minds and spirits in order to continue our journey with optimal attitudes.

Adjusting to the Argentine Lifestyle

We pried ourselves away from the Argentine equivalent of heaven and continued south to Salta, a medium-sized city with an interesting blend of old traditions and modern comforts. Men sell fruit off carts placed strategically on the corners of streets lined with stately townhouses. We stayed in the elegant home of a local woman and continued to indulge in first-world luxuries, namely, the latest *Harry Potter* and *Lord of the Rings* movies on the big screen. Christopher was really hankering for some English-speaking entertainment, and honestly, Fran and I were happy to accommodate his request. One of the theaters was housed in a shopping mall the Argentinians adorably referred to as simply the "shopping." For example, when giving directions, they would say, "Go left at the 'shopping' and continue on down the street." The mall rivaled those found in North America, providing a sharp capitalist contrast to the indigenous street markets to which we had grown accustomed.

While Salta was a comfortable and easily navigable city, we struggled to adjust to the new schedule. Argentinians rise around 8:00 a.m., go to work, take a long lunch break and siesta from noon to 4:00 p.m., return to work until about 9:00 p.m., and then eat and party all night long. As a result, big breakfasts and late afternoon-early evening meals usually are not available, and dinner doesn't start until after 9:00 p.m., with the local crowd filling restaurants by about midnight. Try as I might, I just could not get used to skipping breakfast, taking a big daily nap, and eating a very late, very wonderful dinner. Instead, we ate a late breakfast, tried to find something to do during siesta, snacked around six, and nodded off during dinner.

In the process, I gained about ten pounds, especially after discovering the Argentine *asado*. Often translated as a barbecue, the term does not do it justice. Several different cuts of meat, along with savory vegetables, are served either on a small grill placed on the table or cooked up over a large open grill in which the lucky customer chooses his or her own cuts of meat. Fran and I have eaten steaks all over the world, but Argentine beef is hands-down the best we have ever tasted. Not only is the flavor incredibly rich, but some slices are so tender they can be cut with a spoon. No joking. Another heady find was the *tenedor libre* (literally "free fork"), an all-you-can-eat extravaganza of salads, fruits, cheeses, desserts, and the delectable *asado*, washed down with delicious Argentine wine. Even the supermarkets consistently stocked a wide selection of fruits and vegetables and several types of blue cheeses. This was my kind of country! The food alone was enough to understand why Murray, our American friend from CIWY, spent so much of his yearlong vacation here.

As evidenced by the high quality of food and wine, the standard of living in Argentina contrasted dramatically with our first three countries. The feel of the cities, as well as the architecture, stores, and landmarks, are very European. In fact, Daveed complained that if he had wanted to see a European city, he would have stayed home. We, on the other hand, were thrilled with the experience of being in Europe for less than one-third of the actual prices. While the peso had previously matched the U.S. dollar, the recent economic crises in 2002 caused it to drop to one-third of its previous value. As a result, the exchange rate of pesos to the U.S. dollar was 3:1 when we were there in 2003. At first glance, menu prices appeared comparable to American standards (e.g., $15 for a bottle of wine in a nice restaurant). However upon closer inspection, the menu reflected Argentine pesos, bringing that bottle of wine down to US$5. With the quality of everything still so high, we almost felt guilty about taking advantage of the low prices. But plenty of locals seemed to appreciate our business, so in some ways it was a win-win situation.

Not only is the environment very European, but approximately 85 percent of the gregarious Argentine people descend directly from European ancestry as well, which again differs from the other South American countries. For example, the vast majority of the Bolivian people are indigenous or *mestizos* (a mix of native and European blood). Wherever we went in Bolivia, we saw dark-skinned people in their traditional outfits, creating an adventurous and exotic travel experience. The downside was that we were obviously foreigners and treated as such, becoming potential targets for aggressive sales reps and thieves. In Argentina, most of the population appears European, and we blended into the crowd. Due to the devaluation of the peso, many Argentinians chose to vacation in their homeland instead of going abroad during their summer vacation. They often stopped us to ask for information or directions in Spanish, and appeared surprised when our broken, accented responses gave away the fact that we were indeed *extranjeros*.

We made similar mistakes in our assumptions regarding the ethnicity of the Argentinians. When we arrived in the northern town of Cafayate, we entered a hotel and began the usual negotiations for a room. We went to look at our options, and the owner asked a woman in the lobby to explain that the price also included the use of the kitchen facilities. She approached us and, in flawless English, apologetically explained that the owner had asked her to interpret. I looked at her and instantly became discouraged, wondering if my Spanish was still so bad that he needed some other "gringo" to help us out. We took the room and later, while relaxing in the sunny central courtyard, I struck up a delightful conversation with the same woman. I discovered that she was born and raised in Argentina.

Frankly, we did need some assistance with our Spanish because the Argentine accent made for some communication difficulties. They pronounce "ll" and "y" with a "j" sound (rumored to have given "Che" Guevara his nickname) instead of the more typical "y" sound. As a result, I had trouble understanding even simple words like *calle* (street). In my head, I had to translate the Argentine word into recognizable Spanish, and then into English, and of course by then I was totally lost in the conversation. In contrast, Christopher picked it up right away. Once he translated for me; "He's saying '*calle*,' Mom. You know, 'street!' He wants to know what street our hotel is on!" I felt simultaneously belittled and proud. It was clear that his auditory processing was much better than mine. On the other hand, our American accents rendered our speech difficult to understand as well, as evidenced by a chance meeting with an Argentine woman at a bus station. As an English teacher, she wished to practice the language with us, so we chatted while waiting for the bus to come. I asked her if the bus was comfortable. She had no idea what I meant. I repeated myself several times. Still no luck. Finally, I said *cómodo* ("comfortable" in Spanish). "Oh!" she exclaimed, "you mean, 'com-for-ta-ble,'" carefully stressing each syllable. I realized that, with my American accent, I was pronouncing it "comfterble." She had me repeat the word a few times so that she could accustom her ear to the American pronunciation, and we went on to discuss the differences between American and British accents. Fran and I had already noticed that some English language schools specifically advertised their courses as either "British English" or "American English." We also discovered that, in reading the British version of a *Harry Potter* novel, it took us a while to "cotton on to" certain words and expressions.

An Ironic Twist

The small, charming town of Cafayate is situated amongst scrubby desert vegetation and arid mountains, surrounded by painted hills and productive vineyards. We took advantage of the warm weather and strolled around the main square, lined with cafés and handicraft

A bicycle built for three in Cafayate

stalls. An elaborate bouncy play structure was erected on one side of the square, demanding Christopher's attention. As we waited our turn, some of the local children began talking to us and asked us where we were from. When we replied, "the United States," their eyes grew very big. "*¡Es muy peligroso allí! ¡Los torres gemelos!*" ("It's very dangerous there! The twin towers!"), they exclaimed and then excitedly went on to talk about all the shooting and crime that they had witnessed in American-made movies and on the news. We assured them that while parts of our country could be dangerous, we lived in the safe and delightful city of Portland, Oregon. They seemed unconvinced. As the conversation drew to a close, Fran and I marveled at the irony of our discussion. First my father and brother had warned us against traveling to Argentina due to bad press, and now we were confronted with the same media-driven stereotypes about the United States amongst the Argentine children.

We found the people throughout Argentina to be incredibly warm and welcoming. Like the woman at the bus stop, our "interpreter" at the hotel, and the children at the play structure, they all went out of their way to talk to us. As we were dining in one of those delightful cafés in the main square, a couple at the table next to us leaned over to strike up a conversation. "We can tell that you are not from around here..." began our exchange, and before we knew it, they were inviting us to their home in Tucumán for a "real Argentine *asado*." Though we hadn't really planned on stopping in Tucumán, we couldn't pass up such a wonderful opportunity. We exchanged information and made plans with our new friends, Alejandro and Lali, to meet there later in the week.

While Cafayate turned out to be a wonderful vacation spot, we were primarily interested in sampling the local wines. At Helados Miranda, we prepped our palates with ice cream made from Cabernet Sauvignon and Torrontes, or red and white wine grapes, respectively. Delicious! Feeling fortified and adventurous, we rented a three-seated bicycle to tour the area, which was definitely an exercise in family cooperation. After obtaining a map of the wineries from the very helpful tourist information stand in the central square, we slowly pedaled our way to the nearby wineries. Bodega La Banda had an enjoyable selection for tasting, but we were less impressed with the mass-produced wine at Bodega Domingo Hermanos. And despite our best

Folkloric festival at Finca Las Nubes, Cafayate

efforts, we missed Bodega La Rosa entirely because it kept changing its tasting room hours. Having gained some confidence and balance on our bike, we followed the suggestion of a woman in the tourist office and laboriously rode for a few miles over a hilly dirt road to a little local festival at Finca Las Nubes (Farm of the Clouds). When we finally arrived at the winery, the festival was in full swing. Accompanied by Spanish guitarists, several little boys dressed like gauchos, the masculine Argentine cowboys, were performing with young girls in voluminous, flowing skirts reminiscent of flamenco dancers. With their typical welcoming nature, the locals fussed over us. The children invited us to dance, and the announcer acknowledged us several times over the microphone. Caught up in the festive atmosphere, we had to tear ourselves away to reach the winery before it closed. Fortunately we made it, because Finca Las Nubes turned out to be our favorite winery of them all. The full-bodied, rich wines are crafted from start to finish by hand. After a quick tour and some samples, we relaxed outdoors at an elegantly set table amidst the grapevines, fully enjoying a delightful glass of wine and some regional goat cheese. Luckily the way back was downhill, or we might be there still!

A Traditional Asado

But we had a date to keep in Tucumán, so we ventured on south to the humid city. Our new friend, Alejandro, met us at our hotel and then arranged for a taxi to take us to his house the following evening. I chatted with his wife, Lali, in their cool adobe home while Fran watched Alejandro salt and barbeque the meat on their grill over an open fire. Thrilled to have some young company, Christopher ran around playing with their three adorable children. As we all sat down to the feast, Alejandro pointed out that he had personally gone to the butcher to choose the best cuts of meat. They both agreed that Lali would not have gotten the quality or price that Alejandro had received. Obviously, this type of machismo still pervades South America, even in a country as progressive as Argentina. The meat was cooked to perfection, and as we savored the meal, we considered ourselves extremely fortunate; due to the economic crises, our hosts explained that they could afford *asado* only on special

Elegant architecture in Córdoba

occasions. Our topics of conversation ranged from politics to finances to our dreams for the future. After thanking our hosts profusely for an absolutely delightful evening, Fran and I again marveled over the warm hospitality of the Argentine people.

A Change of Plans

The double-decker bus to the bustling town of Córdoba provided the best public transportation experience imaginable, with clean, spacious, reclining window seats, fully functioning bathrooms, three movies in English, free coffee and treats. The excellent quality of the buses extended throughout our stay in Argentina. While we initially balked at the fact that we had to buy three seats because they would not allow Christopher to share ours for free, Fran especially appreciated being able to stretch out his legs. His knees were still bothering him from some of those previous unpleasant rides with Christopher confined to his lap. Upon arrival we checked our email at a nearby Internet café, and we suddenly received word that our friends George, Mark, and Brenda would be flying into Rio de Janeiro, Brazil, for the world-famous Carnival celebration. We hadn't seen them since graduate school over ten years ago and longed to reconnect. However, our original plan was to continue south along the west coast to Patagonia, and then up the eastern shore, placing us in Rio sometime in late March or early April. What a dilemma! Should we reconfigure our "trip of a lifetime" to meet our friends or simply stay the course?

At first, the choice was very difficult. The original route made much more sense, with short bus rides and a comfortable pace. But by then, we had habituated to traveling. Everything was new and different every day, so the early excitement of being in a foreign environment had waned. Furthermore, while we had just tasted some great wines, more wine-tasting and similar sightseeing plans were on the agenda for the next month. We compared the fun we were guaranteed to have with our friends during arguably the biggest party in the world with our current itinerary involving more of the same types of experiences. The decision became increasingly clear, and we began to formulate an alternative route. Only two summer months remained in Patagonia in which the weather would be comfortable, the roads open, and tourist facilities available, so we needed to visit the area before Carnival. Knowing that the Argentine buses were efficient and incredibly comfortable, we were much more receptive to spending over a full day (28 hours) on the bus driving directly from Córdoba to Patagonia. The new proposal would afford us a full month of sight-seeing there before heading back north to Trelew, a town midway up the eastern coast, and flying on to Rio. As we talked about some of the attractions we would soon encounter in Patagonia and what a shame it would be to miss our friends during such an internationally acclaimed event, we became increasingly excited about our updated travel plans.

The cost of a holiday in Rio during a high-season venue such as Carnival warranted careful consideration. Unlike previous vacations, we had been keeping a detailed account of our daily expenses in a special journal. Not only did this book help us track our financial affairs, it also served as a travel diary and reference guide for hotels and restaurants as well. Approximately every two weeks, Fran reviewed the budget and, after calculating our total expenses, he ensured that we had the correct amount of money in our possession. We recorded exactly how much cash we had on hand and where it was stashed in our belongings; this crucial evidence strengthened our case when we were robbed towards the end of our trip. We also kept track of bank withdrawals and credit card costs, emailing this information regularly to my mother so that she could compare it to our bills back in the States. Taking inventory of our financial situation, Fran determined that we had only spent a total of $12,000 in the previous six months, which included most pre-trip expenses as well as the unplanned trip to the Galápagos Islands. Having spent far less than our $100 a day budget, we felt we could afford this unanticipated indulgence. We hurried off in pursuit of a travel agent to see about plane tickets to Rio.

Our travel agent, Marta Baulina, was very accommodating. Tickets from Trelew, Argentina, to Rio de Janeiro, Brazil, cost a reasonable US$300 per person. As we purchased the tickets, Marta gently reminded us that Brazil required visas for U.S. citizens. She steered us towards the Brazilian consulate to obtain the necessary documents. The helpful staff at the consulate processed the visas as quickly as possible, explaining that the high cost of over US$100 per person was due to the elevated expense for U.S. visas. Increased security at home had caused a reciprocal rise in their fees.

While our primary focus was on conducting errands in preparation for our trip to Rio, we still managed to squeeze in some sight-seeing. Córdoba is a comfortable, clean, efficient city with some beautiful colonial buildings and a lively university atmosphere. Beginning in front of the Cathedral, we joined a free guided walking tour of the elegant urban architecture, and we also built in some kid-friendly time with Christopher at a nearby zoo. While visiting the small neighboring town of Cosquín, we chanced upon a folkloric festival there, which provided us with a unique opportunity to enjoy some local art. We finished up our errands, which included finding an apartment in Rio over the Internet, obtaining and mailing off a cashier's check in U.S. dollars for a security deposit, and making arrangements to meet with our friend, George, in Rio. Overall Córdoba was a great place for us to get organized and geared up for the rest of our trip. We bought bus tickets as far as Trelew, climbed aboard for the 17-hour journey, and embarked on our revitalized adventure.

CHRISTOPHER'S COMMENTS

Hello, it's me again. Pretty much the only thing I remember about this part of Argentina is the luxury place. First we got into this town which we didn't like called Jujuy. Everyone says they like Jujuy but they meant the state not the city. So we hated the city of Jujuy because it was bad and gross. So Mommy and Daddy called this luxury place that they had heard about. Then they were debating because it cost US$60 a night, and our normal budget was US$15 a night. So they finally figured out to try it for one night, and if it wasn't worth it, then we would leave. We went there and we stayed there for a whole week, when we were only going to stay there for one night.

I liked it for lots of reasons. I'll list some of the reasons. First I liked that there was a pool. Second, I liked that you could have a special private spa room overlooking the mountains. I liked that place because I liked doing somersaults in the tub under the water. Third, they would let us get movies and watch them on an overhead projector-like thing, and me and Daddy watched Sword in the Stone. Also sometimes Mom or Dad would do stuff like get a massage or go to the pool or something, and I was left alone to organize my Harry Potter cards. I did a graph of my cards. The final thing was that I liked the food there. We got a free breakfast, and dinner didn't cost that much for really, really yummy stuff. That is what I remember of this part of Argentina.

TRAVELER'S TIPS

1. Be prepared to present copies of your medication prescriptions at border crossings. Make sure all of your medications are in correctly marked containers.

2. Prepare for "culture shock" by recognizing that it can result from the accumulation of sensory overload and stress over long stretches of traveling. Combat burnout by planning a "vacation" at regular intervals. Pamper yourselves and do nothing. Kids love pools and luxury!

3. Be willing to change your original itinerary to accommodate a new opportunity or simply to create more excitement in your trip.

4. Ask about visa requirements before buying plane tickets or making other arrangements.

RESOURCES

LA QUIACA

La Frontera

Belgrano y Siria

Shared bath, clean but noisy for US$15 a night. Restaurant on premise serves decent food. Run by nice folks who helped us recover Christopher's turtle necklace after accidentally leaving it there by sending it on a bus to the station in Jujuy.

Termas de Reyes Hotel-Spa

Tel: (0388) 4922522-4278000
www.termasdereyes.com
info@termasdereyes.com

Totally luxurious five-star resort with large outdoor pool heated with mineral water; spa downstairs includes private soaking tubs accommodating up to three people upon request. Our elegant room contained a huge bed, balcony, and private bath that filled with mineral water for a special introductory offer of US$60 per night, buffet breakfast included. Room service, poolside service, and excellent restaurant on the premises serves fillet mignon among other delicious main courses.

SALTA

Maria Carmen Rodó de Tôffoli Hospedaje

Mendoza 915
Tel: 0387-4320813

Very friendly woman rents out private rooms in her beautiful home. Rooftop terrace, use of kitchen, and semi-private bath for US$13 a night.

CAFAYATE

El Hospedaje

Camila Quintana de Niño esq. Salta
Tel: (03868) 421680

Clean comfortable triple with private bath opening into a large courtyard and use of kitchen facilities for US$13 a night.

Stop at the very friendly tourist office in the main plaza for a map and information about the local **wineries**. They can also recommend a place to rent bicycles. Our favorite winery was:

Finca Las Nubes
El Divisadero (camino al Rio Colorado y Pinturas Rupestres)
Tel: 03868-422129
japmounier@yahoo.com.ar

Not only were their wines wonderful, but they also set a picnic table for us amidst the grapes.

Make sure to try the **wine-flavored ice creams** at:

Helados Miranda
Ave. Güemes Norte 170
Tel: 03868-421106

TUCUMÁN

Hotel Versailles

Crisóstomo Alvarez 481
Tel: (0381) 422-9760/61/62/63
Fax: (0381) 422-9764
hotelversailles@ciudad.com.ar

Beautifully furnished lobby in 18th century French style. Clean double with AC, TV, and private bath for US$11 a night. Breakfast included.

CÓRDOBA

Hotel Quetzal

San Jerónimo 579
Telefax: (0351) 4229106

Reasonable hotel with AC, TV, and private bath for US$13 a night.

Vera Cruz Viajes y Turismo

Marta Baulina
"Paseo del Fundador" Obispo Trejo 29 - Loc. 4
Telefax: 4237695/4272139/4220666

Very helpful Spanish-speaking woman who organized our roundtrip flight from Trelew, Argentina, to Rio de Janeiro, Brazil, via Buenos Aires. Very informative about how to obtain our visas at the Brazilian embassy in Córdoba, as well as how to take a taxi between airports in Buenos Aires.

Kid-friendly activities include a free walking tour of the elegant old buildings downtown, leaving daily from the Cathedral, as well as the **Jardín Zoológico Córdoba (zoo)**, Rondeau 798, Telefax: 0351-4244880.

Chile
Argentina
From Córdoba
To Rio
Península Valdés
Trelew
Gaiman
El Calafate
Torres
Del Paine
Puerto
Natales
Rio Gallegos
Punta
Arenas
Ushuaia
Puerto Williams

CHAPTER 6

PENGUINS IN PATAGONIA

"To those of us who think of ourselves as penguins!" Readers may agree that this was a strange way to toast each other at our wedding, but then again, it truly was an odd mixture of penguins, big 80's hair, and the Grateful Dead. When Fran and I ordered our wedding accessories back in 1988, we chose an adorable pair of penguins to adorn the matchbook covers. However, the store screwed up our order and extended the theme to the napkins as well. No matter, we loved the motif. The problem occurred when my mother wanted to top the cake with a traditional bride and groom. Rejecting anything too conventional, I argued that the cake wouldn't match the napkins. My mom responded that the cake was supposed to be a "reflection" of us. Little did she know that she had just given us one of our all-time favorite quotes. It is true. We don't have wings, we love the ocean, we eat a lot of seafood, and at times, we bray like donkeys. I think it's safe to admit; we really do think of ourselves as penguins.

And so began the lifelong pursuit of our fine feathered friends. We managed our first peek at the tiny, blue fairy penguins on a small island off the coast of Australia. But our search started in earnest in South America. We had taken a boat to observe them in the Galápagos Islands and again trekked off shore in Peru to see more. But when we arrived in Patagonia, we hit the mother lode.

Primal scream therapy, penguin-style

Confronted with our first real deadline of the trip, we now possessed tickets for a flight on February 28, 2003, from Trelew, Argentina, to Rio de Janeiro, Brazil. After firming up our Carnival plans in Córdoba, we only had about four weeks in Patagonia to fit in as much penguin-time as possible before flying to Rio. We needed to abruptly adjust to a strict timeline following six months of free-form traveling, and we set off, determined to make every moment count.

Penguins Bite

From Córdoba, we sped down to Trelew on a roomy, clean, double-decker bus. Situated on the top level, we were thrilled that our comfy front row seats afforded us a panoramic window view. However, our initial anticipation slowly faded away as the route carried on for hours through desolate, brown landscape. Almost totally devoid of houses or other signs of habitation, the monotonous pampas stretched over barren plains and gentle hills for miles with only a few tufts of shrubs and grasses in sight. The vast majority of wildlife consisted of cows and sheep, interrupted only occasionally by an exciting glimpse of ñandús (also called rheas, flightless birds that look like small ostriches) and guanacos (brown and white llama-like animals most closely resembling vicuñas). The Antarctic wind blew freely over the flat terrain, chilling us to the bone whenever we ventured outside and eliciting testimonials from the locals about its awesome power to break windows and knock over homes during winter storms.

Once a Welsh settlement, the nondescript town of Trelew (pronounced tre-LAY-oo) served as the jumping off point for our first visit to a Patagonian penguin colony. We easily arranged a tour through a local agency to Punta Tombo, a protected area on the east coast. Disembarking from the van, we gingerly stepped around hundreds of Magellanic penguins, hiding under bushes, feeding their young, and walking to and from the rocky beach up to their nests in the pampas. I loved sitting quietly and listening to the repetitive crunch of their little feet on the pebbly beach. At times a penguin would thrust back its wings, stretch its head up to the sky, and let fly a primal scream. Because their cries resemble those of a donkey, scientists have nicknamed them "jackass" penguins

Insistent penguin babies hassle their mother for food

and speculate that this behavior might be a mating ritual. To me these stressed creatures seemed to be releasing tension. Surrounded by noise and chaos, the penguins were engaged in a constant food-finding mission. The babies hassled their tired parents relentlessly, poking and prodding and chasing them until they ultimately shoved their beaks down their parents' throats for some regurgitated seafood. What an endorsement for breastfeeding! I was so engrossed in my own efforts to photograph these busy little beings that I unwittingly moved too close to a set of penguins hidden under a bush. The protective mother angrily retaliated by biting me in the leg! Luckily, my jeans shielded me from her wrath, but I quickly learned that those sweet, innocent-looking birds certainly can become aggressive when threatened.

As part of our excursion to Punta Tombo, we rested in the well-preserved Welsh town of Gaiman. At a cozy half-timbered cottage plucked straight out of a fairy tale, we sat down to a British high tea served on elegant china. Surrounded by antiques, Fran and I enjoyed the pampering while Christopher scuttled off with some other children to play a Monopoly game. To my surprise, the game came directly from Wales, with unusual spaces around the board labeled in English and Welsh.

While the vast open spaces of the pampas deceptively appear deserted, knowledgeable travelers can uncover many signs of wildlife in the vicinity of Trelew. In addition to our successful quest for penguins, we joined a tour of the Valdés Peninsula to watch the huge sea elephants posturing and establishing their dominance on the Pacific coast. We cheered on dozens of sea lion pups as they braved the waves for perhaps the first time, while dusky dolphins frolicked off shore. Due to Christopher's newfound interest in archaeology, we also investigated two remarkable sites revealing generations of animal remains. Trelew is home to an extensive dinosaur museum with more impressive skeletons and fossils than I have seen in my lifetime. Even more fascinating, visitors are allowed to tour the grounds nearby where scientists have unearthed a multitude of prehistoric bones. As we made our way from the park's entrance up a rocky hill, we were able to trace the earth's climactic transformation through the ages. Grass-eating mammal bones and other evidence displayed at the base of the slope suggest that 40 million years ago a savannah covered the land. As we hiked up the hill, we passed clearly labeled exhibits of fossilized mollusks, dolphins, and even an ancient penguin, documenting how water later covered the savannah. Finally, towards the top of the hill, we saw the more recent signs of glacial movement over the earth, transforming the marine environment into an arid, cactus-spotted landscape. Christopher enjoyed his visit so much that when we returned home, he requested a microscope similar to those shown at the museum, and he attended an archaeological camp through the Oregon Museum of Science and Industry (OMSI).

After exploring the unique flora and fauna of Trelew, our next order of business was to get to the southern tip of the continent as quickly as possible. In the bus station, we spied a small sign advertising a 28-hour ride all the way to Punta Arenas, Chile, right in the heart of Patagonia. Without hesitation we bought the tickets, and the next morning we were on our way. Because this region remains so remote, transportation options are limited and fully booked during the brief summer season when travel is possible. Many Argentinians were traveling locally due to the economic crisis, and throngs of foreigners had also come to take advantage of the unusually affordable prices. Because of this high volume of tourists, we had heard stories of travelers being stranded for days in isolated Argentine townships such as Ushuaia and El Chaltén, near Mount Fitz Roy, before securing a ride out. So upon arrival in Punta Arenas we immediately made travel arrangements within Patagonia.

Punta Arenas, Chile, served as our home base for the next month. A medium-sized port town with a cosmopolitan feel and a pretty view of the Strait of Magellan, Punta Arenas is large enough to provide many modern amenities but remains small enough to allow exploration by foot or public transport. Numbered taxis constitute the most common method of transportation around town. Passengers simply share a cab as it picks them up and drops them off along predetermined routes. We stayed at the conveniently located Hostal Independencia where our hosts, Eduardo and Veronica, gave us extensive information for organizing our entire Patagonian stay and generously assisted us in making travel arrangements.

Eager to experience the sights and penguins of Antarctica, we exhausted every avenue possible, but there was no way to make it to our seventh continent. We asked several locals for suggestions and then spoke with a travel agent at Comapa to see if there was space available on a last-minute cruise, hoping for a low rate. Not only were the cruises fully booked until we left for Brazil, but they cost US$7,000 per person, placing them well out of our budget. We even tried talking to two members of the Chilean navy. After one look at Christopher, who was deep into some Harry Potter fantasy play and waving his arms around wildly, casting imaginary spells, they laughed and told us that their ships were, in fact, for military business. They referred us back to the Comapa tourist office that we had already visited. So despite our best efforts, our Antarctic dreams melted away. Later, we got word from fellow CIWY volunteers, Suzanna and Dan, that by responding to a tiny advertisement in a travel agency's window in Ushuaia, they had managed to score a great last minute cruise to Antarctica. We also heard rumors of another person finding a similar deal in Ushuaia as well. So for those *viajeros* looking for an inexpensive Antarctic adventure, Ushuaia, Argentina, might be a better place to find one.

With Antarctica crossed off our list and still yearning to veer off the beaten path, we looked into visiting Puerto Williams, Chile, the southernmost settlement in the world and accessible only by boat or plane. The Comapa travel agency suggested a cruise, but the schedule and itinerary did not justify the price for us. Instead, we decided to take the weekly ferry provided by the company Transbordadora Austral Broom. We had hoped to travel to Puerto Williams and then cross the Beagle Channel to nearby Ushuaia but quickly discarded this plan for several reasons. First, the ferry from Punta Arenas to Puerto Williams sails primarily at night, rendering it near impossible to see most of the glaciers. Instead, the company strongly encourages passengers to take the return trip from Puerto Williams back to Punta Arenas to fully enjoy the scenery. Second, it is difficult to traverse the international boundary between Puerto Williams and Ushuaia by boat. No regular transportation exists between the two countries, nor are there checkpoints in either location to obtain the appropriate passport stamps. Occasionally, private boats offer to transport travelers for a stiff fee, but we could not rely on this option. So instead, we ultimately elected to fly from Punta Arenas out to Puerto Williams via a Chilean airline called Aerovias DAP and then return to Punta Arenas on the weekly ferry a few days later.

120,000 Magellanic penguins inhabit Isla Magdelena

Once that trip was locked into place, we began constructing shorter journeys to Patagonian sights of interest, especially the homes of our beloved penguins.

Through Comapa we joined a tour to a penguin rookery on the private shore of Otway Sound, a remote, windy inlet where the rocky coastline merges abruptly with the barren pampas. Penguins roamed back and forth between the frigid ocean waters and their hollowed-out dens in the hard brown earth. Wild foxes lounged nearby, barely glancing at us as we scuttled past them. From the window of our van we saw several skunks and local dolphins called *torinos*, a black breed with white markings on top that are surprisingly easy to spot from above the water. Our driver pulled over to give us a closer look at some ñandús grazing by the side of the road. Startled by our presence, the large, awkward birds quickly took off running in a comical zigzag motion reminiscent of the "Road Runner" cartoon. I struggled unsuccessfully to photograph the hilarious scene as Fran laughed until tears ran down his cheeks.

While our previous encounters were quite satisfying, nothing prepared us for Isla Magdelena, the most impressive penguin display in all of South America. Accessible by a popular daily boat tour, the island lies off the shore of Punta Arenas in the Strait of Magellan. After watching several *torinos* frolicking around our ship, we began to observe smaller black creatures gracefully leaping out of the ocean as well. As we listened to the soft plopping sounds that their bodies made upon reentering the water, we slowly realized that we were witnessing hundreds of penguins swimming intently towards their home. Once the ship docked, we disembarked and gazed around in utter amazement. Over 120,000 penguins breed on Isla Magdelena, and these delightful creatures absolutely covered the otherwise bare, hilly little island. Miles and miles of penguins—mommies, daddies, and molting chicks—were busy digging homes, mating, napping, grooming, eating, playing, and of course, braying. Their collective honking accompanied us as we hiked over designated walkways to a lighthouse with a lovely viewpoint. Along the way, signs cautioned visitors to stop for penguin crossings as large groups made their way slowly up the hill from the pebbly beach. Watching in fascination as one lifted its head upward to release a long, loud, mournful cry of distress, I thought about how many times I wanted to

Guanacos serve as the welcoming committee to Torres del Paine National Park

do the very same thing during a particularly stressful day at work. We snapped countless photos and reveled in penguinhood for hours.

"Why Are We Doing This?"

After reluctantly bidding adieu to our braying friends, we headed a few hours north to Puerto Natales, Chile, a smaller, prettier coastal town surrounded by glacial mountains. Eduardo (our host in Punta Arenas) helped us book a room at the Residencial "Don Bosco," a very comfortable family house with soft beds, fluffy pillows, and a full breakfast. Through a local tour company, we journeyed to the absolutely breathtaking Torres del Paine National Park, a sight every visitor to Patagonia must see. Our sunny day presented us with uncommonly beautiful views of the intimidating mountain peaks, sparkling glacial lakes, and enormous glaciers. Walking along a rocky beach, we fought the powerful wind out to Lago Grey (Grey Lake), the freezing water filled with bobbing icebergs so surreal that they looked like Styrofoam props from a movie set. The huge bluish-white chunks had broken off Grey Glacier at the far end of the lake and floated towards the shore. At Christopher's insistence, we scooped some pieces of ice out of the lake and sucked on them, but the biting wind kept us from lingering for long. On the return trip, Christopher admitted that his favorite part of the day was the big plastic replica of the Milodón we had seen earlier. The remains of this sloth-like dinosaur were discovered in a cave near the park, and the gimmicky model commemorates this discovery.

The next day we boarded a boat through the picturesque fiords of the Bernardo O'Higgins National Park. An accordion player on the vessel taught us some traditional Chilean songs, including one with such a catchy tune that we had Veronica (our host in Punta Arenas) teach us the words and we sang it for weeks afterwards. "*¿A donde va la lancha? A Keawe va.*" ("Where is the boat going? To Keawe it goes.") After passing the Balmaceda Glacier, the boat landed, and a short walk led us to the base of the Serrano Glacier. Pushed down by glacial force, the massive clumps of rock and ice loomed over us at the base of the hill. Impressive scenery notwithstanding, the highlight of the outing was our chance meeting with an accomplished American couple, Bonnie Michaels and

Torres del Paine National Park, Chile

Michael Seef. They had recently completed their own year-long sabbatical around the world and had written a book about the experience (see the Resources section in Chapter 1). We eagerly compared notes regarding the process of traveling for a year and made plans to reconnect the following day.

Joining Bonnie and Michael on a hike through the lovely countryside, Christopher badgered us with the usual "Are we there yet, Dad?" sorts of statements. Despite his passion for wildlife, he prefers electronics and computers to more strenuous outdoor activities. Unsatisfied with our responses regarding the length of our trek, he demanded to know "Why are we doing this?" After we explained that we wanted to enjoy the view, get out in nature, and spend some time with our friends, he replied, "Oh, I get it. There really isn't any reason why we are doing this." Unfortunately, it was a lot harder to get him up the hill after that little revelation. Bonnie and Michael did their best to try to interest him in looking for dragons, but he just wasn't buying it. Only after partaking in an elaborate "tea" and a rousing combination of baseball and soccer at the end of the hike did his mood improve.

Due to time limitations, we arranged a long day trip to El Calafate, Argentina, through a tour agency instead of traveling independently. The one-day tour enabled us easily to cross the border in and out of Argentina to visit Glacier National Park, site of the famed Perito Moreno Glacier. Furthermore, the guide also provided us with interesting information about the park, which was originally protected because it contained 40 percent of Argentina's water supply. The park is located at about 50 degrees latitude, which is no closer to the South Pole than England is to the North, and the altitude is only about 1,000 feet high. So why are there so many glaciers? The relentless wind! Originating in Antarctica, the air picks up moisture over the ocean, freezes, and then drops the frozen crystals onto the Patagonian cordillera. Over the years, snow and ice build up until the mass begins to move down the mountain under its own weight, thus forming a glacier. Currently estimated to contain about 600 tons of pressure per square yard, the astounding Perito Moreno Glacier is the size of the city of Buenos Aires and 2,000 feet deep in some areas. Progressing forward at the rate of two yards a day, enormous slices of ice, some as tall as a 20-story building, calve

Icebergs from Grey Glacier, Torres del Paine National Park, Chile

Perito Moreno Glacier, Glacier National Park, Argentina

off into the ocean. We sipped hot chocolate while witnessing this spectacular waterworks and listening to the deep groans and cracks of the monster. Absolutely phenomenal!

Against this glorious backdrop, Puerto Natales gave our social lives a boost. Not only did we enjoy getting to know our new friends, Bonnie and Michael, but we hooked up with some old friends as well. First, Canadians Rich and Cyndi met us for a rich lunch of fresh local seafood. As we made our way through the heaping mounds of shells, they shared a plethora of travel tips and information about the Lake District, a region spanning the Chilean and Argentine border to the north that we had skipped temporarily to accommodate our plans for Carnival. Fortunate to have their recommendations, we utilized many of them later on. We then paused at an Internet café to write to our lovable Dutch traveling buddy, Daveed (perhaps better known as Monkey Ears). Having just jetted off the email and walked out of the café only moments beforehand, we were incredulous to encounter Daveed striding towards us on the sidewalk. Talk about a coincidence! But weirder yet, he asked in a somewhat irritated tone, "Where have you been? I've been looking all over for you!" I began to apologize for not giving him adequate information in our email to find us. "What email?" he replied, "I just figured that you had to be in Puerto Natales by now, and I spent most of the afternoon looking for you!" His conviction in being able to pinpoint our whereabouts was uncanny.

As we celebrated our reunion in the fourth country together, Daveed shared his clever idea for an addendum to the Footprint guide. His supplement would cover all of the "really important" information about each South American town, such as the number of roosters per square meter, their birth and death rates, their life expectancies, and other significant cockerel data. Daveed kept us in stitches as he expanded on this ingenious concept. Trying to lift his spirits from the depths of rooster trauma, we urged him to join us in Rio for Carnival. After extracting a tentative commitment, we were so sorry to leave him. But we had to meet our ferry in Puerto Williams, and we literally did not want to miss the boat!

Back in Punta Arenas, we prepared for our trip to Puerto Williams. The day before we were supposed to leave, my jeans finally gave out. I had been patching them together for months, but while bending over my backpack, I split the bottom right through. Our frequent meals at a great local seafood restaurant called Restaurant La Luna, in combination with all the delectable Argentine food and wine, had ultimately caught up with me. As I bemoaned the demise of my jeans with Eduardo, he suggested that his mother could probably fix them for me. Sure enough, she patched up the bottom so well I pulled them right on and we headed out to catch our plane. Leave it to Eduardo to come up with yet another solution for us.

It's the End of the World as We Know It

Flying high on a crisp, clear day, we peered down at the gorgeous sights on the tip of Patagonia, including Tierra del Fuego. Numerous islands floated on the sparkling blue Pacific, each with mountains, glaciers, and lakes in gemstone shades of sapphire, emerald, and even ruby. I simply could not resist taking photo after photo of the magnificent scenes. Our plane touched down on a tiny runway, and we managed to find a ride with some fellow passengers into town. The southernmost permanent settlement of Puerto Williams is a small, primarily military, outpost, and boasts about two grocery stores and a handful of hostels set up in private homes along two main streets. We bedded down at Hostal Pusaki in a dormitory-style room, and we shared the bathroom across the hall. Due to the lack of tourist facilities, those residents willing to accept visitors generally provide this type of lodging.

Despite its tiny size, Puerto Williams did have a very interesting museum. After examining the large dinosaur bones strewn about the lawn, Christopher enjoyed an interactive educational computer game while Fran and I inspected the displays about the land and the indigenous tribes of Tierra del Fuego, or Land of Fire. We discovered that the explorer, Magellan, had given the region its unusual name when he first had seen the inhabitants' bonfires lighting up the night. Unfortunately, when he and the early missionaries began settling the area, they brought diseases with them. They also imposed their religious beliefs, forcing the native people to live in filthy conditions by wearing clothing and living in houses that were contrary to their way of life. As a result, over ten years the local population decreased from more than 1,000 people down to only 100 survivors. Today only one remains.

The abundant nature around the tiny town afforded ample opportunities for some fantastic ambling through relatively pristine forests with spectacular views of the mountains and the surrounding waterways. Beavers, another species introduced to the island, have damaged some wooded areas. Setting off on a long hike up a nearby mountain, we were concerned about Christopher's tolerance after his negative attitude in Puerto Natales. Fortunately, despite the length of the intense six-hour hike, he finally "got" the point of it, or at least, invented a purpose that suited him. He set his sights on "bagging" the mountain, and afterwards, he reported feeling very proud of himself for making it to the summit. Even more convincingly, he refused to take a taxi home because "that would be cheating, Mom." I certainly did not want to put a damper on his newfound enthusiasm for hiking!

Every week, the ferry operated by Transbordadora Austral Broom transports much needed supplies out to tiny Puerto Williams, passing through the Beagle Channel and the Strait of Magellan, within sight of the Darwin cordillera. As we animatedly discussed the weekly arrival of fresh produce with the local shop owners, we shared their enthusiasm in anticipation of our upcoming journey back to Punta Arenas. The ferry was delayed a day due to weather, but as a result we ended up with a whole room of 16 passenger seats all to ourselves. Apparently everyone else had canceled except a few folks occupying the tiny private cabins. We shared the boat with a lovely Aussie father-and-daughter team, a young local boy venturing off to college for the first time, and the crew. We enjoyed our roomy abode and actually got some sleep.

But we didn't want to nap too long and miss out on any of the extraordinary ambiance. We awoke to witness mammoth glaciers calving and waterfalls cascading over glittering towers of ice. The vast expanses of untouched land spoke of a wild and unspoiled wilderness, and we were truly skimming on the very outskirts of civilization. Besides our fellow passengers, no human inhabitants were visible throughout the trip. A very large whale spouted by, the breathy sound of its spray barely audible in the heavy silence around us. Sea lion pups swam by in search of food, and now and then a stray penguin peeked out of the water. Numerous seabirds, including albatross and pelicans, floated overhead, gliding on the wind currents created by the boat. The utilitarian atmosphere of the working cargo vessel, in contrast to a cushy cruise ship, added to the rugged experience. While we were on the boat for less than 24 hours, our memories from the "end of the earth" will stay with us for a lifetime.

Alighting only briefly back in Punta Arenas, we squeezed in a bus trip to Ushuaia, Argentina. The southernmost city on the South American continent, Ushuaia lies on the north side of the Beagle Channel across from Puerto Williams. Concerned about getting stranded there and unable to make our flight to Rio, we purchased round trip tickets to Ushuaia from Punta Arenas, and then onward from Punta Arenas to Trelew. Over the Internet we arranged to stay with a wonderful woman, Azu, in her comfortable home called Altos de Ushuaia. Proud of her city and its lack of pollution, Azu convinced me to drink a cup of water directly out of the tap, the first of the entire trip. She argued that the water is cleaner in Ushuaia than any other water in the world. True to her word, the water was delicious and did not make me ill. Azu was a little less enthusiastic about the weather, however. She pointed out that she had to remove all of the windows from one side of her hexagonal-shaped house because she feared that they would break in the powerful winter gales. The wind's chronic intensity even in the summer months rendered her stories all the more frightening.

Seeing that we were eager to experience some of the regional forces of nature for ourselves, Azu generously offered to supervise Christopher while we forayed out to a nearby glacier. After all, she had a boy Christopher's age and a big pile of Legos, so who could resist that? Leaving our son in her capable hands, Fran and I took public transportation to the ski lift at the Martial Glacier and began our ascent of the mountain. While we slowly progressed up the crumbly glacial terrain, we chatted with an American woman, Bridget, who made her living sailing tall ships around the world. Struggling to maintain conversation as we trudged up the steep hillside, I was a bit dismayed to discover that after all of our efforts people were sullying the glacier by writing their names on it with rocks. To avoid them, we labored onward and were eventually rewarded with some pristine glacial snow as well as even more gorgeous views of the city and the Beagle Channel beyond. After leaving our new friend, Fran and I took advantage of our time alone to leisurely peruse the Maritime and Penitentiary Museums housed in the old prison building, Presidio, which came highly recommended by Daveed. Just like its host city, this unique museum is chock-full of character as the exhibitions illustrating the lives of various colonists and quirky convicts revealed.

As luck would have it, we happened to bump into our tall ship sailing friend, Bridget, at Tierra del Fuego National Park the next day. Only minutes into our visit we all paused to watch an industrious beaver just a few feet from our soggy path. He gnawed on a twig and then carefully transported it across the water to his dam. Beginning the day on a high note, we went on to view a multitude of colorful vistas. Rocky outcroppings collided with forested land and then gave way to streams and waterways stained in unusual colors by minerals from the glacial runoff. We paused at points along the way to quietly enjoy various unusual birds and their offspring. Ending at the park gift shop, we purchased a little stuffed penguin for Christopher to keep Scabbers, his toy rat, company. When we returned to town to have our passport stamped with *La Ciudad Más Austral del Mundo* (The Southernmost City in the World) insignia, the little penguin promptly dropped out of Christopher's pocket and became lost on a crowded road. We searched high and low for the little guy, questioning any potentially suspicious-looking children along the way. Convinced of its desertion, we then patronized all the stores on the main street trying to find a replacement. One saleswoman even went so far as to arrange for someone to bring another penguin of equal size and value from the park to the store for us. Unfortunately, that person forgot the new penguin on the bus, and it too was gone! Desiring this tangible memento of our adventure in the land of penguins, we finally settled on a larger version and made sure to hang onto it throughout the trip. After all, we penguins have to stick together!

CHRISTOPHER'S COMMENTS

It was cool to see all of those penguins! I remember when they would throw back their arms and go, "Hoooooooonk!" There were also lots of cute babies. But the thing I remember most was when Mom was trying to take a picture of some penguins. She got way too close to one of the penguins' nests behind her. She didn't see it so she didn't know it was there. One of the penguins inside the hole came out and started nipping her and biting her to get her away from his hole. It was really funny!

Then after we saw all of the penguins, we went to this dinosaur museum. I remember there were lots of huge dinosaur bones. I really wanted to take a tour because I wanted to look through the microscopes. And that is how I got my microscope for Christmas! We got to do this hike where we walked around and saw a lot of bones including one prehistoric penguin and a lot of other funky old creatures. Then I decided I wanted to be an archaeologist. After I came home from the trip, I decided to go to an archaeology camp, but it was really hot there. Now I know that I don't want to be an archaeologist if they have to work in a really hot environment. Last but not least, I saw my first beaver at the end of the world, and now I still want to be a vet.

TRAVELER'S TIPS

1. Don't get stranded in the high season. Work from a home base and buy round trip tickets instead.
2. Kids may not enjoy hiking. Try to build up the adventure by giving them a goal to work towards, and if necessary, a promise of a treat for achieving it.
3. Remember, penguins bite!

TRELEW, ARGENTINA

Hotel "Touring Club"

Avenida Fontana 240
Telefax: 425790/433997/433998
htouring@ar.inter.net

This older hotel with an elegant marble staircase contained adequate rooms (although a bit rundown) with private bath and breakfast included for US$13 a night.

Punta Tombo

chubutur@arnet.com.ar

Tour offices in Trelew provide day trips to this nature reserve to see hundreds of Magellanic penguins from September to March. Often included is a stop at the quaint Welsh town of **Gaiman** for a traditional tea.

Valdés Peninsula

www.chubutur.gov.ar
info@chubutur.gov.ar

Tour offices in Trelew also provide day trips to this beautiful nature reserve to see elephant seals, sea lions, and a handful of penguins. A traditional Welsh tea in **Gaiman** is often included.

Museo Paleontológico Egidio Feruglio (MEF)

Ave. Fontana 140
Telefax: 2965 420012
http://www.mef.org.arinfo@mef.org.ar

A fantastic dinosaur museum with numerous life-sized displays and carefully reconstructed skeletons of the prehistoric critters. Visitors can see the scientists at work in the lab, and can arrange a behind-the-scenes tour as well. Christopher absolutely loved it! Entrance fee of US$3 for adults.

Parque Paleontológico Bryn Gwyn

Arrange a visit through MEF. This unique outdoor museum allows visitors to observe fossils in their original location. As visitors climb the hill, they actually move through history by viewing fossils from 40 million to 10 million years ago, learning about the environmental conditions of the time. A must for dinosaur lovers. There is even a skeleton of a 15 million-year-old penguin! Entrance fee of US$1.50 for adults.

PUNTA ARENAS, CHILE

Hostal Independencia

Avenida Independencia 374
Telefax: (61) 227572
independencia@chileaustral.com
indep374@hotmail.com

Clean, friendly family-run hostel with shared bath, TV, Internet, kitchen facilities available, and breakfast included for US$12 per night. Friendly hosts, Eduardo and Veronica, provide a detailed map and loads of information regarding Punta Arenas and other areas of Patagonia.

Restaurant La Luna

O'Higgins #974
Tel: 228555

Fabulous seafood and excellent wine at very reasonable prices, very friendly service.

Isla Magdelena

Book trip through: **Comapa Turismo**
Magallanes 990 (esquina Plaza de Armas)
Tel: (56-61) 200 202/200-203/200-205
turismocomapa@nisa.cl
www.comapa.cl

Probably the largest penguin colony in South America, this island is home to approximately 120,000 Magellanic penguins. Boats to the island are run by Transbordadora Austral Broom and leave from Terminal Tres Puentes (Take a shared taxi, #15, out along Avenida Bulnes). Trip fees are US$30 per adult, US$15 per child.

Otway Sound

Book through any travel agency, such as Comapa above. Lovely nature reserve has a colony of Magellanic penguins, as well as other wildlife such as ñandús, skunks, and foxes.

DAP Aerovias

Sells airplane tickets to and from Puerto Williams, a breathtaking flight; US$213 for the three of us.

Transbordadora Austral Broom S.A.

Avenida Bulnes No. 05075
Tel: 56 (61) 218100
www.tabsa.cl
correo@tabsa.cl

Arranges weekly ferry from Punta Arenas to Puerto Williams, an absolutely spectacular trip through this remote area of the world. The best route to view the glaciers is from Puerto Williams back to Punta Arenas. This company also runs boats out to Isla Magdelena, but tickets can be arranged for the same price through a travel agent in town instead of going all the way out to their office.

PUERTO NATALES, CHILE

Residencial "Don Bosco"

Padre Rossa 1430
Telefax: 412335

Family-run home with excellent beds, shared bath, and breakfast included, for US$12 a night. Provides lots of useful information for tourists.

Buses Fernandez

Armando Sanhueza 745, Punta Arenas
Tel: (56-61) 242313/221429
Eberhard 555, Puerto Natales
Tel: (56-61) 411111
busesfernandez@chileanpatagonia.com
www.busesfernandez.com

Arranges transportation between Punta Arenas and Puerto Natales.

Navegación a los Glaciares, Parque Nacional Bernardo O'Higgins

Turismo "21 de Mayo"
Eberhard 560
Tel: (56-61) 411176
www.chileaustral.com/21demayo
21demayo@chileaustral.com

Small boat trip to observe wildlife and hike to glaciers in the Bernardo O'Higgins National Park, complete with Chilean music.

Sendero Excursión "Sierra Dorotea"

Ilustre Municipalidad de Natales
Oficina de Turismo
Bulnes 285
Tel: (61) 411263

Wonderful hike that begins at a family home, continues uphill to a viewpoint overlooking the town of Puerto Natales, and returns to their house for tea with the family.

Turismo Zaahj

Sergio Zalej e Hijo Ltda.
Arturo Prat No. 236
Tel: 412260 / 411355
www.turismozaahj.co.cl

Tourism agency that organizes trips to El Calafate, Argentina, the massive **Perito Moreno Glacier** in **Glacier National Park**, Argentina, and to the magnificent **Torres del Paine National Park**, one of the highlights in all of Chile with its rugged natural beauty, jagged snow-topped mountains, and wildlife, including the picturesque guanacos.

PUERTO WILLIAMS, CHILE

Hostal Pusaki

Piloto Pardo 222
Telefax: (61) 621116

Family home provides bunk beds, shared bath, and breakfast for US$10 a night per person.

Martin Gusinde Museum

Aragay No. 1
Tel: (56-61) 621043
martingusinde@123mail.cl
pgrendi@hotmail.com

Interesting museum with dinosaur bones scattered in front and lots of information about the area and the fate of its indigenous people.

The local tourist office, **Ilustre Municipalidad de Cabo de Hornos** (mcabodehornos@tie.cl) provides a brochure with information of various local sites, including the **Omora Ethnobotanical Park,** with great hiking trails.

USHUAIA, ARGENTINA

Altos de Ushuaia

Teshne No. 718 (9410)
Tel: 421322/435315/15600263
azu_ush@arnet.com.ar

Comfortable family home with wonderful hostess, great view, bunk beds with shared baths, and breakfast included, for US$14 a night.

Municipal Tourist Board

San Martin no. 674 (Juana Fadul St. is cross-street)
Tel: 0054 (2901) 432000/424550
www.e-ushuaia.com
muniush@speedy.com.ar

Open Monday through Friday 8 a.m. to 10 p.m., weekends and holidays 9 a.m. to 8 p.m.

Very helpful tourist board stamps passports with *La Ciudad Más Austral del Mundo* insignia. Also provides a map of the area and directions to all attractions, as well as a long list of interesting excursions and prices. Make sure to visit the old prison, **Presidio** (Yaganes y Gob Paz), that houses the Maritime and Penitentiary Museums, the **Tierra del Fuego National Park** with its lovely shoreline views and wildlife, including beavers, and take the chair lift up **Cerro Martial** to the Martial Glacier overlooking the Beagle Channel.

Brazil
Praia do Forte
Salvador
Rio De Janeiro
Paraguay
Argentina
Uruguay
To Trelew,
Argentina

CHAPTER 7

CARNIVAL IN RIO

Carnival in Rio de Janeiro is on the destination list of most international party-goers. We were no exception. In pursuit of this goal we spent an inordinate amount of time and effort making arrangements, from the time we bought our plane tickets in Córdoba to the moment that we saw our first big float in the Sambadrome. We finally confirmed an apartment there through a local Brazilian company called Copacabana Holiday, but the whole experience turned out to be much more difficult than we could have imagined. Instead of agonizing over all of the sordid details, I will give readers some useful tips instead.

- Most hotels in Rio charge about US$1,000 for five nights during Carnival. Many do not accept credit cards but require some or all of a cash deposit up front.

- Finding a bank in Argentina that will sell you a cashier's check in U.S. dollars is quite difficult and time consuming. Standing in line at that bank can take two hours or more.

- Mailing a cashier's check from Argentina to Brazil takes a lot longer than six days, despite what they tell you.

- Brazilians will not accept a cashier's check if it does not have the words "Cashier's Check" stamped across the top of it.

- Western Union will not transfer money directly into a Brazilian bank account. Instead, you need to identify a specific person that will pick up the money at a designated Western Union office.
- Money wired from a U.S. bank account to a Brazilian bank account will take longer than three to five working days, despite what they tell you.
- Phone calls to banks in the U.S., Argentina, and Brazil from the southernmost settlement in the world are quite expensive. You can lose a whole day's budget in half an hour making these calls in an attempt to track down exactly where your money is.
- Operators at the end of the world may not know how to make collect calls to the U.S.

So now that I have spelled out all of these handy tips, readers may have just a small inkling of what we went through to secure an inexpensive apartment in Rio during Carnival and successfully send a deposit to the rental company, Copacabana Holiday. A learning experience is definitely what you get when you don't get what you want.

The travel agent in Córdoba was quite concerned about our safety in the airports of Buenos Aires, Argentina. She specifically instructed us to take a taxi from one airport to the other via a company called Manuel Tienda Leon (see details in Chapter 9, Resources, Buenos Aires section). Conveniently located in the airport, this service proved to be an excellent find. Our very friendly driver, Marcelo Salazar, transported us between airports in an immaculate private taxi for US$13. Upon arrival at the second airport, however, we nearly passed out over the excessive airport taxes. Too late we discovered the importance of being prepared to pay these fees in the required currency at the airport. Traveler's checks or U.S. dollars may not be acceptable in such circumstances so one must plan accordingly. After forking over US$80 for the pleasure of utilizing the airport, we continued on to Rio where we had pre-arranged transportation to Copacabana Holiday, our apartment rental company. Since we were arriving on the first night of Carnival, our travel agent coaxed us into spending US$30 for the airport pick-up. Later we learned that our friends had paid US$25 for a regular taxi from the airport to their hotel in Copacabana Beach without any problems, but due to the timing of our landing, it wasn't clear if this option was available to us.

The first glimpses out of the van window revealed a multitude of twinkling lights weaving a glittering trail through craggy, tropical mountains. The accumulated stress of getting to Rio and reserving the apartment began to dissipate as I admired the beautiful city. I craned my neck for a glimpse of Christ the Redeemer, an illuminated statue of Jesus perched high on Corcovado Mountain, and was welcomed by his outstretched arms. We had finally made it!

The chaos of getting an acceptable deposit to Copacabana Holiday, in addition to negative reports from other travelers, forewarned us about the challenges posed by the Brazilian banking system. When we entered the rental company office on Friday night, we needed to immediately pay the balance for our apartment. The company did not accept credit cards or traveler's checks, so an employee accompanied Fran on his quest for appropriate funds. He battled with three different ATM machines before obtaining enough Brazilian reals to cover our expenses. The machines operated on different networking systems so that two of them required Plus cards and the other, Cirrus. After emptying one machine, Fran was forced to make two small withdrawals (each incurring hefty service charges) on a second machine due to the pitifully low maximum limit. He finally hit the jackpot on the third ATM and stocked up accordingly for the weekend ahead. This turned out to be an excellent move. Our American friends told us that because so many machines were drained by the following day, one of them stood in line for hours at an American Express office trying to exchange traveler's checks for cash. Daveed also pointed out that often ATMs are filled only once a week in South America, usually at the beginning of the week. The rapidly disappearing funds affects the maximum amount customers can withdraw during the week, and by the weekend, the machines are often empty. Savvy travelers carry ample cash and never count on being able to access money out of ATMs in small towns or even large cities during times of high volume. And Carnival in Rio is as busy as it gets!

Despite all the hassles, we were thrilled with our clean, centrally located, one bedroom apartment (with a full kitchen, functioning

A typical sight in the street parades of Carnival

cable television, and air conditioner) in Copacabana Beach. Even with a required minimum stay of ten days, the place was a great deal at US$450. The rental company also supplied us with a very important list of safety tips, sights, and Carnival activities, but our top priority was to locate our friends at the Laancaster Othon Hotel. To our sheer delight, their beachfront hotel was right down the street, less than a five-minute walk away. What great luck! We raced to their place but their rooms were deserted, as one would expect on a Friday night during Carnival. Without hesitation, we assumed that they were already out enjoying the nightlife, and we began searching for them in the nearest watering hole. Sure enough, they were partying it up in the bar right next door. Absolutely impossible to miss, George towered over everyone. A tall, dreadlocked African American with a big booming laugh, he exudes happiness all around him. He had kept our visit a secret from the other two long-time friends, Mark and Brenda (hailing from Scotland and West Virginia, respectively). We got a big kick out of surprising them with our presence. Years beforehand, as graduate students at West Virginia University, we had all spent many nights together staying up until dawn, playing "beer pong," singing tunes from 80's sitcoms, and "tunneling" through drainage ditches under the school grounds. Although we hadn't seen them for over ten years, it felt just like old times.

Amidst our joyous reunion, we happily met the rest of the "Traveling Bastards" clan, brothers of East Indian descent, Dilip and Raj. Collectively we made quite a diverse and rowdy bunch. I loved watching the waiters fawn over George, affectionately nick-naming him "Georgón," or "Big George." We cooled off with numerous *caipirinhas*, a Brazilian drink made with *aguardiente*, or sugar cane liquor, crushed ice, sugar, and limes. An icy cold *caipirinha* on a humid tropical shore amidst the best company on earth comes about as close to perfection as I can imagine. We closed down three different restaurants on the beach before finally calling it a night.

We spent the next few days living it up, interspersed with some brief periods of recovery primarily around Copacabana Beach. Rio is a beautiful city, with different urban centers embedded in a collection of lush volcanic mountains jutting up along a spectacular curvy coastline. Much of the tropical rainforest is evident in its parks, gardens, streets,

Sambadrome, Carnival 2003, Rio

A samba dancer relaxes after the big event

and homes. In fact, on the tram up Corcovado Mountain to Christ the Redeemer, we were surprised to spot a big blue Morpho butterfly flitting around the tracks as well as a small capuchin monkey hanging from a tree limb. And as colorful as their homeland, many of the Brazilian people originate from Africa, giving rise to exotic foods and an energetic nightlife filled with samba, the music and dance of Carnival.

Strangely, one can stay in Copacabana Beach during Carnival and almost entirely miss the festival activities. The venues take place in various sections of the city, and visitors need to know the schedule and purchase tickets in advance to see many of the events. Although some revelry and street parties spontaneously erupt around town, the organized Carnival activities are more about pageantry and spectacle. Most of the impressive parades known throughout the world take place in the Sambadrome, a huge outdoor stadium that stretches for several blocks and was built specifically for the festival. While Copacabana Holiday had provided us with some information about Carnival events, we had no idea how to attend them. Luckily, our Canadian friends Rich and Cyndi came to the rescue yet again, recommending that we check with the tourist office on Sunday to see about getting tickets to the Sambadrome parades. If they hadn't tipped us off, we easily could have missed all of the Carnival activities despite being right on popular Copacabana Beach.

Buying tickets to the parade at the Sambadrome evolved into a day-long project. Prodding everybody into action and navigating the local transportation to the building took endurance and skill. After finally locating the correct ticketing office at the Sambadrome, we waited in a long line with hundreds of other hopeful partygoers. Tolerant of our pathetic attempts at Portuguese interjected with Spanish, English, and wild gestures, the friendly folks at the counter helped us obtain the correct number of tickets for only US$3 each. We were thrilled that we were able to get into the parade, and we all gave thanks to Rich and Cyndi for their much-needed assistance.

Hard-earned passes in hand, our group journeyed back out to the Sambadrome on Sunday night for the big event. The magnificent floats, elaborate costumes, frenetic music, and general excitement all commenced around 9:00 p.m. Literally dancing to its own tune, each samba school parades down the block for over an hour with up to 7,000 dancers in elaborate matching costumes, accompanied by magnificently decadent floats so tall that a mechanical crane hoists riders onto them. Our inexpensive tickets afforded us seats on the concrete stands where locals shimmied with crazed exuberance all around us, and even young children shook their hips with perfect rhythm to the beat. Our neighbors pointed out the words for each samba song in our programs, graciously trying to help us sing along in Portuguese. After hours of nonstop fun, Christopher fell sound asleep, and the rest of us experienced something akin to sensory overload. So around 3:00 a.m. we decided to leave although the festivities were only about half over.

Unfortunately, our return trip was a little too eventful. In order to get to the subway, we had to press through the hoards of people hanging out after running the parade route. While we had mistakenly assumed safety in numbers, our group of eight people spread out as we squeezed through the crowd, and soon Mark and Brenda were missing. Thinking that they had just stopped for food, we slowly retraced our steps to join them. Once reunited, we discovered that someone had just tried to pickpocket Brenda! Being a true heroine, Brenda felt the guy's hand in her pack and reached back to grab him. He dropped her things and then had the nerve to lean over and try to pick them up off the ground. Mark pushed him forward as Brenda stepped on the most valuable items. Ultimately she got it all back. Shaken, we regrouped and started back towards the subway. Suddenly, a woman near Fran began shouting and spilled a drink right in front of us. Aware that this distraction tactic is often used by potential thieves, Fran responded "*¡Tranquilo!*" and kept on walking. Laughing, several men began taunting Fran and shouting "*¡Tranquilo*!" at him. The mood of the crowd had definitely turned ugly. Quite scared and hyper-alert, my eyes darted all around us, studying the foreign faces encircling our tiny group and wondering who our allies were. Eight of us were definitely no match for hundreds of locals. I gripped Christopher's hand tightly as we rushed towards the subway. As quick as lightening, sticky fingers zipped open the pocket on Fran's backpack right in front of me. We had locked the main section of the backpack but could not secure the pocket. I shouted at Fran to stop, and once stationary, I examined the contents of the gaping compartment.

It still contained our most important belongings, a map and guidebook pages. I quickly zipped it up and Fran hugged the backpack to his chest. Lunging a few more paces forward, we broke through the crowd and breathed a sigh of relief in the artificial underground light. It wasn't until about two weeks later that we figured out that our small first aid kit was missing. In the blink of an eye, the pickpocket must have lifted the kit so quickly that I didn't even see him do it. Thankful that the first aid kit was the only casualty of the evening, Fran and I laughed and hoped that somewhere in Rio someone was receiving good first aid.

During the remainder of Carnival, we enjoyed more special events, ate some amazing food, and drank way too many *caipirinhas*. At a smaller parade downtown we cheered on transvestites prancing down the street in wild attire, grown men in Pink Panther outfits, and other Brazilians in crazy costumes. We settled into a main square where samba school students gathered all around us. Tiny children as young as four years old wore elaborate attire with glittering pictures of Disney characters painted on their coats. Every night we dined on different exotic local specialties. Following a guidebook recommendation, we managed to locate the tiny hole-in-the-wall restaurant Arataca, specializing in Amazonian cuisine. Considering ourselves quite daring, we tasted an unusual but tasty regional dish reputed to be poisonous if prepared improperly. Fortunately, the *caipirinhas* constituted the only dangerous item on the menu that evening. Around the corner from our friends' hotel, we also discovered the Churrascaria Palace, an all-you-can-eat extravaganza rivaling Argentina's *tenedor libres*, where waiters repeatedly brought long skewers of delectable grilled meats directly to the table and sliced off portions to the customer's specifications. The restaurant offered a choice of ten different fruit flavors of *caipirinhas* to choose from as well, leading Christopher later to ask about Fran's lack of coordination. We took full advantage of this opportunity to educate him about the dangers of alcohol.

Amidst all the festivity, we patronized some local attractions to learn more about the unique Brazilian art, culture, and flora and fauna. The Jardim Botânico, or Botanical Gardens, comes highly recommended for children. Christopher was able to touch the incredible five-foot-wide Victoria Regis water lilies, feed bread to huge sharp-toothed fish, and

Christopher investigates a Victoria Regis water lily in the Botanical Gardens of Rio

watch carnivorous plants catch and digest unsuspecting insects. We drank in the views from the mountains of Corcovado and Sugar Loaf, and made a special point of stopping at the Museu Internacional de Arte Naif do Brasil (International Museum of Native Art of Brazil) near the Corcovado train station. The small museum was full of folk art, including dolls, toys, and colorful paintings, which was quite appealing to little eyes. Building in some beach time as well, we relaxed on the sand and ordered up a fresh drink. The vender chopped off the top of a coconut, tucked in a straw, and we sipped its fresh juice straight out of the husk. We discovered that we preferred Ipanema Beach to the more hectic and trendy Copacabana Beach to the north. At Copacabana we had to simultaneously keep an eye on our belongings, fend off constant harassment by vendors and sand flies, and make sure Christopher didn't get devoured by the powerful waves crashing dangerously close to the shoreline. This multi-tasking did not make for a very restful beach experience, so instead we often relaxed on our friends' hotel balcony and peered down at the thong-clad crowd below.

A discussion of Brazilian highlights would not be complete without a word about their famous swimwear. For every one gorgeous woman in a thong, at least 100 other scantily clad bodies exist that are not nearly so easy on the eye. After standing behind far too many fat, hairy, sweaty, smelly, balding Brazilian men with their guts hanging precariously over the edge of a Speedo, I had seen enough flesh to last me a lifetime. So as Carnival began to wind down, we convinced our group to travel up to Salvador da Bahia, a smaller city about 1,000 miles north of Rio.

If Rio represents the showy, polished, mature older sibling, then Salvador symbolizes the wilder, unrestrained, popular half-sister. Salvador served as the point of entry for most slaves to Brazil and the rest of South America. As a result, this African influence permeates the culture, particularly the spicy food and rhythmic drumming (as featured in the music of Michael Jackson and Paul Simon). In addition to the old slave auction block and the slave church, Salvador has fascinating museums (including the Museu Afro-Brasileira showcasing the history of slavery, and the Museu da Cidade depicting the city's cultural and religious background) devoted to its African heritage. Women in their traditional white turbans and billowing skirts sell food on almost every

The old slave auctioning block, Salvador

street corner. On the coast and in the marketplace, we caught glimpses of capoeira, a graceful, well-choreographed form of martial arts. The recently restored downtown area surrounding Largo do Pelourinho (the former slave whipping post) sports picturesque cobblestone streets lined with painstakingly restored pastel townhouses and cozy shops displaying a rainbow of artwork. From a meticulously kept viewpoint surrounded by a stone wall, visitors can gaze down on the marketplace in the lower, more industrialized section of the town and out to the bay beyond. A funicular connects the two city levels, its entrances besieged by street vendors. In Salvador, Carnival parades still occur in the main streets, instead of being confined to certain venues as they are in Rio. Therefore Brazilians flock to Salvador for a more traditional celebration, and the points of interest are draped in festive decorations.

Unfortunately, the overwhelming quantity of people requesting money, hawking wares, and generally trying to rope tourists into their gig was exhausting. Any attempts to take photos extracted an outstretched hand demanding a stiff fee. Mindful of our friend Raj's strategy to avoid eye contact and keep moving, I made the mistake of stopping on a corner to read a map. A local woman approached me and began tying a ribbon on my wrist despite my repeated objections. I finally resorted to simply ignoring her as I tried to figure out where we were. She then kissed my hand and blessed it before asking for a "donation" for the ribbon. Her humble piety quickly turned to hostility when I refused to give her anything for the unwanted "gift." She spewed forth profanity as we carried on down the crowded street.

For us SESC/SENAC was an exciting find in Salvador. This government-run cooking school offered an extensive buffet dinner with local dishes clearly labeled in English and Portuguese. Savoring the food, we scribbled extensive notes in our guidebook so that later we could identify our favorite dishes on other menus. Bahian cuisine is renown throughout the world for its spicy flavor, prepared with fresh local ingredients such as seafood, coconut milk, and *dendê* (palm oil). After the sumptuous feast provided at a very reasonable price, we attended a folkloric show in the same building. The production featured an energetic cultural mix of capoeira and candomble (a fascinating religion blending African and Brazilian influences), all to the backdrop of a pulsing drum beat. For

SENAC performers move to a hypnotic rhythm

the entrance price we could snap as many photos as we desired, without hassle, including a few somewhat unflattering shots of us trying to shake our hips like the performers.

Eager to check out some sea turtles, our group investigated transportation options to Praia do Forte, a small fishing community about an hour and a half north along the Atlantic coast. Despite being a busy holiday weekend, we stumbled onto perhaps the only open travel agency in Salvador called Olimpia Viagens e Turismo. Through a combination of English and Spanish, the friendly owner, Vismar Henrique, connected us with a private van and driver for the day trip. Our primary objective was to visit Project TAMAR (an abbreviation of "Tartaruga Marinha," or "Marine Turtle"), created by the Brazilian environmental agency of IBAMA in conjunction with the local fisherman and their community to conserve the sea turtles that nest there. Attractively located in a tropical beach setting, the buildings comprising the project headquarters are constructed of natural materials such as bamboo and palm fronds. The organization houses turtles in all stages of development, from eggs warming gently in incubators to the large adult Olive Ridley turtles swimming in clean, uncovered pools. We were hoping to observe sea turtles actually laying their eggs, but the nesting season had already ended. Fran and I inquired into volunteer opportunities but were informed that if we wanted to help the turtles, we should buy a T-shirt. We were happy to oblige.

Following our delightful visit to TAMAR, we made the most of our time in Praia do Forte. Shaded by palm trees, we snacked at a restaurant on the picture-perfect white sand beach near TAMAR's entrance. Christopher explored the tide pools revealed by the crystal clear blue waters. Eager to share our passion for the rainforest with our friends, we headed out to the nearby Sapiranga Nature Reserve, a protected secondary tropical forest. We debated about whether to take a guided tour or hike independently, but after learning that the reserve supports the community by employing the local youth as guides, we agreed to invest in the service. Our young guide provided a wealth of information about the various plants and even made us special bracelets out of a tough native grass. Stopping at the visitor center, we cracked up over two sloths fighting with each other. Neurologically wired to move

Well-choreographed capoeira martial artists

slowly as part of their camouflage in the jungle, the sloths were taking swipes at each other in slow-motion like a bad Hollywood movie. Finding it hard to believe that they could possibly do any kind of damage, I asked if they were just playing around. The guide assured us that they were defending their territory. Definitely not *amigos*!

On the way back to Salvador, I asked the Brazilian driver in Spanish if he could take us to a simple, cheap, authentic restaurant on the beach. He spoke only Portuguese but seemed to get the gist of our request. However, as we traveled further from the beach and closer to downtown Salvador, our group became increasingly concerned about our poor attempts at communication. The driver finally stopped at a place that did not quite look like what we had envisioned. The open-air style restaurant was still fairly close to the beach but in a more urban setting than we preferred. I again tried to get my request across to the driver. He insisted that we wanted this place. We decided to give it a shot, and he turned out to be absolutely right. The gregarious staff served us some of the freshest, tastiest food in all of Brazil, offered in generous proportions for a ridiculously affordable price. We actually checked the figures twice, and the total cost really was less than US$40 for all of us. Obviously the driver knew exactly what he was doing.

Fran, Christopher, and I were enjoying our stay at the Grande Hotel da Barra overlooking the beautiful Barra beach. For US$35 a night, our double room had a private bath, full buffet breakfast, and the use of a large pool attractively decorated with an elaborate tile mosaic. Unfortunately, our friends felt less enthusiastic about their accommodations in comparison to their oceanfront room with lovely balcony in Rio. Despite a higher ticketing price, they decided to fly back to Copacabana Beach for a few more days before going home. We sadly parted ways, amazed that even after ten years we could still finish each others' sentences and think the same (albeit bizarre) thoughts. But all good things must come to an end. So with memories of drums beating, hips jiggling, and a heady mix of spicy seafood and *caipirinhas* lingering on our lips, we congratulated ourselves on having joined our friends to celebrate the breathtaking climax of Brazilian culture, Carnival.

Christopher sips a coconut on Ipanema Beach

CHRISTOPHER'S COMMENTS

We had a lot of fun with our friends in Rio. When I first saw George, I knew it was one of my parents' friends because when Mom and Dad saw him they got all excited and went "Hey!" He was big and had dreadlocks. I liked playing with his Magellan (GPS). I even figured out something that he couldn't do on it. Then I met Raj and I liked playing Game Boy games with him. Then I met Dilip and "Night Train." Everyone called him "Night Train" because he was always a trooper. He walked a lot. Brenda was the only girl there, except for Mom. Every night I would always ask, "Tonight are we going to party with our friends?" I wanted to party with our friends because it was fun! I had a good time. But one night Daddy was wobbly. The next morning, I asked Mommy why Daddy was so wobbly, and she said people should be careful because drinking too much caipirinhas makes you wobbly.

Another night we went to the Sambadrome. The floats were boring, and I read my book most of the time. One float was a big huge person. After the floats my parents made me take a picture with a guy with feathers on his costume.

I didn't like it. It was weird. The next day we went to the Botanical Gardens. I got to touch a big huge lily pad, and I got to see a Venus fly trap eat a fly. The lily pad felt squishy, and when I poked it with a stick I accidentally popped a hole in it. I felt bad because I didn't mean to do it. I enjoyed seeing the gardens and being with our friends, and that is what I liked about Rio.

TRAVELER'S TIPS

1. A cashier's check should have the words "Cashier's Check" stamped across the top of it or it might not be accepted.
2. Western Union will not transfer money directly into a bank account. Instead, you need to identify a specific person that will pick up the money at a designated Western Union office.
3. Money wired from a U.S. bank account to an international bank account may take longer than three to five working days.
4. Americans are accustomed to an excellent postal system. Often letters mailed in other countries take a lot more time to arrive at their destination.
5. Always ask about airport fees when purchasing tickets to determine if they are included in the price. Find out if you will be required to pay them at the airport and what currency will be expected.
6. Never count on being able to access money out of ATMs in small towns or large cities during holidays and other busy times. Make sure to have cards networked on both Cirrus and Plus systems.
7. Find out about holiday activities ahead of time. View the website and visit the local tourist office to stock up on as much information as possible.
8. Walk through crowds with your backpack on your chest.
9. Ignore any distractions, such as people yelling or throwing food or drink on you. This is a ploy to attract your attention while someone else rips you off. Be vigilant and keep going!
10. If you are traveling in a large group, consider arranging a van and driver to visit nearby sights of interest. It may be more cost-effective than taking local transportation and certainly more convenient.

RESOURCES

RIO DE JANEIRO

Copacabana Holiday

Rua Barata Ribeiro, 90 - Loja A
Tel: (21) 2542-1525/ 2543-1477
Fax: (21) 2542-1597
http://www.copacabanaholiday.com.br
holiday@vento.com.br

Rents furnished apartments near Copacabana and Ipanema Beaches. A minimum stay of 10 days during Carnival cost US$450 for a clean one bedroom apartment in a great location, with full kitchen facilities, AC, and working cable TV. They do not accept credit cards and cashier's checks must have the words "Cashier's Check" stamped across the top.

Apa Hotel

Rua República do Peru, 305 - Esquina (corner) de Barata Ribeiro
Tel: (21) 2548-8112
Fax: (21) 2256-3628
www.apahotel.com.br
apa@apahotel.com.br

Our friends, Rich and Cyndi, stayed at this hotel and highly recommended it. Clean, centrally located, and economical, their "apartment" included a bathroom, AC, cable TV, and fridge. They were able to make their deposit via credit card for Carnival, thus avoiding some of the headaches we encountered.

Arataca

Rua Domingos Ferreira 41

Recommended by Lonely Planet, this tiny restaurant features unique, delicious specialties from the Amazon region.

Churrascaria Palace

R Rodolfo Dantas 16B

Great *churrascaria* for the value, with an extensive buffet of salads, meats brought to the table, and ten different fruit choices of *caipirinhas*.

Make sure to visit the Tourist Office, **Riotur** (Av Princesa Isabel 183, Tel: 541-7522) to obtain valuable information on Carnival events and tickets.

Family-friendly activities in Rio include the tram ride up Corcovado Mountain to **Cristo Redentor** (Christ the Redeemer), admiring the colorful sculpture and artwork at the nearby **Museu Internacional de Arte Naif do Brasil** (R Cosme Velho 561), the cable car up **Pão de Açúcar** (Sugar Loaf), and a stroll through the **Jardim Botânico** (Botanical Garden) to observe the carnivorous plants, huge Victoria Regis water lilies, and the hungry sharp-toothed fish.

Andes Sol

Agencia de Viagens e Turismo Ltda.
Gustavo Kirby
Ave. N. S. de Copacabana, 209 – Loja D e E
Tel: (21) 2543-4662
Fax: (21) 2275-4370/2541-0748
andessol@uol.com.br

Gustavo helped us purchase plane tickets to Salvador and reserve a hotel there.

SALVADOR

Grande Hotel da Barra

Av. Sete de Setembro, 3564 - Porto de Barra
Tel: (71) 264-8600
Fax: (71) 264-6506
www.grandehoteldabarra.com
reserva@grandehoteldabarra.com.br

Reserved through Gustavo at Andes Sol, this hotel overlooks a clean, safe beach (Barra) and has a pool surrounded by lovely tile work. Spartan but clean rooms include private bath, AC, TV, some with small balconies, and large buffet breakfast for US$35 a night. We felt this was an excellent value for a triple, but our friends were less enthusiastic about it.

SESC/SENAC

Largo do Pelourinho, 19
Tel: (71) 322.8273

Catering school provides dinner buffet with 40 local dishes labeled in English and Portuguese, as well as an exciting on-site folkloric show featuring demonstrations of capoeira, candomble, and fabulous drumming.

Olimpia Viagens e Turismo

Vismar Henrique
Praça José Anchieta No. 15, Centro Histórico
Telefax: (71) 321 2387
Cell: 9153 7048
vismartour@hotmail.com

This travel agency was one of the few open during Carnival. Vismar helped arrange plane tickets back to Rio, as well as a reasonably priced, clean, comfortable van to accommodate our group of eight for a trip up to Praia do Forte, although the driver spoke only Portuguese.

Must-sees in Salvador are the historic center surrounding **Largo do Pelourinho**, the old slave auction site, **Igreja NS do Rosário dos Pretos** (slave church), **Museu Afro-Brasileira** (a museum showcasing the import of African slaves to Brazil), and **Museu da Cidade** (a museum which gives detailed information about the candomble religion).

PRAIA DO FORTE

Projeto TAMAR

Tel: (71) 676-1045

www.projetotamar.org.br

This extensive project, established to help conserve endangered sea turtles, will delight family members of all ages with its informative video and interesting exhibits of turtle eggs, babies, and huge tanks filled with the adult sea turtles, as well as its great beachside restaurant and gift shop selling interesting mementos to raise funds for the turtles. Gorgeous tropical beach and tide pools provide hours of exploration and relaxation.

Reserva da Sapiranga

Tel: (071) 99811896/99898268

www.fgd.org.br

ecoturismo@fgd.org.br

This private nature preserve has great walking trails through an Atlantic rainforest as well as some native animals, including sloths and exotic birds being rehabilitated back into the wild. Local kids serve as guides in an education effort to make conservation viable for native families.

Chile
Argentina
Uruguay
Mendoza
Valparaíso
Isla Negra
Santiago
Buenos Aires
Talca
From Rio
Pucón
Valdivia
Volcán Osorno
Puerto Varas
Puerto Montt
San Martín
Villa La Angostura
Bariloche
Isla Chiloé
Castro
Esquel
Trelew
Gaiman

CHAPTER 8

PUSHING THE LIMITS IN THE LAKE DISTRICT

Our return back to Argentina was like coming home. We felt safe, pampered, and welcomed everywhere we went. From Trelew on the Atlantic coast, we immediately headed west to the Lake District on the Chilean border. We spent the next several weeks following a very circuitous route through five countries altogether (Argentina, Chile, Uruguay, Paraguay, and Brazil), crossing multiple borders and the entire continent twice before working our way north towards the Amazon Basin. In fact, ultimately we collected over 20 Argentine stamps in our passports. Whenever other *viajeros* questioned our odd itinerary, we would simply respond "Blame it on Rio!" Reconnecting with our dear friends amidst an exuberant atmosphere was certainly worth any inconvenience, and we never regretted our decision to meet them there.

Shared by Argentina and Chile, the Lake District contains glorious glacial lakes ranging in color from sparkling turquoise blue to deep emerald green, snow-capped Andean mountains, and many different kinds of trees and vegetation. Interestingly, much of the scenery reminded me of Oregon, although the wide variety of indigenous plant life was unusual. The region abounds with national parks, each offering a unique look at its own ecosystem and special types of trees. For example, in the Alerces National Park (Parque Nacional Los Alerces) outside of Esquel, the towering Alerces trees stretch up to 100 feet tall and date as far

The Old Patagonian Express

A restored Welsh flour mill in Trevelin, Argentina

back as 3,000 years ago. Near Bariloche lies the Arrayanes National Park (Parque Nacional Los Arrayanes), the only place in the world with growing conditions that cause the Arrayanes vines to develop into distorted cinnamon-colored trees. The vines obtain nourishment from the water of the Nahuel Huapi Lake, and as a result, feel very cold to the touch. These eerily twisted trees reputedly inspired Disney's fantastical forest in the animated movie, *Snow White.* Perhaps even more strange, the jagged, geometrically-shaped leaves of the araucaria, or monkey puzzle trees, resemble an Escher sculpture. For three weeks we explored this hiker's paradise, rambling over pathways through its diverse wooded areas for hours.

The comfortable, clean little town of Esquel provided a wonderful base for our initial forays into the Lake District. Through local companies, we arranged day tours to the surrounding national parks and regional sights, including a lovely series of waterfalls. On a trip to the Welsh town of Trevelin, we witnessed a demonstration of a carefully restored flour mill, dated over a century old and powered by its original water wheel. Christopher was particularly intrigued by the elaborate mechanics involved in producing a small handful of flour. Following in the footsteps of famous travel writer Paul Theroux, we took a ride on the Old Patagonian Express. Though now used exclusively for transporting tourists from Esquel to the countryside, the train passed through painted arid landscapes and a small lake full of pink flamingos. At a rest stop, Christopher loved the opportunity to pull the train's whistle before returning back to town.

A Perfect Day

In contrast to Esquel's flat, frontier-like appearance, Bariloche resembles a village in the Swiss Alps, with its stone and half-timber architecture, clock tower, and restaurants serving Alpine specialties. After a delicious meal of raclette and cheese fondue, Christopher tried his first chocolate fondue, and found it very much to his liking. In the main square, we indulged his love of animals by posing for a family photo with a Saint Bernard carrying fortifications in a keg under her chin. Christopher received an appreciative lick on his nose from her pup. We

A perfect day in the Lake District

then consulted the nearby tourist information office to find out which mountain peak offers the best lookout point, and on their recommendation we rode a gondola to the top of Cerro Campanario. Brilliant sunshine illuminated a spectacular panorama of deep blue lakes punctuated with woodsy green valleys and snowy mountain peaks. Relaxing in the sun, we blissfully soaked up the warmth until Christopher's stomach began complaining of hunger. At the base of the mountain we boarded the local bus to a nearby brewpub called Cerveceria Blest, where we satisfied his appetite with some excellent pub grub and sampled our first decent dark beers of the entire trip. The day was absolutely perfect from start to finish. The fabulous view under the warm sun high up in the cordillera made for one of my most memorable moments of the trip.

Many Argentinians highly recommended the Seven Lakes Drive outside of Bariloche. The guided tour meanders through quaint little alpine villages and wooded landscapes, stopping at a total of seven lakes before reaching the final destination of San Martín de los Andes, a beloved lakeside vacation spot. The return trip over the Andes and down the opposite side affords a different viewpoint, as the lack of water gives rise to a more arid mountainous landscape.

We enjoyed the picturesque little town of Villa La Angostura so much on our Seven Lakes Drive tour that we decided to invest some more time there. We stayed in the rustic cabin home of a local family, and made plans to explore the Bosque de Arrayanes (Arrayanes Forest) in the Parque Nacional Los Arrayanes. The park is located on the tip of a peninsula, so we arranged to take a boat there and then planned to hike 15 kilometers (about ten miles) along the peninsula back to town. We prepped Christopher extensively for the walk, emphasizing the Disney connection to the bizarre trees as well as the possibility of encountering some wildlife. We reassured him that we would walk slowly to accommodate him and built up the adventure as a real challenge. To our complete delight, Christopher was psychologically ready for the task and, in fact, looking forward to it. The hike was a beautiful and relaxed four-hour event through old growth forest, complete with a picnic lunch in a secluded place deep in the woods. By the end of our journey, Christopher was very proud of his accomplishment. He even went so far as to insist that we walk another two kilometers (a

A monkey puzzle tree

little over a mile) back to town instead of taking the bus. "No cheating, Mom! We need to walk the whole way!" We were thrilled to see him developing an appreciation for physical activities as well as an interest in the out-of-doors, as opposed to his usual American diet of computers, TV, and Game Boy. The only casualty of the day was the loss of Fran's Leatherman tool at our picnic spot, but not even Christopher was up for trekking all the way back to retrieve it. From then on, our son began measuring everything against that distance. When contemplating another hike a few days later, Christopher commented, "It's only four kilometers away? That's not far! We did 15 kilometers, remember?"

After thoroughly exploring the Argentine side of the Lake District, we contemplated our options to cross over into Chile. We had hoped to take a scenic tour via Lago Todos Los Santos involving a combination of buses and boats, but the popularity of this trip amongst wealthy tourists had pushed it right out of our budget at US$120 per person. Instead, the friendly man at the bus station in Villa La Angostura informed us that our only inexpensive alternative lay in taking the bus to Puerto Montt, Chile. On the bus we befriended another American couple who had boarded the bus earlier in Bariloche, and they were under the impression that the bus was actually going to Puerto Varas, Chile. We were very excited about this possibility, because Puerto Varas was rumored to be much nicer than Puerto Montt.

In a rare instance of feeling disappointed at being correct, we glumly watched the bus circumvent Puerto Varas and pull into Puerto Montt. Sure enough, it proved to be a nasty, fishy, port town. We secured a tiny room with shared bath near the waterfront, and immediately began planning our escape during lunch. We happened upon a second floor restaurant overlooking the waterfront and happily wolfed down large bowls of *curanto*, a scrumptious local stew of seafood, meats, and potatoes. Coincidentally, our new American friends ended up at the same restaurant. With guidebooks and memorabilia spread all around our tables, we offered them advice about their upcoming trip to Patagonia. I handed out business cards, maps, timetables, and other helpful brochures I had accumulated along the way. They appreciatively teased me about being their personal travel agent. I was just happy to "pay it forward." Our backpacks were full of the same kinds of useful paraphernalia that Rich

The Alpine city of Bariloche, Argentina

and Cyndi had shared with us down in Puerto Natales in anticipation of our present travels throughout the Lake District.

Exploring Mapuche Territory

The next day we successfully fled Puerto Montt to the tranquil island of Chiloé. The crisp, clear day enabled us to disembark our bus and wander around the ferry linking the island to the Chilean mainland, where we delightedly watched seabirds surfing the air currents and the torino dolphins leaping through the waves. The Mapuche people indigenous to Chiloé and other parts of Chile were never conquered by the Spanish, and for that reason, they tenaciously retain their cultural identity. This stronghold is evident in the people, language, and lifestyle. We relaxed for a couple of days at the comfortable, family-run Hostal Mirador in the island's small capital of Castro. Fran and I both enjoyed the fantastic view of the bay from our room, and Christopher had a great time playing on the computer with the family's children. We enjoyed many meals of fresh seafood on the water's edge and wandered around admiring the *palafitos*, pastel-colored houses built on stilts to accommodate the changing tides. Struggling to recall the Spanish word, I affectionately nicknamed them "profiteroles," as their shimmering reflection in the water at twilight made them almost good enough to eat. We spent a peaceful day at the deserted beach in Quellón, and the clear weather allowed us to see across the bay to the snowcapped Andes on the mainland. That night, we treated ourselves to some English movies on a rented VCR. We were fascinated by the movie, *Alive*, about the Uruguayan Rugby team's ill-fated flight and subsequent ordeal surviving in the mountains, not far from the very place we had just seen earlier that day.

Our American friends' confusion about the bus route served to fuel my desire to go to Puerto Varas, a picturesque little lakeside town with a strong German influence. Being of German heritage myself, I have a strong affinity towards the culture and can't seem to get enough of the beautiful half-timbered architecture. The arresting view from Puerto Varas across Lake Llanquihue to Volcán Osorno, a perfectly cone-shaped snow-covered volcano, is one of the most photographed visions of Chile.

Palafitos *on Chiloé Island, Chile*

Volcán Osorno, Puerto Varas, Chile

Upon our eagerly anticipated arrival, a Chilean woman suggested that we rent a car to circumnavigate the lake. We easily located a travel agency (TravelSur) willing to lend us a vehicle for US$35 a day. After nine months of public buses, Fran drove for the first and only time on our entire trip. How delightful to have ample opportunity to explore the area and appreciate the stunning landscape, which even included some of the waterfalls and lakes that were a part of the expensive bus-boat tour we were forced to forgo. In Frutillar, we stopped at the open-air Museo Colonial Alemán, or the German Colonial Museum, and admired the replicas of two colonial houses, a waterwheel, and even a working blacksmith shop. We learned more about the trials and tribulations of the first German settlers in the area. Unlike other places in Argentina and Chile, these brave men and women immigrated in the 19th century to develop the land and, therefore, were not Nazi war criminals on the run. At Christopher's suggestion, we watched the blacksmith imprint our nickname, "Rumsky," on a horseshoe for a souvenir. We then drove up to the snow line on Volcán Osorno and ate a picnic lunch. Christopher had fun holding the large, deceptively light-weight lava rocks high up above his head and trudging through the volcanic debris. After wearing himself out, he slept in the backseat as Fran and I marveled at the violet and rose-colored swirls created in the clouds by the setting sun.

Somewhat reluctantly giving up the private vehicle for our customary public transportation, we journeyed north through the Chilean countryside. Taking advantage of a brief pit stop in the town of Valdivia, we visited the fish market for lunch. The market backs right on the Valdivia River, where vendors clean their fish and throw the guts to the eagerly awaiting sea lions lined up in the water. Their loud, insistent demands for food contributed to the ruckus in the busy marketplace. After watching the sea lions vying for their meals, we perused the food stalls packed with interesting sea creatures and kelp before heading back to our bus. Our route wound comfortably through some lovely forested areas as we worked our way towards our destination, Pucón. Filled with log cabins and cozy restaurants, this woodsy little town is rapidly becoming an adventure traveler's paradise. Even the bus barn was adorable; we all agreed that its construction of local timber and attractive landscaping rendered it the nicest station we had encountered on our

The German town of Frutillar, Chile

Sea lions awaiting a handout behind the fish market of Valdivia, Chile

entire trip. Nearby, we found an inexpensive, family-run hostel newly built in the same alpine style, and we spent a relaxing day exploring the town. Inspired by the fish market, we discovered a sushi restaurant on a main street and savored the tasty fish.

In pursuit of some family-friendly adventures, we followed Rich and Cyndi's suggestion to stay at a Mapuche farm located a few miles outside of Pucón. Although the prices were slightly higher (at US$27 a night) than our usual budget, we all reveled in the warm family atmosphere, interesting excursions, and excellent food. In addition to a nighttime trip to some natural hot springs, our friendly host, Peter, took us horseback riding through the beautiful countryside. We ate a delicious picnic lunch in a private forested spot next to a gurgling brook. Christopher particularly loved the farm life and participated in a variety of activities there. He learned how to successfully milk the cows after the first few tries landed on his pants. He also went fishing and "wandered around after the guy trying to see if I could help him do any farm things." Although we were planning to leave after two days, Peter encouraged us to climb Volcán Villarica, an active volcano approximately 9,000 feet in altitude (about 2,800 meters) overlooking the town. He stressed the rarity of being able to climb an active volcano, particularly with the availability of a tour company that provides all the transportation and equipment to do so at a reasonable price. He even offered to have his Mapuche mother-in-law watch Christopher during our trek. We just couldn't refuse this unique opportunity!

"Con Dolor"

The day started out cloudy, and there was some concern that the trip would be canceled due to the wind. In fact, some companies did not run their tours that day. However, once we approached the base of the volcano, the sun broke through the clouds, and the guides decided that the weather was adequate, so we commenced our climb. Unfortunately, part of the gear that they gave us included very heavy boots similar to those used for skiing. This footwear was required to tread through the slippery snow and fasten on the crampons (which ultimately we did not even need). The moraine at the bottom of the mountain was very soft

Our quest: to climb the active volcano of Volcán Villarica

and sandy, so that for every three steps forward, we literally slid two steps back. After battling the moraine for an hour in those damn boots, both Fran and I were struggling. Fran's flat feet were very uncomfortable and already developing blisters. I was getting quite winded despite being in relatively good shape between working out at the gym and walking all over South America. Luckily we were accompanied by a supportive group made up of two Chilean guys and an Aussie couple who cheered me on. One of the Chileans gave me some advice about tackling the mountains in a zigzag manner, which worked quite well, but he also made some disparaging remarks along the way, such as "Americans think they are the best, but now look at you, last on the mountain," which wasn't quite so helpful. Concerned, the Aussie asked Fran if he was planning to walk the rest of the way using the strange sideward stance he had adopted to try to cope with his boots. "Something like that," he responded, trying to remain upbeat despite the growing pain. We rested at a chairlift station and fortified ourselves with lunch. I had never been so happy to eat slices of apple in my life.

When we started out on the glacial ice, our guide, Pedro, demonstrated how to use our ice picks and fall appropriately so we would not slide backwards down the mountain. I tried to maintain my position at the end of the line, taking advantage of my companions' footsteps on the glacier. I was not having much luck creating my own steps in the hard ice with the ski boots. I wasn't heavy enough to be able to pack it down effectively, and my repeated attempts to produce toeholds by kicking at the ice seemed only to hurt my feet. Traversing the mountainside in switchbacks, our group slowly made our way up the approximately 5,000 foot (1,500 meter) gain. At one point I was completely exhausted and insisted on stopping to rest near some rocks. I seriously considered whether or not I could continue. Pedro chose that moment to tell me about a rock that had tumbled down the mountain about two weeks beforehand, striking another guide in the head. He was seriously injured and in a coma for two days. "The weather conditions were the same as they are today," he said, looking anxiously at the wind. "Great, now you tell us!" was my first reaction, but at least it got me up and moving. At that point there was clearly no backing out.

Bagging the summit

As we neared the peak, I again had to rest and ingest a few more slices of apple. Pedro tried to encourage me onward, telling me that we only had about 40 more minutes to go. We had been climbing for about four hours, so the thought of almost another hour's worth of work did not make me very optimistic. Pedro took my backpack, and I tried to show my appreciation by propelling myself onward. He radioed the folks below, and I overheard him saying that we were approaching the summit. "*Sí, sí, vienen.*" ("Yes, they are coming.") He paused, chuckled, and added, "*Con dolor.*" ("With pain.") I smiled in spite of myself. He was exactly right about that! About ten minutes from the top, I began stumbling over the sharp, black lava rocks encircling the rim. Pedro and the others were cheering for me, shouting "You're almost there; you can see it!" With my nose dripping incessantly, I wheezed and choked on the sulphuric fumes spewing out of the volcano as well as the fine black dust blowing up around us. Pedro suggested that I wear my gas mask. I put it on, but forcing the air through the mask was more effort than I could muster, and I became quite lightheaded from the attempt. After falling over twice from the lack of oxygen, I gave up on the mask and my legs as well. I crawled the few remaining yards over the sharp volcanic rock until the ground leveled out. I had bagged the volcano! Wahoo!

The hard-earned view was spectacular. Through wisps of cloud, the surrounding hills, valleys, and checkerboard farmland stretched on for miles. I felt as if I was observing the miniature homesteads and tiny vehicles from a plane instead of on land. Even better, we could see the reddish glow inside the crater and watch the sulphuric gases pouring out of its sides. But I only had about five minutes to enjoy the amazing sights. Pedro continued to worry about the wind. He strapped on my gators and returned my backpack. "Luckily it will be easier going down," I commented hopefully. I rationalized that, if nothing else, at least gravity would be on my side. However, Pedro disagreed, indicating that the hike downward would be just as difficult due to the rocks and the wind. Feeling extremely discouraged, I came close to tears, but obviously there was nothing I could do but get going.

Pedro was right; at least initially, the descent was awful. Our boots clashed with the hard, sharp, angular lava rock, causing my feet and ankles to contort in unnatural ways. After struggling with the rocks for

Fran shows off his sliding technique

about a half hour, we came to the snow slides carved through the glacier. Now the fun would begin! Pedro showed us how to glide safely down the mountain using the ice pick as a break. Having grown up in Syracuse, New York, I felt confident in my abilities to sled through the heavy snow. I eagerly emulated Pedro's graceful slide but again was thwarted in my efforts. I was not heavy enough to zoom down the slopes like the larger men. Wet snow accumulated under me so that I had to keep pushing myself forward with my arms and legs, leaving me exhausted and defeating the purpose of the slide. Pedro even pulled me along a little bit with his ice pick to try to build up enough momentum to get me going. No luck. "Rats!" I shouted in frustration, "I can't even do the damn snow chutes!" Thankfully, Fran offered his assistance by carrying my backpack. Refusing to accept failure, I developed a turtle-like approach where I sped down the slope on the center of my back, curled up in a little ball. Completely ignoring our guide's ice pick technique, I whizzed merrily down the mountain. Poor Pedro was a little freaked out and shouted at me to stop, but I felt completely in control. I showed him that I only had to put my legs down to stop myself. Thrilled that I finally got something to work out right, I happily made my way through the snow against a backdrop of literally breathtaking views. We then slogged and slid through the sandy terrain at the base of the mountain, which really was infinitely easier going down than up. When we eventually arrived back at the van, I felt a heady sense of accomplishment. I had truly pushed myself beyond my limits. I took particular delight in noting that I finished the trek several minutes before the Chilean who had teased me during our ascent. Despite my temptation to say something, he looked so battered by the time he reached the van that I thought better of it and held my tongue.

While we waited for the Chileans at the van, I asked Pedro if any families had ever brought along their children. He indicated that only one European family had attempted the climb, and the father carried his daughter on his back all day. Unbelievable. I was so glad we had left Christopher back at the farm. Though I had bruises on my shins and toes for weeks and two of my toenails turned black and fell off, it was still pretty amazing to be able to climb an active volcano.

"Here Lives the Devil"

After about three weeks in the Lake District, we continued north through Chile, stopping in Talca and Santiago for some serious wine-tasting. Peter helped us reserve a room at a beautiful B&B called Casa Chueca in Talca with luxurious beds, private bath, gorgeous grounds, and even a pool. We soaked up the dry sunshine while Christopher had fun following the llama and other animals around the lovely flowering gardens. Again the price, US$30 a night, was higher than we were accustomed to paying, but we had limited hotel options in Talca, and we were determined to try their wines.

Most Chilean wineries strive to create a memorable and personalized experience for their guests. Instead of holding set visiting hours in their tasting rooms for drop-in customers, wineries typically require their visitors to make an appointment ahead of time and pay for a guided tour and private tasting. Furthermore, because the wineries are often not accessible by public transportation, visitors need to utilize expensive taxi services. Fran and I accepted these extra expenses and time constraints to taste some of the region's best wines.

In Talca, or the Maule Valley, we visited two very different wineries. Built by a well-known American company, Kendall Jackson Wine Estates, the elegant Viña Calina (Calina Winery) utilizes state-of-the-art technology to showcase their uniquely Chilean wine. We tried the 2001 Chardonnay, the 2000 Cabernet Sauvignon, 2001 Merlot, and 2001 Cabernet-Carmenère. The French oak gave some nice structure to these wines, as the balance between fruit, tannin, and the vegetal terroir was delightful. Our favorite was the rich tobacco and spicy flavor of the Cab-Carmenère blend, which had received 90 points in the December 2002 edition of the *Wine Enthusiast*. We were disappointed at not being able to bring several bottles home, as the same bottle of wine in the United States costs over twice as much. Our second winery, Viña Domaine Oriental, or Casa Donoso, began as a family-run bodega (winery). Its reliance on traditional methods within a centuries-old hacienda contrasted nicely with the modern elegance of Viña Calina. Domaine Oriental offered a wider variety of wines, with several grades ranging in quality from basic table wine to their Ultra Premium label. While they employ traditional methods to age some of their wines in American and French barrels, they also use a unique style of placing oak chips into the tanks during the fermentation process to impart the wood flavor to their Linea Classica (Classic Line). We found their very drinkable wines to be somewhat softer and fruitier than those at Viña Calina. The casual, family atmosphere made for a delightful tasting experience.

The vibrant, upscale, capital city of Santiago was next on our wine-tasting circuit. We opted to save some money by staying a bit out of town at SCS Habitat, or Scott's Place, where we had a room to ourselves with shared bath and breakfast. As advertised in his numerous fliers and the Footprint guidebook, Scott provided an absolute wealth of information, and we quickly learned to consult him before venturing out on our own. Scott helped us organize two trips to local wineries. First, we took a taxi to Viña Cousiño-Macul. Located on luxurious sprawling green grounds within the greater Santiago area, the land has been producing wine for almost 500 years. The small museum, therefore, contained some very interesting centuries-old relics of wine-production. Furthermore, their grapes are harvested from old vines imported from Europe in the 18th century before the phyloxera blight. While the phyloxera aphid has destroyed most of the old vines in the United States and Europe, the South American vines have avoided the deadly insect. Wines made from these very grapes are showcased in their Antiguas Reservas and Finis Terrae lines. We tried three reserve wines, the 2000 Chardonnay, the 1999 Merlot, and the 2000 Cabernet Sauvignon. Using primarily French and some American barrels, their wines were oaky and tannic with some complexity, a nice nose, and a lingering finish. The trip was informative and the wines, delightful.

Saving the best for last, we eagerly sought out the most anticipated winery of the entire trip, the granddaddy of them all, Viña Concha y Toro. Producing an astonishing 100 million liters of wine a year, Concha y Toro is the largest wine maker in Chile and the biggest exporter to the U.S. market and worldwide, sending their wines to 90 countries altogether around the globe. The founder, Don Melchor, arrived from Bordeaux in 1883, and the winery continues to have French connections, forming an alliance with French wine baron Philippe de Rothschild in 1997. Sipping an outstanding Chardonnay, we strolled

Looking for the Devil in the Casillero del Diablo, Concha y Toro Winery

Christopher dances out a tune in Santiago

through the grapevine-covered arbor way and around the glorious gardens. Our tour group then moved indoors, and we descended past dusty bottles dated over a century old to the famed Casillero del Diablo (Devil's Cellar). Apparently, after frequently finding bottles of red wine missing from his cellar, Don Melchor began telling his workers, "Here lives the Devil." Being very superstitious, the locals believed him and subsequently avoided the area so that no wines were ever stolen again. Using eerie music and strategic lighting, the cellar continues to give off a spooky vibe. As we began to make our way to the tasting room, we turned around just in time to see a shadow of the Devil himself at the gate! Christopher certainly got a kick out of it. With so many wines to choose from, the tasting room offered samples ranging in price from the least expensive vintages of Casillero del Diablo and Trio (US$5 a bottle) to the exclusive Don Melchor and Almaviva lines at US$50 a bottle. We stuck with the Trio 2002 Chardonnay, 2001 Merlot, and 2001 Cabernet Sauvignon. The name, Trio, pays tribute to the delicate combination of climate, soil, and wine-making skills necessary to produce a good wine. Despite no oak on the Chardonnay, the natural grape yielded a wonderfully toasty, buttery flavor, while the reds proved to be complex and full-bodied, with cherry tones and rich finishes. Devilishly delicious!

After all that wine-tasting, we had to build in some quality kid time, and the Museo Interactivo Mirador (MIM) really fit the bill. This interactive museum for children enabled Christopher to dance a tune on a 10-foot keyboard just as Tom Hanks did in the movie *Big*, encase his entire body in a gooey soap bubble, and create artistic masterpieces with a pen suspended from the elevated ceiling. We also really enjoyed the elegantly displayed pre-Columbian art at the Museo Chileno de Arte Precolombino. In the afternoon, we rode the *teleférico* (cable car) to the top of Cerro San Cristóbal, a tall hill on the edge of town. While the ride was fun, we were disappointed with the view of heavy smog pressing down on the city, very reminiscent of Los Angeles, California.

Ready for some fresh ocean air, we took a day trip to the home of the famous Chilean poet, Pablo Neruda, in the tiny coastal town of Isla Negra, just south of Valparaíso. In contrast with sunny, warm Santiago, the fog on the Pacific Ocean lowered the temperature in Isla Negra dramatically. Despite the chill, we enjoyed Mr. Neruda's unusual home,

Crossing over the Andes, the filming site of Seven Years in Tibet

Niño y vino

which was full of odd items perfect for entertaining an inquisitive seven-year-old boy. We easily boarded a bus along the main road to Valparaíso but watched in dismay as the fog thickened outside our windows. By the time we got off the bus in the city center, we were shivering in our T-shirts and shorts. A sympathetic fellow passenger informed us that she had seen many tourists go through the same experience. Fran graciously lent Christopher and me the clothes literally off his back; I zipped his pants' legs onto my own, and Christopher wore his long-sleeved shirt. We set off at a rapid pace in search of some hot food. We quickly strode by interesting views of tiny, colorful houses jumbled together on the steep hills, connected by narrow walkways and moving stairways. Ultimately, we found a very nice, upscale restaurant, appropriately called Bote Salvavida (literally, "Life Saver" or the Spanish term for a life preserver) overlooking the dock. We ate sumptuous rich seafood stew while watching the huge hydraulic cranes loading and unloading long ocean liners. We lingered over lunch, enjoying the warmth and pleasant atmosphere in our box seats to one of the best hydraulic shows in the world. While Viña del Mar was originally on the itinerary, we abandoned that plan in order to return to much warmer and sunnier Santiago.

From the capital, we boarded our last Chilean bus, crossing back over the Andes into Mendoza, Argentina. We were excited about returning to Argentina, as the Chilean prices for comparable goods and services were consistently higher, and the friendly Chileans were no match for the impossibly gregarious Argentinians. Our mountainous route wove through the breathtaking scenery where they filmed the movie *Seven Years in Tibet* starring Brad Pitt. When we arrived in Mendoza, a young woman approached us at the bus station. She showed us photos of an apartment close to the center of town and offered us a free ride there. She looked harmless enough, and we agreed to come see the place. For US$12 a night, it turned out to be a great deal, and we resided there for several days over the Easter holiday, or Semana Santa. Economic pressures resulted in many Argentinians opening their homes and apartments to tourists, which worked out very well for our family. We also found a large all-you-can-eat *tenedor libre* (called Las Tinajas, meaning large earthenware jars) close to our apartment. Eating there became a nightly ritual and directly contributed to my purchase of a larger pair of jeans.

In Mendoza, a moderately sized European-style town best known for its wine-making tradition, we found wine-tasting more accessible and inexpensive than in Chile. Public buses leave regularly from many places in Mendoza to outlying wine-making regions, and visitors can walk from one winery to another without needing an appointment. In fact, the popular Ruta del Vino y el Olivo, (Wine and Olive Route) is shown on a handout easily obtained from the tourist office. We visited several wineries in this area and were consistently impressed with the quality and price of the wines, as well as the diversity reflecting the ethnic mix of the country. We first stopped at Bodegas Lopez, a large winery founded by a Spaniard named José López Rivas, who arrived in Mendoza at the turn of the century. Visitors flooded the tasting room as we waited for our tour through the huge facility, and we passed the time posing by several six-foot bottles of wine. On our visit, we learned that in Argentina one winery might bottle its wines under a variety of labels to signify differences in quality, vintage, crops, and vineyard locations of the harvested grapes. Bodegas Lopez produces well over 20 labels, and we tried the 2002 Carona Lopez Chardonnay and the 2002 Bodega Lopez Malbec. Unfortunately the wines available to visitors during the tour tasted fairly mass-produced, being young with a sharp edge to them.

We fled the crowds at Bodegas Lopez and found the wines more to our liking at the smaller, locally-owned Bodega Cavas del Conde. Producing small volumes of high quality wines, their reds (including a Cabernet Sauvignon, Malbec, and Merlot) are often put on French oak and tend to be fruity with a soft finish. Bodega La Rural/Viña San Felipe boasts a wine-making and carriage museum full of old artifacts, which were of interest to Christopher. The wide variety of wines made in the traditional style, including some Italian wines under their Rutini label, offer something pleasing for almost any palate. We enjoyed the 1998 San Felipe Museo Malbec, with its lingering rich flavor and touch of spice, as well as the oaky, buttery 1998 Museo Pinot Blanco. Having already toured several wineries and hoping to avoid the occupants of the ominous tour buses out front, we headed directly to the tasting room at Antigua Bodega Giol. Their wines were particularly delicious and unique, especially their Moscato and Mistela dessert wines. We snuck into a side door to ogle the over 20-foot tall, ornately carved wine barrel with the Giol insignia (a bull), and Christopher played with the life-sized metal bull out front. On our way back to the bus stop, we couldn't resist pausing at yet another interesting wine museum, the Museo Nacional del Vino y la Vendimia, or the National Museum of Wine and the Harvest Festival, also full of old wine-making paraphernalia and information about the area, as well as some Italian varietals available for tasting.

While going to the wineries themselves was certainly *vale la pena* (worth the effort), our best tasting experience actually occurred right in downtown Mendoza at La Cava del Mercado Central (the Cave in the Central Market). While wandering around looking for food and a dry haven to escape the heavy afternoon rain, we were approached by a young, attractive couple asking if we would like to try some wine. Before we could say "*¡Por supuesto!*" ("Of course!"), we were chatting away in Spanish with our delightful hosts and sipping probably the best wine of the entire trip. The Cave features handcrafted wines made by small local wineries lacking the resources to run their own tasting rooms. Taking careful inventory of our wine preferences, our hosts opened bottles particularly suited to our palates. Cecilia was especially helpful in her analysis of the Syrahs from the Ruggeri family. She indicated that one bottle was like Mel Gibson, while the other, Sean Connery. We bought a glass of Mel and took home a bottle of Sean. For only US$4 a bottle, he turned out to be quite a cheap date.

Wine-tasting is not the only attraction in Mendoza; we participated in many other family-oriented activities there. The convenient tourist bus provided several choices for sight-seeing, and we particularly liked the city tour to the Monumento Ejército Libertador, a huge statue commemorating the Argentine liberator General San Martín, which overlooks the entire city from its location high on top of the Cerro de la Gloria. The bus tour also included a trip to the Museo del Area Fundacional, an archaeology museum with Plexiglas floors revealing a work-in-progress excavation, and the Serpentario, a snake museum which really caught Christopher's interest. Unafraid to venture out alone in Mendoza, I indulged myself in some shopping trips as well. The leather goods were exceptional and I splurged on a fuchsia leather coat and matching miniskirt, as well as exquisite leather boots and matching handbag. Much to Fran's chagrin, I was too afraid to send them home in the mail, so we (or rather, he) lugged these items around in our backpacks throughout the rest of our trip.

Our Family Transformation through Life on the Road

Unfortunately, the pace of our new schedule was decidedly hurried in comparison to our first six months of traveling, and the frequent packing and unpacking, the pressure of meeting buses and making deadlines, and constant togetherness certainly had its stresses. Being inseparable 24-7 meant that we knew more than we wanted to about each other, and small quirks became blown out of proportion. Christopher and I would constantly hassle Fran about his tendency to use the bathroom right when we were walking out of the door to get started with our day. He also had an irritating habit of going on an errand to get something in the late afternoon and then returning home with the local brew instead of the original necessity. While I tend to make decisions quickly, Fran took much longer to make up his mind about our itinerary and often needed to draw out the route and think about it for several hours before committing to a plan. I would get impatient and hated to see valuable time ticking by when we could be taking action; Fran disliked feeling pressured into these decisions. I also heard complaints from Fran about my "micromanaging" or my insistence on keeping things neat and always in their place. We bickered over which seats to choose on the buses when the best ones (over the driver on a double-decker or to the right of the driver with a window view) were taken. We argued over where to eat and whether we should find a place to stay with food preparation facilities, as I tended to enjoy going out while Fran was longing for his own cooking. Being joined at the hip is enough to strain the most stable of marriages.

Furthermore, in the midst of all the fashion-conscious beautiful Argentinians, rumored to have the highest number of cosmetic surgeries in the world, I was frustrated with how I looked. I had gained quite a bit of weight, and all of my ill-fitting clothes were literally falling apart. The jeans that had begun to rip in Ecuador were just a series of threads by this point, sewn precariously together by patches. I finally broke down and bought new jeans in Mendoza, but they were just not the same as my comfortable pairs from home. My hair was growing out so that streaks of gray were showing, and my skin was often covered with bug bites and acne due to climate changes. Shaving body hair in cold, cramped, sometimes dirty showers was a real chore, but I still kept at it as best I could. Before the trip, I thought I would not be troubled to keep up my appearance but, rather, do as the locals do and maybe even neglect American obligations such as shaving my legs. However, I discovered that 36 years of vanity was not about to change that quickly. I found myself trying to explain to people we met on the road that I really didn't look that way at home. Despite reassurances that I looked fine, I still felt self-conscious about my decidedly travel-worn appearance.

At times, long-term traveling was difficult for Christopher as well. During our city tour to the archaeology museum, I watched Christopher gaze longingly for several minutes at a large group of children on a field trip. He looked so lonely and homesick that it nearly broke my heart. I rushed over to hug him, and we talked about how much he missed his English-speaking friends. Generally a shy, introverted child, he found it difficult to initiate conversations in English, let alone a foreign language, no matter how much we encouraged him. He definitely missed out on peer interaction while on the road.

As we came to understand the psychological effects of a year-long journey together, hindsight indicates that scheduling a break in the later months is at least as important as doing so earlier in our trip. Had we to do it over again, we would have planned for more relaxation time at regular intervals (e.g., every two to three months) throughout the trip. Initially, we made the mistake of treating the year as an endless amount of time to travel and went at such a relaxing pace that we were scrambling to compensate for lost time later on. The further we moved into our trip, the more our time limitations became apparent, and the more stress we experienced about our perceived deadlines. Furthermore, while we had originally thought of activities such as Spanish lessons and volunteering as a break, we definitely should not have viewed any type of volunteering as a vacation. Typically, it constituted at least as much work as traveling and needed to be treated as such.

However, despite the drawbacks, we were having the time of our lives. Nothing can compete with the freedom of waking up and creating your own day, full of exotic adventures, handcrafted to your personal interests. I loved the anticipation and exhilaration of experiencing places that I had heard about and dreamed of for years. I relished the connections made with people from all over the globe and the fascinating cultural and historical insights these chance encounters afforded. The challenge of learning and practicing Spanish consistently appealed to my intellect and growth as a person. The minor inconveniences and self-consciousness I felt paled in comparison to the advantages of our highly coveted time off.

Despite our minor irritations with each other, we thrived as a family and became increasingly close through daily teamwork and adjustments around each other's unique interests and talents. What a gift to be able to spend so much quality time together, sharing fascinating adventures, laughing over crazy situations, and delighting in each other's company. Traveling together constitutes an interactive process of transformation from self to group. Each of our personal strengths was enhanced because our entire family relied on them. For example, Fran tirelessly transported all of our heavy luggage, fixed and jury-rigged things, and carried out all kinds of mundane tasks without ever complaining. Christopher dubbed me "The Rememberer" as I frequently needed to use my memory in recalling dates, times, and places. I typically organized and scheduled our activities, especially as I was the most fluent in Spanish. Fran and I both counted on Christopher's ability to pick up Spanish phrases and remember spoken words better than either of us, and just having him along opened up all kinds of conversations with local families. While we each developed our unique talents through our contributions to the family, we all collectively became excellent problem-solvers and organizers.

Furthermore, through the process of self discovery, I also gained a greater understanding of my own weaknesses and how they interacted with those of my family. I learned to be much more patient and tolerant, and became increasingly self-sufficient and confident in taking on just about any challenge thrown my way. To assuage my irritation over some trivial quirk, I reminded myself about all of the wonderful qualities my husband and son have to offer or joked about some recent funny event.

Amazingly, Fran and I have developed such a similar style of traveling over the years that we were almost always in complete agreement about our daily activities and trip itineraries. However, traveling with a child dramatically changed our approach. By remaining open-minded, we all came to appreciate each other's interests and sought out activities that would appeal to everybody, including Christopher. For example, Fran and I planned trips to specific wineries of potential interest to children due to a museum or some other special on-site attraction, and we allowed him ample time to observe anything that caught his eye or to simply run around. We learned so much about each family member's personal areas of interest that these topics evolved into our family's collective areas of expertise. Christopher's love of animals brought us to some of the most fascinating places on the continent, and we all learned a tremendous amount about the delicate ecosystems there.

Although Christopher struggled with homesickness, his intellect and knowledge of the world blossomed. He experienced first-hand what most American children are only able to read about in books. He became increasingly outgoing and struck up engaging conversations and relationships with people of all ages. He even collected email addresses of friends that he had met totally on his own. I felt intense pride at seeing my son master the Spanish language. His ability to understand and remember Spanish vocabulary became so refined that I would often tell him to remember certain words that we heard in passing, because I knew I wouldn't be able to recall them later on. His excitement about archaeology and the natural world, particularly animals, intensified, and he became increasingly invested in planning our daily outings and, eventually, our overall trip itinerary. It was thrilling to see him develop a passion for traveling, one of the greatest gifts that Fran and I could give to him.

CHRISTOPHER'S COMMENTS

My favorite part of the Lake District was Bariloche. I had my first chocolate fondue there. It was the best! It had everything—strawberries, oranges, and bananas. I didn't really like the bananas. Also in Bariloche I saw one of those big dogs with a barrel under its chin. It had a little puppy that was so cute! It kept licking me and licking me and licking me while we were trying to take the picture. It was so cute I could barely let go. We also saw these cool trees called the monkey puzzle trees. I don't know why they called them that but it was cool because it was a cross between a cactus and a pine cone. I would recommend Bariloche because it was a nice town and had a lot of fun things for kids.

TRAVELER'S TIPS

1. Collect brochures, timetables, business cards, and other paraphernalia to pass along to other travelers.

2. Always keep a business card from your hotel on you and your child to facilitate your safe return at the end of a long day.

3. Consult the hostel owner regarding your plans to solicit insight and information.

4. In some countries, you *can* take advantage of people who approach you at bus stations offering rooms in their homes. Ask others if this is a safe and acceptable option. Inspect the photos carefully and trust your judgment. You may stumble onto an excellent deal!

5. Be aware of the way travel will stress family relationships. Take time to be alone and pursue your own interests. Try to be patient and sympathetic, and focus on each other's strengths. Refer to your original goals and pacing agreements in order to gain consensus. Plan for more relaxation time towards the end of your trip.

6. Try to create opportunities for your kids to spend time with local children. Stay in family-run hostels and homes with children present to take advantage of naturally occurring interactions. Bring along toys that encourage involvement with others.

7. Help your child remain connected with friends at home through the Internet.

RESOURCES

ESQUEL, ARGENTINA

Dirección de Turismo (Tourist Office)
Av. Alvear y Sarmiento
Tel: (02945) 45 1927/ 453145
www.esquel.gov.ar
turismo@esquel.gov.ar

The very helpful tourist office provides maps and extensive information about exploring the area around Esquel.

Elena Rowlands
Rivadavia 330
Tel: 452-578

Recommended by Footprint, clean comfortable room in family home with shared bath and breakfast for US$10 a night.

Patagonia Verde E.V.T.
9 de Julio 926
Tel: (02945) 454396

This agency arranges great boat and hiking tours of the gorgeous **Los Alerces National Park**, the local waterfalls called **Nant Y Fall**, and the Welsh town of **Trevelin** with its century-old, functioning flour mill run by a water wheel.

Viejo Expreso Patagonico (Old Patagonian Express)

The train, affectionately known as La Trochita, delights young and old alike; just ask at the tourist office in Esquel for directions to the train station and the schedule. Fee is US$5 for adults, free for children.

BARILOCHE, ARGENTINA

Residential Rosán Arko
Güemes 691
Tel: 423109

Recommended by Footprint, clean, comfortable room in family guesthouse with private bath and kitchen facilities for US$17 a night.

Cerveceria Blest
Av. E. Bustillo Km 11.600
Tel: (02944) 461026

This brewpub poured quite possibly the best beer in all of South America, served alongside delicious food in a cozy atmosphere.

The Tourist office said that the best view is from the top of **Cerro Campanario**, accessible by cable car, and we are inclined to agree. Near the tourist office in the **Centro Cívico Plaza**, keep on the lookout for the St. Bernard dogs and the interesting **Museo de la Patagonia**. Also, make sure to take the **Siete Lagos (Seven Lakes) tour**, offered by several agencies for about the same price. The tour of seven Argentine lakes will include a trip to **San Martín de los Andes** (Secretaria de Turismo, Tourist Office, Tel: (02972) 427347/ 425500, munitur@smandes.com.ar), the **Nahuel Huapi National Park**, and **Villa La Angostura**.

VILLA LA ANGOSTURA, ARGENTINA

Secretaria de Turismo (Tourist Office)
Av. Siete Lagos 93
Telefax: (02944) 49-4124
www.villalaangostura.gov.ar
turismo@villalaangostura.gov.ar

Sra. Isolina
Las Mutisias 59
Tel: 494282

Recommended by Footprint, this rustic home includes an outhouse and shared kitchen facilities for US$10 a night.

Los Amigos del Lado Sur
Los Taiques 55

Lovely restaurant with delicious food and extensive wine list.

Huemul II

Runs boat trips to **Los Arrayanes National Park**. Can make reservations at its office near the boat launch at Puerto Angostura or at:

Hotel Angostura
Telefax: (02944) 494224/ 494233
www.hotelangostura.com
www.laangostura.com
info@hotelangostura.com

PUERTO MONTT, CHILE

Residencial El Talquino
V. Pérez Rosales No. 114
Tel: 253331
Cell: (09) 6445868

Family-run, small room with shared bath and breakfast for US$8 a night.

CASTRO ON CHILOÉ ISLAND, CHILE

"El Mirador" Hospedaje
Magaly Bohle
Sotomayor extensión Barros Arana 127
Tel: 633795 – 095796793
maboly@yahoo.com

Great family atmosphere, very clean and nicely furnished, with fantastic sea view, TV, private bathroom, access to the kitchen, and breakfast, all for US$20 per night.

Family activities include a visit to the ***palafitos***, the cute pastel-colored houses on stilts by the water, as well as an easy bus trip to the clean, deserted beach at **Quellón** with a lovely view of the Andes in the distance. Watch for dolphins when on board the ferry to Chiloé from the mainland.

PUERTO VARAS, CHILE

Trauco Cabañas & Camping

Imperial 433
Telefax: 65-23 62 62 / 65-23 33 25
www.turismotrauco.cl
ctrauco@surnet.cl

Funky place with camping and apartments, a bit run-down but functional with hot water and cable TV for US$18 a night.

TravelSur

José Manuel Molina
San Pedro 451
Telefax: 65-236000
www.interpatagonia.com
travelsur@travelsur.com

Rented us a car for US$35 a day.

We highly recommend that families rent a car to drive around **Lake Llanquihue** and up the picturesque **Volcán Osorno**. Stop in **Frutillar** to visit the **Museo Colonial Alemán de Frutillar** (Museum of German Colonization), with interesting exhibits for kids and adults including a real-life blacksmith in action.

If your travels take you north to **Valdivia**, make sure to go to the **fish market** on the coast and look for the sea lions waiting for a handout!

PUCÓN, CHILE

Hospedaje Victor Gallegos

Palguin 705
Tel: 443525
www.victor-gallegos.Bizhosting.com

Cozy, family-run guesthouse with shared bath and central room with cable TV and use of kitchen facilities for US$5 per person. Close to bus station.

Sushimania

Fresia 477

Make sure to check it out if you need a sushi fix!

Kila Leufu Guesthouse

Margot Martinez and Peter Krinner
Tel: (56) (09) 7118064
www.kilaleufu.cl
margotex@yahoo.com

Great family guesthouse on working farm with Mapuche hut, about 30 minutes from Pucón. Comfortable, clean triple room with breakfast and shared bath for US$27 a night. Can purchase all meals and wine on site. Hosts will arrange activities such as horseback riding, biking, fishing, trekking, hot springs and climbing an active volcano.

TALCA, CHILE

Casa Chueca Guesthouse

Kati or Franz
Tel: (56) (71) 1970096
Cell: (56) (09) 419 0625/ (56) (09) 837 1440
www.trekkingchile.com
casachueca@hotmail.com

Beautiful ranch-style guesthouse with gardens, pool, pet llamas, and open patios. Very comfortable, clean rooms with private bath and breakfast for US$30 a night. Arranged wine-tasting tour for us.

Wine Route of Valle del Maule

www.sernatur.cl
wineroute@entelchile.net

Viña Calina

Representative: Dinelly Pino V.
Fundo el Maitén
Camino Las Rastras Km. 7
Tel: (56) (71) 263126
Fax: (56) (71) 263127

www.calina.cl
info@calina.cl

New state-of-the-art winery owned by Kendall Jackson Wine Estates. Wines include Chardonnay, Cabernet Sauvignon, Merlot, and Cabernet-Carmenère. Must call to set up appointment for tour and tasting. US$6 per person tasting fee.

Viña Domaine Oriental—Casa Donoso

Fundo La Oriental, Camino a Palmira Km. 3.5
Tel: (56-71) 242506
Fax: (56-71) 242091
www.casadonoso.cl
courrier@casadonoso.cl
ereinero@casadonoso.cl

Traditional winery within beautiful centuries-old hacienda. Wide range of whites and reds available for tasting. Must call to set up appointment for tour and tasting.

SANTIAGO, CHILE

SCS Habitat or Scott's Place

San Vicente 1798
Tel: (56) (2) 683 3732
scshabitat@yahoo.com

Basic accommodations with shared bath and full breakfast for US$5 per person. Located 15 to 20 minutes by bus from city center. Scott has a wealth of information about the city and surrounding areas, and can set up tours to wineries.

Viña Cousiño-Macul

Avenida Quilin 7100 Peñalolen
Tel: (562) 351 41 00
Fax: (562) 284 15 09
www.cousinomacul.cl
vtaparticular@cousinomacul.cl

Centuries-old vineyard with interesting relics from wine-making times gone by, located on well-manicured grounds within city limits. Wines include Chardonnay, Merlot, and Cabernet Sauvignon. Need to set up an appointment for a tour and tasting.

Viña Concha y Toro

Avenida Virginia Subercaseaux 210 in Pirque,
27 km SE of Santiago
Tel: (56-2) 476 5269
Fax: (56-2) 853 1063
www.conchaytoro.com
rpublicas@conchaytoro.cl

Best known and largest exporter of all the Chilean wineries. Extensive tour of the lovely grounds includes the famous Casillero del Diablo, complete with spooky effects that are fun for kids of all ages. Extensive wine-tasting includes a range of whites and reds. Reservations for a tour and tasting are strongly encouraged. Tasting fee, US$6 per person.

Museo Interactivo Mirador (MIM)

Punta Arenas 6711, La Granja
Tel: 294 3955

New children's science museum with loads of fun, unique interactive exhibits.

Other must-see sights around Santiago include the ***teleférico*** (cable car) from Av Pedro de Valdivia Norte to the top of **Cerro San Cristóbal**, as well as the **Museo Chileno de Arte Precolombino** at Bandera 361, *esquina* (corner) Compañía, www.precolombino.cl.

Also, make sure to visit **Fundación Pablo Neruda** at Isla Negra overlooking the Pacific Ocean, with its interesting collection of objects that appeal to kids and adults alike. Following an easy bus hop north along the coast, we had great fun exploring **Valparaíso** and eating at the upscale, delicious, **Bote Salvavida** right on the dock with a great view of the boats. Remember to bring warm clothing no matter what the weather in Santiago!

MENDOZA, ARGENTINA

Las Tinajas

Lavalle 38
Tel: 0261-4291174/75
www.lastinajas.net
mendoza@lastinajas.net

Great *tenedor libre* (free fork, or all-you-can-eat) restaurant with wide array of *asado* (grilled meats), salads, desserts, etc. for very reasonable prices.

Bus Turistico (Tourist Bus)

Direccion de Turismo Municipalidad de Mendoza
9 de Julio 500
Tel: 0054261 4495185/6
Av. San Martin y Garibaldi
Tel: 00 54 261 4201333-4238745
turismo@ciudaddemendoza.gov.ar

The tourist office sells bus tickets for a highly recommended city tour, which stops at the **Monumento Ejército Libertador**, an impressive statue paying tribute to General San Martín, high on top of the Cerro de la Gloria in the Parque Gral. San Martín, the **Museo del Area Fundacional** (an archaeological museum highlighting the history of Mendoza), and the **Serpentario** (snake museum).

Ruta del Vino y el Olivo

Departamento de Turismo
Departamento General de Desarrollo Económico
Ozamis 914 Maipú
Tel: 0261 497 7437
economaipu@nysnet.com.ar

Ask at the helpful tourist office for this brochure of the wine routes, and the buses available to get there. The wineries in this area are about six miles from Mendoza.

Bodega Cavas del Conde

Dorrego s/n (5513) Coquimbito, Maipú
Telefax: 154544953
turismo@cavasdelconde.com

Locally owned and operated for approximately 100 years, this bodega bills itself as a "boutique" winery that focuses on the production of small volumes of high quality wines. Fruity wines (Cabernet Sauvignon, Malbec, and Merlot) with soft finish; some put on French oak, others not.

Antigua Bodega Giol

Ozamiz 1040, Maipú
Tel: (0261) 4976777

Popular large winery; many tour buses stop here to observe unique traditional wine-making facilities including an elaborately carved barrel over 20 feet tall and the iron bull out front. Delicious wines, including dessert wines (Moscato and Mistela).

Bodegas Lopez

Ozamis 375 Gral. Gutierrez, Maipú
Tel: 0054-261-4811091
Fax: 0054-261-497 3610
www.bodegaslopez.com.ar
lopezmza@bodegaslopez.com.ar

Very popular with a busy waiting room, six-foot tall bottles of wine nearby, and frequent tours of the grounds. Wines available for tasting on the tour included a Chardonnay and a Malbec, which were young with bright fruit and a sharp edge to them.

Bodega La Rural/Ruttini/Viña San Filipe

Montecaseros s/n, Coquimbito, Maipú

Traditional bodega with interesting wine and carriage museums. Wide range of wines for tasting included Pinot Blanco and Malbec.

Museo Nacional del Vino y la Vendimia

Located on Ozamis, on the Ruta del Vino y el Olivo

Interesting museum with historical information about the area and wine-making paraphernalia. Wines available for tasting included some Italian varietals.

La Cava del Mercado Central

Representative: Cecilia Anahi Martinez
Entry: Gral. Paz, Las Heras
Tel: 4256904

This tasting area in the Central Market showcases wines from small local vineyards. The delightful representatives poured excellent wines at exceptional prices. Our two favorite winemakers were:

Finca Aguinaga de Medrano

La Legua s/n medrano Junín, Mendoza
Tel: 0261-4235819
fincaaguinaga@hotmail.com

Their unoaked Merlot 2002 was rich and full of fruit.

Los Vinos de la Familia Ruggeri

San Martin 1650 (5507) Luján de Cuyo
Telefax: (54-261) 498-7376
bodegaruggeri@ciudad.com.ar

Their 2000 Merlot, 2000 Syrah, and 2001 Syrah were very rich and flavorful, with nice tannins and structure. Cecilia likened two of these wines to Mel Gibson and Sean Connery.

Unfortunately, we do not have any information regarding our accommodations in Mendoza as we were approached by a family looking to rent their private apartment—clean, comfortable, great location—for US$12 a night. The best we can do is to encourage you at least to consider the same possibility if approached at the bus station. Ask lots of questions and check out the pictures and location; if it looks like a good deal and the family looks safe, go check it out!

Brazil
Paraguay
To São Paulo
Asunción
Ciudad del Este
Foz do Iguaçu
Puerto Iguazú
Encarnación
Posadas
Colonia Carlos Pellegrini
(Esteros de Iberá)
Salto
Mendoza
Argentina
Uruguay
Colonia
Buenos Aires
Montevideo
Punta del Este

Chapter 9

NIGHTLIFE AND WILDLIFE IN AND AROUND BUENOS AIRES

Bidding farewell to the fertile vineyards of Mendoza we again traversed the country to Buenos Aires, big apple of the south. The city is well known among *viajeros* for its vibrant energy and intense nightlife, where young and old eat at midnight and party until dawn. What an exciting place to be! We began with a tour and a musical performance at the world famous opera house, Teatro Colón. Acting ranks high among Christopher's many interests, and therefore, the behind-the-scenes tour was particularly meaningful for him. He loved the huge sets as well as the elaborate costumes ranging from spooky masks to platform boots. Later that evening, it was my turn to be delighted as the show featured a clarinet soloist. I had played the clarinet for years, and I marveled at the amazing acoustics enabling the music from a single instrument to fill the entire concert hall designed to seat 2,500 people. We then took advantage of the famed bar scene by watching a tango show at the oldest tango bar in the city, Bar Sur. The tiny candle-lit room contained only about ten small tables around the dance floor and provided such an intimate setting that we were even invited to participate in the show. Although I am not very coordinated, how could I refuse to dance with a gorgeous Argentine man? The passion of the tango is so well-known that it is almost cliché, but once experienced, it is an absolutely exhilarating experience. The music and movement left me breathless and crying out

The passion of the tango

for more. Christopher was even caught up in the moment as he continued to try to dip me for months afterwards with very limited success.

We spent our days eating in trendy restaurants and absorbing the fascinating history of the city. We joined the Manzana de las Luces (roughly translated, "City Block of Light") cultural tour to explore the oldest colonial buildings in Buenos Aires, including the underground tunnels connecting them. Constructed by the Jesuits, this area represented the city's intellectual center in the 17th century. That afternoon we admired the European and Latin American artistic works at the Museo de Bellas Artes (Museum of Fine Arts) and followed up with a visit to the Museo de Motivos Populares Argentinos José Hernández (the José Hernández Museum of Popular Argentine Motifs), which houses a wide array of Argentine folkloric art including crafts, silver work, and attire from the native people, European colonists, and gauchos (Argentine cowboys). The rest of our time we tracked down various connections to one of my favorite leading ladies, Eva Perón, often simply referred to as Evita. The life of this actress, who became the wife of the Argentine president Juan Perón during the 1940's, has been immortalized in a Broadway musical and a movie starring Madonna. We toured the Casa Rosada, a rose-colored government building at the heart of the city in the Plaza de Mayo, where Evita (and later Madonna) made her famous speech. We visited her tomb in the Duarte family mausoleum at the Cemetery of the Recoleta and checked out a new museum called Museo Evita. Devoted exclusively to the life of Evita, this museum is housed in a building which originally contained one of her public works programs. The displays indicated that not only did she start many similar projects to help destitute women and children by providing them with health care, housing, and job training programs, but she was also instrumental in bringing about women's right to vote in Argentina. She truly was an incredible woman. How sadly predictable that the musicals primarily focus on the negative aspects of her life rather than all of her good work. Long live Evita!

Straight out of a fairy tale, the drawbridge and lighthouse of Colonia

A tranquil setting overlooking Río de la Plata, Colonia, Uruguay

South America's Best-kept Secret

Uruguay lies just across the river, Río de la Plata, from Buenos Aires. Easily accessible by boat from the city, the tiny country serves as a popular destination for vacationing Argentinians and Brazilians. Beach resorts, hot springs, sprawling haciendas (ranches), and European-style colonial cities encompass just a few of the delights that Uruguay makes available to its visitors. The extremely friendly and laid back people speak easily understandable Spanish and often English as well. Similar to Argentina, the food and wine are exceptional, and the quality of life is excellent. Furthermore, the local currency is heavily tied to the Argentine peso, rendering everything very affordable for us lucky U.S. citizens. As in Mendoza, a local woman offered us a room in her home upon our arrival at the pier, and after one look, we took advantage of this opportunity. Unlike in Peru, following touts in Argentina and Uruguay worked out well for us. We loved every minute spent in Uruguay, and wished that we had planned to spend more time in this little-known holiday hot spot.

Ranking in our top ten favorite places in all of South America, the walled city of Colonia resembles a fairy-tale land of cobbled streets lined with historic stone buildings and cafés overlooking tranquil waterways. The Barrio Histórico (Historic District) has been declared a UNESCO World Heritage Site, and a 17th century drawbridge adds to the charm. Even the trash collection method appears quaint, as horse-drawn carriages remove the rubbish. We dined on a leisurely lunch of tasty *parrilla* (barbecued meat) and seafood on the terrace of La Luna while gazing out at the river. We surveyed the view from the top of the Faro (The Lighthouse), and explored the interesting local Municipal Museum next door, where the fossils and taxidermal animals delighted Christopher.

We would have loved to remain in Colonia for a couple of weeks, practicing Spanish and absorbing the historic atmosphere. But with no time to spare, we hopped on an eastbound bus, and in two quick hours, we arrived in the capital city of Montevideo. Amidst the pretty colonial buildings, we chose the cheapest hotel we could tolerate right downtown. After meandering about the city, we discovered a luxurious 18th century French-style restaurant at the top of the Radisson Hotel in the

Plaza Independencia. Sipping on drinks and taming our late afternoon cravings with some delightful snacks, we played several games of Harry Potter and watched twilight commence over the port and the river beyond it. The very friendly service even came with a big smile despite our wet and disheveled appearance. With an unbelievably low price of approximately US$15 for all of us, a light evening meal there became a daily habit. The following day we rode the bus out to Punta del Este, the up-and-coming high-class playground of the jet set. The drive along the river passed by peaceful coastal towns, which ultimately we preferred to glitzy Punta with its harbor filled with enormous yachts.

Wishing to exchange the rain for more comforting waters, we cruised north from the capital to Salto, a resort destination popular for its numerous hot springs. Because the damp and dust of our cheap Montevideo digs had become a health hazard for me, we splurged and stayed at the centrally located Hotel Los Cedros in a clean, modern, very comfortable room with a balcony overlooking the street below. The friendly staff in the lobby introduced us to the equally gregarious owner of La Caldera, a restaurant down the street. Because of the autumn drizzle, he graciously offered to transport us there in his car, and we gratefully accepted. The cozy, restored brick building with a wood-burning fireplace was very inviting, and his delightful family served us sumptuous *parrilla* and wine. For more pampering we spent the following day at the Termas del Dayman, trying out their collection of clean, tiled pools, ranging in depth from shallow to deep and heated with mineral water to various temperatures. Families abounded, and we thoroughly enjoyed the ability to relax while keeping an eye on Christopher, splashing around delightedly in the water.

Unfortunately, due to the rain, the dust from our Montevideo hotel, the stress of constant motion, and what I later learned to be allergies, I became increasingly ill with some disconcerting ailments. I developed a sinus infection that eventually did not even respond to Afrin, the potent nose spray I had brought along for emergencies. I also acquired an awful form of bronchitis that left me gasping for breath after a short walk down the block and gave me coughing fits every time I laughed. After attempting to outlast the illness, I ultimately broke down and obtained antibiotics in Salto. The medicine helped to alleviate my sinus symptoms, but the raspy cough and breathing difficulties persisted. Because SARS (a life-threatening respiratory illness) had broken out in Asia and Canada, my bronchial infection was especially problematic. Whenever we crossed a border we were required to fill out a little card questioning whether we had visited infected areas, experienced any bronchial problems, or received any medical treatment for such issues in the previous two months. Those unfortunate souls answering yes to any of those questions had to stand in a separate line where a medical professional loomed ominously with latex gloves. Eager to move through the system, we always put "No" on the card, and I did my best to breathe easy throughout the process.

Snail Eggs

Despite my lingering health problems, we carried on in pursuit of a nature reserve called Reserva Provincial Esteros del Iberá (Marshes of Iberá Provincial Reserve) tucked into the panhandle of Argentina. After hearing our enthusiasm for the animals in Bolivia, a fellow American traveler named Eric highly recommended that we visit the marshes despite their remote location. Excessive rains flood the bright red earth (known locally as the *tierra colorada*), causing floating plants and reeds to build up over time and become dense enough to allow only animals and birds to walk on them. Thus an ideal environment develops for a wide variety of fowl and aquatic life. True to Eric's word, getting to the reserve proved to be difficult, and our guidebooks were of little help. Because of the limited tourist facilities, we made transportation and sleeping arrangements ahead of time with the Ñande-Reta Inn, located in the tiny town of Colonia Carlos Pellegrini on the banks of the marshes. To get there, we crossed the border from Salto to Concordia, Argentina, and changed buses to proceed on to Mercedes, Argentina. Then a jeep picked us up at the Mercedes bus station in the late afternoon for the four-hour drive to the inn.

Providing just a tease of the abundant wildlife to come, the setting sun brought many interesting animals out of the rustling grasses flanking the crimson dirt road. We spotted lots of birds, a few snakes, and even a rodent or two. Upon arrival, we worked with the innkeepers

Preparing to set out on the Iberán marshes

to arrange forays into and around the marshes by foot, canoe, and horseback, Christopher's new favorite method of transportation. Our boat enabled us to get so close to the large capybara rodents that we could hear them chewing greedily on the reeds. We also glided silently by several caimans at rest with their mouths hanging open in the warm sun and witnessed two river otters scurrying along a small island as they played with a freshly caught fish. Our knowledgeable guide demonstrated how vast islands of lovely purple lilies floated on the water due to air sacks underneath the plants. As he lifted one out of the water, he discovered a cluster of bright reddish-orange eggs, each about three to five millimeters in diameter, amongst its roots. I was shocked when he informed us that these tiny rubbery balls were snail eggs. I had no idea that snails lay eggs!

Later we hiked in the forest adjacent to the marshes with a guide required by the government to ensure that the reserve remain protected. Our guide knew the habits of the resident animals, and we were subsequently rewarded with close-up views of armadillos, foxes, deer, and howler monkeys. On our way out of the forest, we encountered large groups of capybaras munching on the lawn surrounding the park headquarters. Our guide laughingly told us that they welcome the overgrown rodents; they keep the lawn so neat and trim that the park rangers never need to cut it themselves. Despite the transportation difficulties, the expense, and our time constraints, our visit to the amazing reserve and the luxurious lodge was worth every effort, and we were very thankful to Eric for the tip.

From the inn, we hired a jeep to take us north to Posadas, a small, pleasant city on the border between Argentina and Paraguay. Our Argentine driver tried to convince us to stay in Posadas, indicating that it was far safer and cleaner than the Paraguayan town of Encarnación directly across the border. Still, we insisted on going to Encarnación because we hoped to take a bus to the Paraguayan capital city, Asunción, the next morning, and we thought that it would be easier to buy a bus ticket to Asunción from within the country. Our driver generously offered to take us across the border, which turned out to be quite an ordeal in itself. Unfortunately, it was just a foreshadowing of things to come.

Paraguay—the good

The bad, and the ugly

Bribes at the Border

Our first eye-opener occurred when the border officials notified us that U.S. citizens now needed a visa to enter the country, to the tune of US$45 apiece. They gave us two options; we could go to an embassy somewhere in Argentina to obtain the visa, or they could put a stamp in our passport which would be valid for 10 days, but they would not give us any change or a receipt of the transaction. They then interrogated us extensively about why we wanted to enter the country, and appeared very skeptical about our sight-seeing interests. We got the impression that they did not think there was much of value for visitors, and started questioning our own motives! Not wanting to waste the time and effort we had expended to get there, and still determined to see the country, we paid the bribe of US$135 in cash, which was tossed into an empty drawer at the immigration counter. After talking to our jeep driver about the delay, he shook his head sadly and warned us that this type of corruption was typical in Paraguay. In fact, on lists of the most corrupt countries in the world (e.g., Transparency International), Paraguay consistently ranks in the top ten. We had just learned why.

With the necessary visas stamped into our passport, we crossed over into the run-down, nasty town of Encarnación. The negative experience at the border set the tone for our stay in Paraguay, which we generally found to be unpleasant and unfriendly. Simply walking on the filthy crumbling sidewalks and avoiding the vehicles chugging clouds of dark smoke into the air was challenging. The following day we bravely forged ahead to the capital, Asunción. The ride afforded some nice views, as the red earth and bright red brick of the homes contrasted strikingly against deep green foliage and beautiful tropical flowers. However, most of Asunción was also dirty and dusty. The people at our hotel never cracked a smile despite our best efforts at being friendly towards them. "Breakfast," consisting of stale hot dog buns and instant coffee, started each day off on the wrong foot. Furthermore, we struggled to find our way around the city. Our guidebooks were of absolutely no help; it seemed as if the writers had not set one foot in the country. One of the maps had a stairway going right through the center of town. We asked several locals but no one had any idea why that might be. Moreover, every single recommendation that we followed was either closed down or nothing like the guidebook description. While this is typical of most South American cities, it was unusual for us to have absolutely no luck at all.

Despite these problems, Asunción did have a positive side. In an attractive downtown area, we managed to find the Panteón Nacional de los Héroes, a monument commemorating war heroes and child soldiers, as well as the Museo Etnográfico Andrés Barbero, a museum full of native artifacts. After our discouragement over the poor recommendations in the guidebooks, we chanced upon a restaurant serving a delightful blend of French and Paraguayan dishes called San Trope. Our waitress was decidedly the kindest person that we encountered in Paraguay, and we returned to her place every night without fail. We also emptied our pocketbooks on several wonderful mementos at the tourist office. Paraguayans from all over the country gather there to share their wonderful handicrafts, and we bought anklets, necklaces, bracelets, and other trinkets from the indigenous tribes in the jungle. A saleswoman described how her family raised exotic birds and harvested the feathers to make these unique body adornments. She assured us that her people do not harm the birds and strive to preserve the species for future generations. These treasures hang on our living room wall today.

Another positive outcome was that I received very good health care there. While my sinus infection had cleared up after the first dose of antibiotics, my bronchial troubles continued. I emailed my mom, a nurse, and she suggested that Zithromax might be more successful. With this information in hand, we headed off to the health care clinic. After listening to my chest, the doctor seemed quite alarmed and immediately ordered an X-ray and some type of nebulizer treatment. At each step of the process he repeated the cost of each procedure and made absolutely sure that I was willing to pay. The entire bill amounted to under US$50, and I appreciated his consideration of our financial affairs. He prescribed the same antibiotics my mother had recommended, as well as some cough medicine. In a few days, my bronchial infection had greatly improved. Thank goodness, no SARS! After this forced hiatus, we fled the capital as rapidly as possible to Ciudad del Este on the eastern border and into Argentina to see the spectacular Iguazú Falls.

Politics en Route

While traveling, we remained somewhat isolated from international events due to our lack of access to the media. Still, we eventually learned of the U.S. invasion of Iraq in an Internet café. Typing away on our computers, we abruptly heard the familiar voice of George W. Bush declaring "If you're not with us, you're with the terrorists!" This sound bite elicited loud gasps of shock from us as well as others working at their respective terminals. While the comment could have been taken out of context, the implication was that anyone who didn't support Bush's policies was as bad as the people that flew planes into the World Trade Center and the Pentagon. Without fail, every South American we met felt angry at Bush's international agenda. They viewed the war with Iraq as an imperialistic attempt to gain access to oil. Memories of the Chilean man's taunts on the active volcano came back to me. "You Americans think you are the best" resounded in my ears.

It was disheartening to see local people's smiles and open expressions of welcome turn to concern when we told them our nationality. We tried to distance ourselves from any association with the Iraq war by stating that we were simply, *Norteamericanos* (North Americans), but people always insisted on determining exactly where we were from. We considered telling people we were Canadians like one American traveler we met who wore maple leaf memorabilia all over his belongings. However, the SARS epidemic and resulting immigration challenges during border crossings discouraged us from doing that as well. So instead, we routinely responded, "We're from the United States, but we didn't vote for Bush and we don't support the war." Following that clarification, people would immediately open up. Interested in discussing political issues, they typically emphasized the universal South American sentiment that the war was *por petrol* (for oil). One woman looked as us with fear in her eyes and asked earnestly, "We don't have any oil here. Do you think they would still try to take over Argentina?"

At about the same time, we began receiving reports of the military coup that had recently occurred in Venezuela. Fellow *viajeros* coming from the capital city of Caracas said it was "crazy" and shared rumors that people were being abducted directly out of the airport. Because our

The mighty Iguazú Falls

return plane tickets flew out of Caracas, we were alarmed. With negative feelings running high against the U.S., we were potentially prime targets for problems. We contacted the airlines to determine whether we should change our point of departure. The airlines reassured us that if the need arose, they would assist us in making the necessary arrangements at that time. While we had originally planned to travel for about a month in Venezuela, we had no idea what we would encounter there following the coup. We decided to change our itinerary to include a trip to the Guianas and possibly the Caribbean, instead. Fran started some Internet research about Trinidad and Tobago and became increasingly excited about relaxing on the beaches there before going home.

"Poor Niagara!"

Our final stop in Argentina was the world-famous Iguazú Falls, reputed to have made Eleanor Roosevelt exclaim, "Poor Niagara!" Throughout Argentina, locals frequently asked us if we had seen this amazing natural wonder and travelers had consistently raved about it. In reality, the falls truly are a sight to behold, dwarfing any other falls in the Americas. Flat plateaus create a long series of drop-off points, as the water tumbles from one level to the next before swirling into the bottommost river and beyond. The intense spray creates dazzling rainbows, and tiny swifts fly straight through the rushing water to their nests behind the falls. Along the shores, lush tropical vegetation teems with wildlife. Upon entering the park, we were immediately surrounded by hundreds of brilliantly colored butterflies. We trod carefully on the stone walkways, trying to avoid stepping on several large, hairy banana spiders. The park rangers informed us that they were migrating. We also encountered an extended family of coatis on a trail descending to the falls. After seeing what they did to the volunteer's leg at CIWY, I jumped up onto the railing to get out of their way, but I still managed to snap a few photos.

While the falls themselves were absolutely breathtaking, we had even more fun the next day in the rainforest bordering the water. Our "short" nature hike through the jungle extended to the entire day. We stopped to watch three different groups of monkeys pass all around us

The annual banana spiders' migration

A coati explores the falls

in search of food. We saw a myriad of birds, including a woodpecker that looked just like Woody, the beloved cartoon character. On a brief rest stop near the river at the end of the trail, I spied a thin, bright green snake dangling silently from a nearby tree. The snake was well-camouflaged, and I was very glad that I checked the area thoroughly before sitting down. Still charged after such a wonderful day, we took a special night tour to a lookout point at the top of the falls called the Devil's Throat (La Garganta del Diablo). Guided only by the light of the full moon, we passed over walkways suspended above the rushing water and peered out into its raging flow as it thundered over the massive edge.

We devoted a third day to exploring the Brazilian side, which provided a broader view of the entire series of falls. The footpaths enabled us to venture closer to the rushing water where we got soaked by the spray. Afterwards, we visited the nearby Parque das Aves (Bird Park) to enjoy the wide variety of birds, including toucans, flamingos, ibis, spoonbills, and rheas (the ostrich-like birds of the pampas). Returning to Brazil on the following day, we toured the Usina Hidreléctrica de Itaipu, the world's biggest hydroelectric power plant. The dam produces 95 percent of Paraguay's electricity. Our visit consisted of a bus tour around the dam as well as a movie, in English, detailing its history. Down the road, the project also instituted a museum describing the government's protection efforts of the local flora and fauna when constructing the dam. After soaking in the entire Iguazú experience, our entire family was inclined to agree with Mrs. Roosevelt. "Poor Niagra" indeed!

In addition to the remarkable ecological sights, we even enjoyed our stay in the small Argentine town of Puerto Iguazú, a clean, friendly place with a broad range of eating and sleeping options. While dining out on our last night there, we "watched" a televised soccer match between Argentina and Brazil. In reality, we became much more engrossed in the boisterously cheering, chair-waving, ceiling-thumping, excited fans around us than in the game itself. Outside, the clear night bestowed a magical view of a rare lunar eclipse. We left our seats at regular intervals to venture outside and admire the moon as it slowly turned black and then deep crimson. Sighing with the knowledge that we would soon be leaving this phenomenal country, we breathed in the memorable night, combining natural wonder with the exuberance of the Argentine people, thus providing a fitting end to our time in fabulous Argentina.

CHRISTOPHER'S COMMENTS

We saw a lot of animals at Iguazú Falls. There were birds flying right in and out of the water. When we were climbing the stairs on the path, a whole family of coatis came over on one of the rails. They were just walking along. Mom got really scared, but I wasn't. I just slid to the side of the path. When me and Dad went down to the water, Mommy saw a green snake. Mommy yelled for us to come back, and we saw the green snake too. The snake was long and skinny, not a big one. Then it went away. I liked Iguazú Falls.

TRAVELER'S TIPS

1. Check current visa requirements before arriving at a foreign border.
2. When deciding on a family-friendly destination, look at the Transparency International website to investigate the corruption of a country.
3. You will probably need to pay for medical expenses out of your own pocket on the road. Always ask the cost and be prepared to pay for it in cash. Keep receipts in order to submit them to your travel insurance company.
4. Stay aware of the political climate of the country you plan to visit. Change your plans if necessary.

BUENOS AIRES, ARGENTINA

Manuel Tienda León S.A.

Driver: Marcelo D. Salazar
Tel: (54-11) 4496-6089
In Buenos Aires: 15 4496-6089
marcesalazar2002@yahoo.com.ar

Exceptional service between airports in Buenos Aires; make sure to look for the counter in the airport. Apparently will do city tours as well.

Hotel Europa

Bartolomé Mitre 1294 esq. Talcahuano (1036) Capital Federal
Tel: 4384-8360
Telefax: (011) 4381-9629
www.eurohotel.com.ar

Reasonable accommodations with private bath in a great location near the Obelisk and Opera House for US$10 a night, although a recent peek at their website shows rates have increased dramatically.

South American Explorers Clubhouse

Jerónimo Salguero 553
Tel: 4861-7571
Cell: 54-911-5113-9861
www.samexplo.org
baclub@saexplorers.org

Great resource for members; this clubhouse was not opened during our trip. See Chapter 1 Resources section for more details.

Bar Sur

Estados Unidos 299, San Telmo
Tel: 4362-6086
www.bar-sur.com.ar

www.centroculturaltango.com.ar
info@bar-sur.com.ar

Perfect, intimate setting to view, and perhaps participate in, the passion of the tango, as well as other traditional Argentine entertainment. Dancers may also give private lessons.

Teatro Colón (Opera House)
Pasaje Toscanini 1168
Telefax: 4 378-7132/ 33
visitas@teatrocolon.org.ar

Fascinating behind-the-scenes look at costumes and sets is included in the tour of this grand establishment. Try to see a show if possible!

Manzana de las Luces
Perú 272
Tel: (54-11) 4331-9534/ 4342-6973
www.manzanadelasluces.gov.ar

Interesting tour of excavated tunnels and other underground and above-ground cultural areas of interest, including colonial buildings dating back to the 17th century.

Museo de Bellas Artes
Avda. del Libertador 1473

Contains works of European masters (Monet, Rodin) as well as influential Latin American artists.

Museo de Motivos Populares Argentinos José Hernández
Avda. del Libertador 2373 (1425) Capital Federal
Telefax: (0541) 4803-2384
www.museohernandez.org.ar
museo_hernandez@buenosaires.gov.ar

Houses a wide array of Argentine folkloric art including crafts, silverwork, and attire from the native people, colonial period, and gauchos. Attractive displays are appealing to children.

Fans of Evita (Eva Perón) will want to see the **Casa Rosada** in the Plaza de Mayo and her grave at the **Cemetery of the Recoleta**. Also, don't miss the new:

Museo Evita
Lafinur 2988
Tel: 54 11 4807 9433/ 4809 3168
institutoevaperon@arnet.com.ar

Displays clothes, memorabilia, and film clips of Eva's good deeds, such as bringing about women's right to vote and providing homes for destitute women to learn marketable skills.

COLONIA, URUGUAY

Colonia is easily reached by boat from Buenos Aires and can be visited in one day. We highly recommend that you take the time to visit this magical place!

Familia Abot Silveira
Coronel Arroyo 525—entre (between) Artigas y Rivera
Tel: (052) 23016

Large, clean room in family home with private bath, TV, fridge, and hot plate for just US$10 a night.

La Luna Restaurant
Gral. Flores 43 Esq. (corner) Del Comercio, Barrio Histórico
Tel: (099) 145364

Great *parrilla* (grill), seafood, paella, and drinks with a rooftop terrace overlooking the beautiful shoreline. Reasonably priced!

Wander around the **Barrio Histórico** (old town) and see the **drawbridge**. In the Plaza Mayor, go up to the top of the **Faro** (The Lighthouse) and visit the nearby museum, **Museo Municipal**, which contains rooms of stuffed animals and cool fossils, as well as historical items and native handicrafts.

MONTEVIDEO, URUGUAY

Hospedaje del Centro

Soriano 1126 esq. (corner) Gutierrez Ruiz
Tel: 9001419

This colonial building, once beautiful, has fallen into disrepair, now dusty and noisy due to housekeeping in the courtyard. Safe, centrally located, with private bathroom for US$6 per night.

Radisson, top floor restaurant

Plaza Independencia

We stumbled onto this restaurant in an attempt to see a view and get out of the pouring rain. While we expected it to be out of our budget, we were very pleasantly surprised at the prices (under US$15 for snacks and drinks). The food and wine were excellent, the view wonderful, and the service, delightful despite our unkempt appearance. We spent several late afternoon hours playing cards here. Highly recommended!

SALTO, URUGUAY

Hotel Los Cedros

Uruguay 657
Tel: (0059873) 33984 – 33985
Fax: 34235

Because I was ill, we decided to splurge a little on a hotel, and we were so glad we did. Large, very clean, comfortable, modern triple with balcony, AC, TV, small fridge, and breakfast included for US$22 a night.

La Caldera

Uruguay 221
Tel: (073) 2 46 48

Within easy walking distance from Hotel Los Cedros. Gorgeous renovated colonial building with brick walls and wood-burning oven. Fabulous *parrilla*, pasta, and fish for very reasonable prices. The exceptionally friendly owners even gave us a ride to the restaurant from our hotel!

Termas del Dayman

Information available through the Tourist Office:
Intendencia Municipal de Salto, Division Turismo
Uruguay 1052
Tel: (073) 34096 –25194
Fax: (073) 35740
imstur@adinet.com.uy

These hot springs are easily accessible from Salto; most hotels and the Tourist Office can tell you how to take the bus there. The grounds are beautiful with several pools of various sizes, depths, and temperatures. Very family-friendly with changing rooms and snacks. Bus and entrance only US$3 a day for all three of us!

RESERVA PROVINCIAL ESTEROS DEL IBERÁ (Marshes of Iberá), ARGENTINA

Ñande-Reta Inn

Colonia Carlos Pellegrini
Tel: 420155
pnoailles@usa.net

Recommended by Footprint, this beautiful family-run inn has very comfortable, clean rooms with private bath, breakfast, and dinner for US$70 a night for a triple. Staff will arrange transportation to and from the inn, boat and canoe tours of the marshes, and other day trips into this wonderful area, where wildlife abounds, including capybara, monkeys, storks, caimans, deer, and reptiles.

ENCARNACIÓN, PARAGUAY

We do not recommend Paraguay for families. Check out the Corruption Index published by Transparency International at www.transparency.org. Our taxi driver also strongly recommended staying on the other side of the border in Posadas, Argentina, for safety and sanitary reasons. We do too. If you do find yourself in this town, here is our recommendation:

Hotel Itapúa

C A López y Cabanas
Telefax: 5045

Near the bus terminal, convenient but unpleasant location. Tolerable room with private bath and TV for US$10 a night.

ASUNCIÓN, PARAGUAY

Secretaria Nacional de Turismo

Palma 468 esquina (corner) Alberdi
Tel: (595 21) 441 530/ 450966
Fax: (595 21) 491 230

Contains indigenous handicrafts for sale, including necklaces made out of seeds from the rainforest and lace clothing, a specialty of the area.

Hotel Miami

Mexico 449 c/25 de Mayo
Tel: 444 950

Very unfriendly service, tolerable room with private bath, TV and "breakfast" (instant coffee and one hotdog bun) for US$17 a night.

Bolsi Restaurante

Estrella, 399 Esquina (corner) Alberdi
Tel: (59521) 491-841/2

Excellent buffet.

San Trope
Plaza Uruguay

Comfortable, family-friendly atmosphere. Delicious French and Paraguayan food for very reasonable prices.

Sanatorio Migone Battilana
Eligio Ayala No. 1293
Telefax: 498 200
Fax: (595-21) 205 630

If you need to obtain medical care, we highly recommend this facility. Clean, caring, professional, reasonably priced.

Farmacia Oliva
Oliva 681
Tel: 453 169/ 453 170 / (0971) 202 281

Handled our prescriptions for five medications quickly and competently.

Panteón Nacional de los Héroes, a statue dedicated to child-soldiers, on the Plaza de los Héroes, and the indigenous artifacts at the **Museo Etnográfico Andrés Barbero**, España 217, are worth a look.

IGUAZÚ FALLS (ARGENTINA AND BRAZIL)

Albergue Residencial "Uno," Puerto Iguazú, Argentina
Fray Luis Beltran 116
Telefax: 03757-420529
iguazu@hostels.org.ar

Popular basic accommodations among backpackers, triple with private bath and breakfast included for US$10 a night. Provides ample information regarding falls and environment.

Take the time to explore both **Argentine and Brazilian** (www.cataratasdoiguacu.com.br) **sides** of the falls, as well as the **night hike** illuminated only by the full moon. Make sure to do the **nature walk** on the Argentine side; we saw troops of monkeys, butterflies, snakes, and banana spiders.

Usina Hidreléctrica de Itaipu (Itaipu Dam), Brazil

Av. Trancredo Neves, 6720
Tel: +55 (45) 3520-6999
Fax: (45) 520-6622
www.itaipu.gov.br

The hydroelectric dam tour includes a fun bus trip through this huge facility as well as a movie (in English) to get all the information. The museum up the street focuses on the dam's impact on local flora and fauna. Both are highly enjoyable for children.

Parque das Aves (Bird Park), Brazil

Rodovia das Cataratas Km 18

Great bird sanctuary with flamingos, ibis, spoonbills, rheas, and toucans galore.

Bosque Zoológico Guarani (Guarani Zoo), Brazil

Near the Terminal Urbana (bus station) in Rua Tarobá

A nice woodsy place with some well-kept animals.

Really Turismo, Brazil

Cristina Gomes
Rua Xavier da Silva 649
Telefax: (45) 523-6822
cristina@reallyturismo.com.br

English-speaking travel agent that assisted us in purchasing plane tickets from São Paulo to Manaus.

Home
Trinidad and Tobago
Caracas
Venezuela
Guyana
Suriname
Georgetown
Galibi Reserve
Paramaribo
Cayenne
French Guiana
Brownsweg
Boa Vista
Manaus
Brazil
Bolivia
Paraguay
São Paulo
Foz do Iguaçu
Argentina

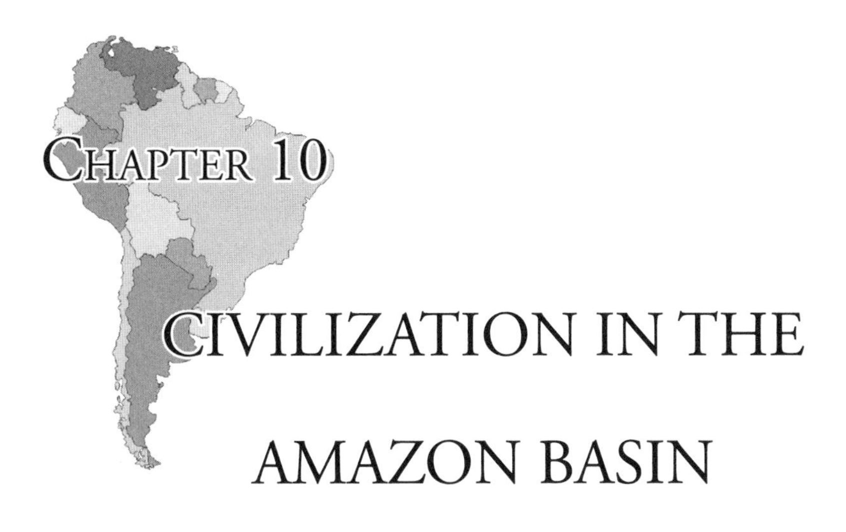

Chapter 10

Civilization in the Amazon Basin

We sadly recited our traditional goodbye song as we crossed over the Argentine border for the 20th and final time. "Goodbye, Argentina, we loved you!" Our direct bus to São Paulo, Brazil, was the ultimate in luxury, with soft reclining seats rivaling any American La-Z-Boy back home. I was already impressed with the quality of the sumptuous steak dinner and Argentine wine, but when the conductor came around with a bottle of cognac, I thought I'd died and gone to heaven.

A man at the border offered to change our 300 Argentine pesos (worth about US$100) into Brazilian reals. Until this point, we had often been carrying around as many as four currencies, including Argentine pesos, Brazilian reals, our emergency stash of U.S. dollars, and whatever else was the local currency (e.g., Chilean or Uruguayan pesos or Paraguayan guaranís). I was eager to finally deal with only one foreign currency, so I wanted to exchange them. However, Fran was unhappy with the rate. We bickered about this for a while until the opportunity passed. Regrettably, it turned out that we should have gotten rid of the pesos while we had the chance. We wasted countless hours trying to exchange that money over the next several months. After weeks of searching at home, I finally found an office in Texas that would accept it for exactly the same amount that we had been offered at the border. It

The Japanese market in São Paulo, Brazil

seemed that the further we got from Argentina, the less people wanted anything to do with their pesos.

The one positive outcome of the peso fiasco was that the person working in the São Paulo tourist office thought we were Argentinians. When I asked why, he said, "Because you came in speaking Spanish and trying to exchange pesos." I was so incredibly happy that someone had mistaken me for a Latina woman, especially one from so fine a country as Argentina. That interaction started off our time in São Paulo on a positive note. While our whole intention of going there was solely to catch a plane to Manaus, we actually quite enjoyed South America's largest city. Thanks to yet another travel tip from our Canadian friends Rich and Cyndi, we stayed near the Praça da República, a lively central square packed with musicians, craft vendors, and art displays. Families strolled through the lovely flowering gardens while young children ran around pointing at the turtles swimming leisurely in ponds filled with water lilies.

Presenting an unusual blend of vastly different cultures, São Paulo hosts the largest population of Japanese citizens outside of their homeland. After a quick trip on the outstanding subway system, we explored the huge Japanese Sunday market. We melded into the fascinating ethnic mix of Brazilian and Japanese people on the streets, passing by storefronts advertising Oriental wares in Japanese and Portuguese. We paused to watch a teenage sumo wrestling competition on the sidewalk before settling down to eat some fresh sushi. To further expand our cultural awareness, we boarded the subway again to the Barra Funda Metrô station to see the Memorial da América Latina. The huge building, designed by Oscar Niemeyer, houses perhaps the most impressive exhibit of Latin American handicrafts in all of South America. Entire rooms are dedicated to the textiles, tools, and other items produced by the native people of specific regions across the continent. The colorful displays and life-sized models presented a virtual reality tour of the many wonderful places we had already visited throughout our trip.

Our final stop in São Paulo was the world-famous Butantã Snake Farm, where we saw at least 30 species of poisonous snakes, many indigenous to the area. Placards on the walls described the milking process used on the premises to make five different kinds of snake serum, as

Opulence in the heart of the jungle, Teatro Amazonas

well as antidotes for lethal spider and scorpion bites. At the end of the process I wasn't sure if I felt better or worse about the potential of snake bites in Brazil! But it still didn't deter us from heading right into the heart of snake country, Manaus.

"I'm All Sticky, Mom!"

While not necessarily attractive, the fascinating city of Manaus ekes out an existence whereby the wild and unruly jungle threatens to gobble up man's feeble attempts to establish a presence. Turn-of-the-century European opulence rises and crumbles amidst the leafy clutches of overgrown vines. Traces still remain of the elaborate buildings constructed by the wealthy rubber barons in the late 1800's with expensive imported materials. Development continued until the rubber boom ended by 1920, and today green foliage and modern, functional, concrete structures grow up among this decaying, decadent architecture.

Because our plane landed in the wee hours of the morning, we prearranged a hotel and transportation from the airport. While somewhat overpriced at US$32 a night, our centrally located hotel included a small indoor pool and buffet breakfast, and we were especially grateful for our private bathroom and refreshing air conditioning. As we hit the street on our first day out, the humidity engulfed us like a tidal wave. Christopher complained, "I'm all sticky, Mom!" Feeling quite uncomfortable myself and carrying two weeks worth of stinky laundry, I responded somewhat unsympathetically, "You're going to have to get used to it. We will probably feel like this for the rest of the trip!"

After dropping off the nasty bundle at the cleaners, Fran and I laughingly reminisced about the trepidation we had expressed to our travel doctor back in Oregon about the rainforest. If only he could see us now! We felt so comfortable and at peace there. The serene natural environment and melodic sounds of the forest helped clear my busy head of the noise and stress of daily life. I even came to welcome the humidity as a signal that we would soon be reentering that fascinating mix of lush pristine foliage and exotic creatures. While the humidity was fairly overwhelming initially, we got used to it after a few days of acclimatization.

Our first task in Manaus was to organize a day trip to see the Meeting of the Waters, where the black Rio Negro and muddy brown Rio Solimões collide to form the mighty Amazon, the most voluminous river on earth. The very friendly folks at Green Planet Tours conduct daily tours to this natural phenomenon, and also provide a wealth of information about other sights in Manaus and transportation options out of the city. Despite the pouring rain, we boarded the boat and immediately huddled up with the small group of passengers in our efforts to avoid getting soaked. We made an instant connection with an Italian writer named Eli, who had journeyed up the Amazon River from the Atlantic coastal town of Belém. He raved about the opportunity to observe the locals engaged in all aspects of life on the water. We had considered taking the same trip, but were discouraged from doing so after hearing about Daveed's horrific experience in the Peruvian Amazon Basin. (His hilarious rendition of this trip from hell can be found in Appendix C.) Packed onto an overcrowded vessel, Daveed's hammock was besieged on all sides by other hammocks and livestock. Bored with the same scenery after a few hours, Daveed finished his book on the first day and then went mad with frustration as the slow-moving boat missed its destination deadline time and again. Exasperated, he insisted that the boat pull up alongside another going in the same direction, and, after dangerously crossing over a small plank connecting the two vessels, he took up residence on the other boat. As luck would have it, his new boat broke down, further extending the "three-day" trip. He eventually docked after almost a week on the water. With Christopher in tow, we decided that several days on a river boat might not keep any of us entertained enough, and we didn't really have time for any unexpected delays. We settled on the day trip instead and were satisfied with that decision.

Eli also shared a terrible story in which he was mugged while making a phone call from a pay phone on a busy street in Rio. In the middle of the day, the two thugs held him up at knifepoint and cut his backpack right off his back, slicing his arm in the process. We were shocked and dismayed to learn that no one even tried to help him and added it to our long list of safety concerns about Brazil. Compared to that experience, our stolen first aid kit was small potatoes.

Despite the drizzle, the intersection of the two tributaries creates a clearly visible jagged line that stretches for miles down the Amazon before blending together. Our vessel crossed back and forth over the meeting place, giving us all several vantage points from which to view the incredible natural phenomenon. We then traveled upriver, taking time to observe the activity of daily life on its banks. Green Planet Tours had constructed a small floating lodge on an isolated section, and we stopped there for a lunch of healthy local dishes. Accompanied by a guide, a few of us took a small canoe out to give piranha fishing another try. I am sorry to report that the results were no better than the first go-round in Bolivia.

Back on solid ground, every day felt like a new adventure in Manaus, full of fascinating activities in which we learned more about the seemingly endless wonders of the Amazon Basin. We got a closer look at the local seafood in the bustling Municipal Market downtown. After examining rows of unusual fish for sale, a kindly old fisherman showed Christopher how to clean his catch and carefully extricated two small shiny bits of bone for him to keep. A short walk away, the Museu do Índio (Indian Museum) and the Museu do Homem do Norte (Museum of Man from the North) both offered interesting insights into the daily life of the Amazon people, their artistry, and their handmade products derived from nature. An easy bus ride out of town brought us to the Instituto Nacional de Pesquisas da Amazônia (INPA), a botanical garden and animal reserve that serves as home to giant river otters, manatees, monkeys, caimans, sloths, and agoutis (large jungle rats with long, thin, almost deer-like legs). Arriving at feeding time, we had the opportunity to see the giant river otters breaking shells to extract the fresh fish. Christopher insisted that we take our time observing these adorable creatures; he was just the right height to look them straight in the eye. Huge water tanks held freshwater manatees, enabling close-up contact with these elusive creatures. We commemorated the encounter by purchasing a small, wooden hand-carved manatee for my father at the enticing gift shop. Just as we were leaving the park, we saw our first free-roaming sloth sitting hunched over in the top of a tall tree. He looked strikingly like that loveable Star Wars character, Yoda, as he surveyed the park from his perch. Tearing ourselves away to hop on a

The Meeting of the Waters

Life on the mighty Amazon

taxi to the nearby Museu de Ciências Naturais da Amazônia (Natural Science Museum of the Amazon), we found elaborate displays of the wide variety of fish and insects native to the Amazon. In the back of the well-kept museum lies a swimming-pool-sized aquarium containing several arapaimas, also locally known as the *pirarucú*, the world's largest freshwater fish. These prehistoric-looking creatures can grow up to 15 feet long, have greenish-red bodies like trout, and abruptly change shape from a vertically slender torso to a horizontally flat head. As one drifted indifferently by us, its large mouth gaped open so wide it could have easily swallowed a basketball whole. In the gift shop, the Asian owners sell the inch-long scales for use as a natural fingernail file. Christopher decided to add one to his ever expanding collection of rocks, feathers, and other goodies.

Contrasting dramatically with the disorderly jumble of the rainforest, the world-famous Teatro Amazonas is painstakingly constructed of rich local hardwoods as well as rare marble and hand-painted tiling imported from Europe. After touring the lavish facilities, we scored three balcony seats to an opera based on the classic tale of Cinderella. We donned our best clothes, including my skirt of Argentine leather, and stepped out for a night of high culture. While Christopher thought his first opera had a bit "too many notes," Fran and I reveled in the surreal experience of witnessing a professional performance surrounded by such luxury in the middle of the humid Amazon Basin.

After all of this exciting, yet sticky, exploration, Christopher was ready for a day of relaxation. We celebrated his eighth birthday by allowing him to spend it any way he wanted. Quite predictably, he decided to stay in his sweats all day, run the air conditioner full blast, and play numerous games of Harry Potter. As a special birthday bonus, he even won a few rounds!

The Scoop on the Guianas

From Manaus, we traveled overland to the tiny Brazilian town of Boa Vista, a nondescript place where we caught our flight for Georgetown, the capital of English-speaking Guyana. We had to go to Guyana first in order to obtain visas from the Surinamese consulate to enter this neighboring country. Our guidebooks indicated that the overland trip from Boa Vista to Georgetown required hitch-hiking and could take as long as two weeks. Although we are not typically ones to turn down such an adventure, we gave it a miss in the interest of time. Later we were very thankful for making this choice after we talked with two young travelers while waiting at the Surinamese consulate. They complained about the discomfort of their journey on dirty buses and in the back of pickup trucks. They said that from the road they couldn't see anything beyond the wall of dense green foliage lining the road, which got old after a few hours. They indicated that if they had it to do over again, they too would fly.

Few travelers visit the three small countries known collectively as the "Guianas" (i.e., Guyana, Suriname, and French Guiana) because they are difficult to access and relatively expensive in comparison to the rest of South America. Located on the northeastern coast of the continent where the Atlantic Ocean and Caribbean Sea come together, the Guianas are separated from their neighbors by acres of largely uninhabited, dense jungle. While their isolation renders them an attractive off-the-beaten-path destination, even for adventurous South American *viajeros*, they generally do not have a lot of the typical tourist amenities, such as inexpensive hostels or bank machines. They also do not have a regulated public transportation system. Instead of scheduled bus routes, vans leave from a designated point once they reach capacity. As a result, passengers can wait up to six hours in the hot steamy vehicle before departure. Furthermore, no stores or facilities, including medical centers, are open on weekends. The few stores that do exist have very limited options because most products are imported. Our guidebooks again were not much help and, in fact, contained misleading information that was so far from reality we again questioned whether the authors had actually gone to these countries. In hindsight, we should not have relied on the guidebooks but tried to get as much information over the Internet as possible before we arrived. Instead, as in Paraguay, we trudged around looking for large landmarks that were nonexistent (and no one had ever heard of them), restaurants that had gone out of business, hotels that had closed down or become brothels, and fictitious transportation. The guidebooks also did not consistently report Labor Day in their list of national holidays. This holiday plagued us throughout the trip, landing on the same weekend that we arrived in each of the three countries. Most services were shut down for three to four days, stranding us with little money, food, information, and sight-seeing options. What unlucky odds!

Not Everybody Survives Guyana

Sadly, our overall impression of Guyana was not favorable. The crime rate is high, the capital felt dangerous and very tense, and many of its inhabitants behaved in an aggressive and hostile manner. Faced with no tourist information counter or bureau of exchange, we emerged from the small airport to a literal mob scene. We were immediately distinguishable from the dark-skinned locals, and touts swarmed all over us. Insisting that they could take us downtown cheaply, the vendors resorted to shoving each other aside and even threatening their competitors with sticks in an effort to get our business. We countered with information from our guidebooks, stating that we planned to take bus #42 to the city center for about US$1 each. Suddenly, everybody drove bus #42. We glanced around wildly for a tourist information bureau, a bus stop, or something to help us make an informed decision about getting downtown, all to no avail. Giggling "Run away! Run away!" as in our favorite Monty Python movie, we retreated back into the airport to catch our breath and regroup.

A soft-spoken taxi driver followed us, showed us his identification badge, and insisted that he could take us downtown for US$15, with a stop to exchange money along the way. We showed him the guidebooks and asked about the buses. He clarified that the vans we were seeing really were the buses, and on closer inspection, we could just make out the number "42" painted on the sides. He then directed us to a sign on the wall that listed the regulated fares to the city center, which were the equivalent of about US$5 per person. We asked why the guidebooks said that it would be US$1. He laughed and asked us how old our information was. One of the books we had bought en route when it had been released, so we thought it was less than two years old. He said it was much older than that, and he couldn't remember a time when fares had

A glimpse of Guyana

been that low. Normally we did not rely so heavily on our guidebooks, but in the absence of any other information or allies, we were literally grasping at straws.

As we again braved the open air outside the airport, another driver of bus #42 approached us and attempted to convince us to ride with him for US$5 a seat. I asked him, "Why should we cram into your van when we can take a taxi with this guy?" "How much is he charging you?" the driver asked. "Fifteen dollars," I answered. "Well, then you should go with him!" he responded and left us gaping after him. By that point, the airport traffic had cleared out. The taxi driver pointed out that everyone had departed, and there were no more flights that day. In a few minutes, he warned, we would not have any ride downtown at all. We would be stuck walking for over ten miles with all of our things in the sweltering heat, easy targets for thieves. So we reluctantly agreed to get into his old, beat-up car, which certainly did not look like any taxi we had taken earlier on our trip. Every bone in my body screamed, "How crazy is this? Getting into some random guy's car in the middle of nowhere?!" But, in my gut, I honestly felt that he was a good guy. All of the information he had given us so far had been accurate. And by that point, we had run out of options. The advantage of a "bus" would have been safety in numbers, but they had all left. While he loaded our stuff into his trunk, I scrutinized his name tag, memorizing his name and identification number in case we managed to survive some horrible fate and lived to report the information to whatever authorities may prevail in that God-forsaken place.

As he gently coaxed his car along the dirt road towards town, the taxi driver said, "Welcome to Guyana!" We all laughed and began to loosen up. He then started describing his life growing up "in the bush." His most memorable story was about an anaconda eating his friend's dog. We listened in rapt fascination as he explained how the snake vomited up a substance and disengaged its jaws to ease the poor animal down its throat. He talked about feeling simultaneously sad and mesmerized by the situation, unable to leave because "it wasn't every day I see something like that." Christopher in particular asked a lot of questions about that incident. The taxi driver patiently responded to each one, making a deliberate effort to speak American English so that we could understand him. We chatted about his wife and family, and he showed us their photos. Before we knew it, he had stopped at somebody's house to exchange money because all of the banks were closed due to Labor Day. Again I thought about how going into some stranger's home with a wad of cash goes against all travel advice about safety I've ever read, but with the banks closed and ATMs nonexistent, we needed some way to get money. Fran courageously went inside while Christopher and I waited anxiously in the car. I breathed a sigh of relief when he eventually emerged carrying some Guyanese bills. He said that, again, the guidebook was so out of date that the folks inside laughed at him when he tried to lobby for a better exchange rate. We should have looked up the exchange rates earlier on the Internet, instead of having to take their word for it. Luckily, the exchange rate was fine.

As we drove away from the house with our cash, our driver cautioned us about Georgetown, saying that the petty crime rate was very high and our skin color made us attractive to thieves. He commented, "I see you have a neck pouch, and you, sir, are wearing your wallet in your pocket." Both of these statements were true. He urged us not to wear them, leave all of our valuables in the hotel, and just carry around the minimum amount that we would need. "Keep it lean and flat," he recommended, patting his pockets, "and hopefully you won't have any problems." He then took us to the first hotel listed in the guidebook, but it was full. We suggested another from the book but he discouraged that choice, saying that he frequently saw "crazy" people go in and out of there, and he thought that it was very dangerous. He asked what type of place we wanted, and we tried to describe an inexpensive, reasonable option. He brought us to the Palace de Leon Hotel, which exactly met our specifications. While all of the prices in Guyana were much higher than we had anticipated, our huge room with air conditioner, television, and a balcony in a beautiful, safe, Caribbean-style building for US$40 a night was a great deal. Our taxi driver turned out to be a wonderful resource, helpful and honest in all of our dealings with him, and we were extremely fortunate to have met him. As he prepared to leave, I tipped him and expressed my gratitude, using his first name. He looked startled and responded, "I didn't ever tell you my name!" I winked at him and indicated, "I'm not quite as naïve as you might think!" He still looked surprised as I waved goodbye. Of course, now I can't remember his name anyway, so I doubt it would have done much good in an emergency. But thankfully, all's well that ends well, at least for the first day.

The rest of our short stay in Guyana was more of the same craziness, all set in a very hot and humid backdrop. Our hotel hosts looked concerned and issued safety warnings to us whenever we ventured out of the hotel. The streets themselves presented navigational challenges, as the town lies below sea level and ditches full of rotting garbage and tropical debris surrounded all the buildings. Fran recalled a newspaper article reporting that a giant anaconda had been found in one of these waterways. Broken boards and bits of odds and ends were scattered haphazardly across the trenches in a desperate attempt to create some type of "sidewalk." One false move could cause a hapless visitor to plunge several feet down into the putrid filth. With an eight-year-old child, this possibility was particularly frightening. The occasional quaint 19th century white wooden houses and flowering plants did little to assuage our negative impressions. Georgetown, Guyana, is absolutely not a family-friendly place.

Walking around town in the heat and enduring constant harassment from locals trying to sell us something proved so unpleasant that we did not do much sightseeing. Our forays outside of the hotel consisted primarily of waiting in the courtyard of the Surinamese consulate and standing in long lines at the bank. While we encountered people that were friendly and curious about us, we struggled to communicate with them. Although the Guyanese national language is English, the grammatical structures and vocabulary of the local Caribbean dialect differs from American English so much that we literally could not understand a word anybody said. For example, at the Botanical Gardens, a caring staff member made a substantial effort to speak slowly and clearly to Christopher. When he didn't understand her, she repeated her statement to Fran and me several times and pointed to the ground. Eventually, we heard something like, "I be telling that he be slide," and we finally grasped that she was trying to warn Christopher not to slip on the wet surface. This statement was her best attempt at translating her dialect into American English. We found it very ironic that as native

English speakers we wished to be back in a Spanish-speaking environment so that we could better converse with the locals!

The helpful staff at the consulate quickly processed our visas and provided us with the name of someone ("Bobby") who reportedly could take us to Suriname. Although the border was only a few hours away, no public transportation was available. Because we didn't speak the language, we asked the kind hotel staff to call and arrange for "Bobby" to meet us at 4:00 a.m. the next day. At the designated time, we paid the fare, approximately US$40 for all three of us, and squeezed into the crowded van. Bobby proceeded to pick up the rest of the passengers around town. At one place, he woke up the security guard and demanded that he go inside to rouse the customer. Somehow an argument ensued and escalated to the point where Bobby grabbed a stick from behind the driver's seat. He began threatening the guard with it, shouting something about him sleeping on the job. The rest of the bus laughed and seemed to take it in stride. We giggled nervously and hoped to make it out of Guyana unscathed. Eventually the unsuspecting rider emerged from the dwelling, and we got on the road.

A couple of hours later, we stopped to board a ferry across a river. Although we were still in Guyana, some passengers began exchanging money with a man who approached the bus. We did not find a working Internet in Georgetown so we still did not know the exchange rates. We didn't want to rely on finding an ATM somewhere on the way to our destination of Paramaribo, the capital of Suriname, so we asked the other passengers if the exchange rate was acceptable. They seemed encouraging and we figured that if the locals were swapping money, we would too. It turned out to be a good decision because we never encountered a working ATM in Guyana or Suriname. As we finished up our transaction, things somehow heated up again. Bobby got out his stick and started to wave it at the money-changer. We couldn't tell if Bobby had a particularly hot temper or if this was typical behavior. The nonchalant demeanor of the others seemed to imply that it was par for the course in a Guyanese day.

We crossed the river without incident and found ourselves in the final stretch to the border. As I was silently willing the bus forward over the pock-marked dirt road, Fran caught a glimpse of a dead victim of a hit and run accident from the dusty window. The young man was well-dressed, and at first glance looked as if he had been on his way to work. However, upon closer inspection, his head was tilted at an unnatural angle and his eye jutted out of its socket onto his cheek. Fran was very distressed, not only upon seeing the dead man, but also at the lackadaisical attitude of the pedestrians walking around him. Having enough bad memories of Guyana, I was thankful that Christopher and I missed that terrible sight. The disturbing image haunted Fran for weeks.

Suriname, a Tropical Escape

Our second ferry successfully crossed the river dividing Guyana and Suriname, and we emerged victorious on the other side. In the absence of effective communication, we had presumed that the van would just drop us off at some border town, and we were madly scouring our guidebooks, trying to figure out how to get to Paramaribo. Imagine our delight when Bobby continued to drive us all the way to the capital city. Despite his volatile temper, Bobby had given us a great deal and excellent door-to-door service. Our spirits continued to soar as we took in the beautiful scenery in Suriname. Red dusty earth contrasted dramatically with brilliant green tropical foliage against an intensely blue sky. While the Guyanese route was full of potholes and other obstacles (both alive and dead), the roads improved considerably on the Surinamese side. Occasionally we passed a handful of indigenous people living in grass huts by the side of the road. The tidy huts rested on well-kept grounds that remained neat and swept clean of jungle debris despite the children and livestock running around. When we arrived in Paramaribo, Bobby asked us for our final destination and we quickly flipped through our guidebooks. Shaken by our Guyana experience, we decided to splurge on the Eco Resort. We had done so well financially that we were still well within our annual budget, and we rationalized that we could pursue less expensive accommodations the following day if the resort was not worth the money.

This time, the guidebooks came through for us; the Eco Resort was so wonderful we stayed for several days. Our extremely comfortable room contained two big beds, an enormous private bathroom with

A bird song competition on the Presidential Palace lawn of Paramaribo

lots of hot water, a balcony, a fridge, air conditioner, television, use of a safety deposit box, and a big buffet breakfast (which served as our main meal of the day) in a beautiful tropical garden setting for US$78 a night. As we rushed joyfully into our room, Christopher lay down on the bed and sighed with satisfaction. "Look at this!" I shrieked, holding up a washcloth. "When was the last time you saw one of these???" Our Mickey Mouse washcloth, like so many of our belongings, had become so threadbare that we could see through it in spots. It also had a nasty habit of becoming somewhat slimy after being trekked around in a plastic bag without drying properly for days at a time. But perhaps best of all, Eco Resort guests had access to the facilities at the luxurious Torarica Resort next door, which included a large swimming pool, several hot tubs, sports equipment, tropical garden with small zoo, and poolside bar and restaurant service. We spent some blissful afternoons lounging by the pool, decadently sipping overpriced fizzy drinks and working on our tans. Christopher had a great time practicing his rapidly developing swimming strokes, observing the zoo animals, and relaxing in the hot tubs with us. The Eco Resort was also conveniently located near the city center and the Presidential Palace, where we witnessed a bird song competition early one Sunday morning. Two caged birds were placed on poles opposite one another on the palace lawn, and judges meticulously recorded every time each bird "sang" on a blackboard erected next to each cage. We thought it hilarious to see all these rough-looking macho men daintily carrying their caged songbirds around town. What a wonderful national pastime!

Our hotel was also right next door to STINASU, the Foundation for Nature Conservation in Suriname. This government-run agency ensures that the wonderful Surinamese flora and fauna remain protected and accessible to everyone. Their dedicated staff customizes trips for visitors to nature reserves and offers a variety of service packages ranging from only the basic necessities to all-inclusive guided tours. They assisted us in making transportation and lodging reservations for Brownsberg National Park and gave us maps and information about eating options so that we could explore the park independently. STINASU staff also arranges volunteer opportunities, connecting willing participants with groups doing research in the rainforest and on the beaches. We took advantage of this opportunity as well, making plans to volunteer with the sea turtles at Galibi Beach. The Eco Resort allowed us to leave most of our belongings and valuables safely behind on our outings so that we only had to carry a change of clothing and other essentials with us when exploring Suriname's abundant natural beauty.

In stark contrast with Guyana, we found Suriname to be absolutely fabulous. Formerly a Dutch colony, the country fluctuated under British, French, and Dutch rule so that an old-world European-style influence permeates the tropical Caribbean atmosphere. The Dutch brought over African slaves, and after they were emancipated, the colonists recruited indentured servants from Indonesia and India to develop the area. These foreign cultures meld peacefully with the existing indigenous lifestyle so that the tiny country boasts an astounding ethnic diversity. Christian churches, Hebrew temples, and Muslim mosques occupy the same street. Restaurants offering a wide range of spicy, exotic cuisines proliferate all over the city. The friendly people are warm and welcoming, and while Dutch is the national language, English is widely spoken. Set amidst spectacular scenery, including pristine rainforest and beaches full of mangroves, Suriname rates highly as a family-friendly vacation spot.

In Search of the Giant Sea Turtles

Our top priority in Suriname was seeing the huge leatherback turtles, the largest of the sea turtles reaching lengths of eight feet and weighing up to 2,000 pounds. Primarily found at a depth of 3,000 feet, these giants are rarely visible to humans except during nesting time. Surviving for over 100 million years, these prehistoric creatures are in danger of becoming extinct, in part due to poaching and the disappearance of their nesting sites. At the Galibi Reserve, STINASU strives to preserve sea turtles (primarily leatherbacks and greens) by providing the local fishermen with income from participating in research studies counting the turtles' nests and acting as guides for tourists as an economic alternative to poaching the eggs. We made arrangements with STINASU to volunteer at the beach. After missing the season in Praia do Forte, Brazil, we were eager to see them laying their eggs. We looked forward to camaraderie with locals and volunteers while helping out with a worthwhile cause. Furthermore, we wanted to get more of a feel for the rhythms of the place and thought that volunteering would give us ample time to explore the area at our leisure instead of a more expensive and rapid-paced tour. The ten-day minimum commitment ate up a large chunk of our remaining month on sabbatical, but we all discussed the benefits as a family and decided to forgo a trip to French Guiana in exchange for the experience. We extended our Suriname visas, a relatively simple process that required finding the immigration office at the docks and handing over our passports and yellow immunization booklets for the first and only time during the entire year. We purchased our own supplies at a small grocery market and prepared to leave Paramaribo.

The jeep and boat trip to the small beach was very scenic and festive. We covered everything with plastic bags, a smart move because we got absolutely soaked on the motorized canoe ride to the site. Our extremely basic lodging on the beach consisted of a cement room with well-worn cots jury-rigged with mosquito netting. The shower and pit toilet were located in a separate outhouse. Like the ocean water, the brown shower water was filled with silt, particularly after the frequent rains. My first shower left me, my Mickey Mouse washcloth, and my towel, even dirtier than before I attempted it. After that I chose instead to wait for the first signs of rain and then grab my bathing suit, soap, and shampoo to scrub up outside in the downpour. We shared the outhouse facilities and a cooking area with four researchers, two Dutch and two Surinamese young adults, who were working on a separate long-term project. Their project coordinator, also a Dutchman, utilized STINASU transportation and facilities, but received separate funding for research on the leatherback turtles. Their rigorous data-gathering system was organized into shifts and involved scouring designated areas of the beach from dusk to dawn in search of the giants. Once found, the researchers scanned the turtles electronically, tagged them if needed, and recorded information about their health and nests. The voracious bugs, particularly the mosquitoes, attacked these poor researchers mercilessly on their nightly hikes. We were very impressed with the scientific nature of their studies and their devotion to the cause. We loved spending time with this lively group, and in the absence of much other diversions, we were fortunate to have such delightful company. Christopher took advantage

A giant leatherback turtle lays her eggs on Galibi Beach, Suriname

of all that free time to teach them, you guessed it, the omnipresent card game, Harry Potter.

STINASU volunteers typically stayed at the opposite end of the beach with the volunteer coordinator. We remained separate from them due to some space issues that we never understood, and as a result, we never received adequate information about their research mission and objectives. A local man was assigned to us to serve as our guide and research advisor. He stayed with his supervisor and some other locals in a STINASU building near us. On our first night, our guide said that we should get settled in and did not need to worry about going out to see the turtles that night. Somewhat disappointed and confused as to why the research efforts would not occur that evening, we deferred to his judgment and arranged a time to meet the following night.

At about midnight the next evening, our guide knocked softly on our door, and we headed out into the pitch dark. Unable to use our flashlights because of their disorienting effect on the turtles, we stumbled around on the dark beach until our eyes adjusted to the dim light. Engulfed in a cloud of humming insects, we walked tentatively along the coastline making futile efforts to ward off the unwanted companions until our guide started whispering excitedly to us and pointing. Looking in the direction of his finger, we could barely make out a large mound in the sand. As we silently drew closer, the clouds shifted and allowed a sliver of moonlight to illuminate the beach. There, in the silvery glow, lay the monstrous leatherback turtle. With great patience, the huge creature carefully and deliberately constructed her nest, her back flippers delicately curving into massive shovels to scoop out the sand and toss it aside. After the hole was about a foot and a half deep, the turtle stopped the digging motion and began laying her eggs. Our guide very briefly flashed his light on the round, white eggs, resembling gooey ping-pong balls, as they dropped into the hole. Deeply absorbed in her maternal trance, the ancient being remained oblivious to us as we reached out and lightly touched her rubbery shell. We lingered for several moments before continuing on down the beach in search of another nest. We encountered a second turtle dropping the last of her 80 to 100 eggs and observed as she camouflaged the nest by dragging her body around in circles and forcefully flicking the sand into the air with her flippers. Stifling our giggles, we ducked to avoid the airborne granules. Once finished, she hauled her enormous bulk methodically towards the water and slipped away. As she faded from view, we felt incredibly moved by what we had just witnessed. It was almost impossible to believe that these creatures were real and not some fantastical characters from Christopher's *Harry Potter* novels.

Our guide then showed us a notebook where he recorded the number of turtle nests. Having passed several markings in the sand, we were uncertain about how he distinguished between the old tracks and newly formed nests, but we assumed we would learn soon enough. He also warned us not to go out on our own at night. Blindly walking along the beach in the dark could be dangerous; however, if we carried a light, it would disturb the turtles. Given the fact that we had already seen two highly venomous snakes, including a fur de lance sitting on the top step of one of the buildings, we readily complied with his instructions.

We felt very pleased with our guide at that point but things soon took a turn for the worse. He told us to be ready for another trip around 3:00 a.m. Following his directions, we were all up and ready to go, but he never showed up. Disgruntled but willing to give him the benefit of the doubt, we waited for about a half an hour and then went back to sleep. The next morning, we were invited to the supervisor's birthday party at 2:00 p.m. At the appointed time, we looked over at the building but there was no visible activity. We asked the researchers if they planned on attending the party, and they indicated that they were going after lunch. Having traveled for months in South America, we were quite used to time being simply a suggestion. Often events started hours after a designated time, and Latino people did not attend pre-arranged meetings at all if something more important came along. Furthermore, since our guide had stood us up the night before, we assumed that time was not terribly important there either. So we waited, and after about an hour, we saw some people start to gather at the other house so we headed over. Unfortunately, our host appeared quite displeased with us and asked why we had not come over earlier. Surprised and embarrassed that we had not understood the local expectations better, we tried to explain that we didn't see anyone at the party so we weren't sure if they were ready for guests. Our irritated host didn't seem very satisfied with our answer, but the initial tension eventually wore off as a bottle of Jack Daniels circulated among the guests. By the time the researchers showed up almost an hour after we got there, everyone was so relaxed that no one gave them the third degree, just a plate of food instead. The party livened up, but without any other children to play with, Christopher soon grew bored and wanted to leave. Between shots of whisky, our guide indicated that he would meet us that night, and we returned to our room.

Unsurprisingly, the guide did not show up that night either. Clearly Jack Daniels took priority over the turtles. We again shrugged it off as a special event, went back to sleep, and the next afternoon we asked about why he had not shown up the past two nights. He offered no explanation, but made arrangements with us to go out that night. We were thrilled when he arrived at the designated time, and we eagerly set off towards the other end of the beach with him. Our long walk was rewarded by the sight of another leatherback laying her eggs, but we wondered aloud why we were walking so far. Our guide simply responded, "Maybe we will see another turtle, a green one!" We thought it was odd that we were going all the way over to the beach that was already well-monitored by the other volunteers instead of the one we had patrolled the first night. However, we weren't supposed to go off by ourselves so we really had no choice but to carry on. The guide met up with the volunteer coordinator, and they chatted for fifteen minutes in their native language. When we were introduced at the end of the conversation, the coordinator did little more than grunt in our direction. Not feeling particularly welcomed, we followed our guide to the house where the rest of the volunteers were staying. When we arrived, some people asked Fran and our guide to help with a broken boat. They raced off, leaving Christopher and me all by ourselves, sitting under a tree in the dark. Not wanting to scare the turtles, we sat there quietly as bugs and other creepy crawlies flew all over us. Becoming increasingly frightened, we imagined poisonous snakes and dangerous jungle creatures lurking in the pitch black.

Suddenly, we heard a strange noise. Poor Christopher jumped right up in my arms, grabbing me and shrieking, "What's that, Mommy?" in a voice that reflected my own rising panic. We gave up on being brave and began shouting out for Fran. A kindly woman in the house came out to see what was going on and reassured us that everything was all right. I tried to explain that we had been abandoned, but she did not invite us inside to wait. By the time Fran and the guide returned, I was furious. Why was I subjecting my eight-year-old child to sit, defenseless, in the middle of the jungle, in a place with poisonous snakes and bugs carrying all kinds of diseases, without a flashlight or any kind of protection, in the dead of night? We made our way back down the beach towards our room. A stray dog joined us and ended up chasing off the only green turtle Christopher and I saw in our time there. While, admittedly, it was quite interesting to watch the poor turtle move along on its flippers at top speed in the shallow water, I again was angry that our efforts at conservation seemed to be doing more harm than good. Even after I expressed my concern about the dog to the guide, he seemed indifferent and just laughed at the animal's behavior. It wasn't until the end of the walk, after I had complained about our poor efforts at conservation, that he even bothered to take out his notebook and halfheartedly jot down some information. Still fuming but trying to remain optimistic, I agreed to rendezvous later that night to count the turtle nests. The guide also talked about taking us on a hike through the jungle the next day. Skeptical about the chances of our guide showing up, I didn't even bother to wake up Christopher at the designated time. Per usual, he did not show up. Dressed and ready to go, Fran ventured out alone to count the nests.

The next day, Fran and I compared notes about our volunteer experience so far. We were confident that our excursion the previous night was some kind of personal errand, probably an alcohol run, for our guide as opposed to turtle research. I was also very frustrated that we had repeatedly gotten up in the middle of the night only to be blown off time and again. Not only did this routine constantly disturb Christopher's sleep, but he was particularly disappointed when he couldn't go out to look for the turtles. The problem didn't seem exclusively cultural because somehow that lackadaisical attitude did not apply to us when it came time to attend the birthday party. We were getting the feeling that the lame efforts at counting turtle nests were basically a way to give us something to do and, perhaps, the guide as well. Our housemates, the true researchers, were collecting data in a very systematic manner, and we could not see the utility in duplicating their excellent efforts with incredibly shabby ones. Worst of all, we felt that our presence might be having a negative influence on the turtles. We knew that one of the researchers was going back to Paramaribo the next day, and after some deliberation, we decided that we would cut our time short and leave with her since the transportation was already in place through STI-NASU. With a dwindling timeline, we felt that the five remaining days we had designated for volunteering at Galibi Beach would be better spent exploring the rainforest and French Guiana.

We spoke with the supervisor about our concerns and our desire to leave. Rather than exclusively blaming the irresponsible guide, we emphasized our feeling that our presence was not needed for the research and our time could be better spent elsewhere. Seeming unhappy with our decision, the supervisor offered to speak to our guide and encouraged us to stay, but our minds were already made up. He remained cordial, and we felt that we parted on a positive note. We then sought out our guide to explain the matter to him. Speaking clearly in English for the first time, he angrily interrogated us about why we were leaving while a woman sitting near him shot us icy looks. We repeated our concerns about the conservation efforts and the inconsistency of our walks. He remained agitated and did not make any efforts to explain or express any remorse for his contribution to the situation. He never took responsibility for standing us up repeatedly and taking us on a personal errand under the guise of doing research. We apologized for leaving early and did our best to resolve the issue in a respectful manner. We are not the kind of people who normally back out of any obligations, and to do so was very uncomfortable for us. However, it was clear that we were not contributing to the research efforts, and we had already made a substantial donation to the conservation funds and were not asking for a refund of any sort. Trying to make some reparations in the severed relations, we mentioned our interest in the jungle hike. He softened a bit and said that he would like to go in a little while. Of course, he did not.

We expressed our guilty feelings to the researchers, and they reassured us that we were doing the right thing. They said they could take us into the surrounding bush but were not encouraging due to the swarm of blood-thirsty insects and lack of wildlife. Christopher really wanted to play some more Harry Potter with them, so we gave up the hike in exchange for a nice day relaxing with our new friends. They offered to take us with them on their nightly walks, so that evening Christopher and I teamed up with one woman while Fran went on a separate shift. It was fascinating to watch them scan, measure, and tag the huge animals. Unlike our guide, they demonstrated their elaborate tracking records and system of distinguishing old from new tracks and nests. We relished the opportunity to accompany them and felt quite supportive of their excellent work.

Our departure from Galibi the next day was bittersweet. We bid goodbye to our new friends and tried to remain pleasant with the locals despite the obvious tension. On the way back, our canoe stopped at a nearby village for supplies. Speaking to us for the first time since our heated conversation the previous day, our guide asked us if we wanted to come with him into the community. The researchers had not been very encouraging about stopping there either, saying that essentially it was a way for the villagers to try to sell us some trinkets. We did not have any extra spending money with us, and because we were already uncomfortable and did not want to alienate them further by declining to purchase their wares, we decided not to go. He looked disappointed as he left the boat alone and did not speak to us again. The rest of the STINASU staff remained quite pleasant and professional on the return canoe trip.

Like anything that does not turn out as planned, we learned a great deal from our experience. We realized the importance of obtaining as much information as possible about the actual volunteer responsibilities up front, as well as assuming nothing and being punctual regardless of perceived local norms. Just like so many other decisions we made on the road, we tried our best to weigh the pros and cons of each option and determine how best to spend our time. While it was unfortunate that we left amid some hurt feelings, we made the right decision for our family. The problematic volunteer experience certainly did not sour us on STINASU. To be fair, STINASU's volunteer program was clearly still in its infancy and had laudable ideals. The agency had the potential to make very positive changes towards conservation goals with further development, and perhaps is already doing so at the time of this writing.

Fortunately, our change of plans did not seem to negatively affect their feelings towards us, either. They continued to be gracious and helpful in planning our visit to the rainforest.

To our dismay, the Eco Resort was booked when we came back. While Christopher and I aired out on the lovely wicker furniture in their air-conditioned lobby, Fran scoured the town for a room and came up with the only available option in a No Tell Motel. We had lots of fun answering Christopher's questions regarding the selection of television programs, the placement of a see-through window between the shower and the bedroom, and the little contraceptive packet that accompanied the towel. Luckily we kept our sense of humor and managed to find space back at the Eco Resort the next night as we prepared to leave for Brownsberg National Park.

We made plans with STINASU to journey to their lodge in the national park, which is located about two to three hours south of Paramaribo. Arriving early at the designated street corner to secure a spot on the already overcrowded public "bus," we headed off to the village of Brownsweg, consisting of one main road and a small convenience store at the edge of the jungle. We guzzled down soft drinks while waiting at the store until the park vehicle came to transport us to the lodge. Our accommodations at Brownsberg were much nicer than our volunteer lodging at Galibi. The building consisted of a few bedrooms, a common sitting area, a kitchen, and a large bathroom with several shower stalls and toilets. While we brought our own food, we thought it would be fun to eat dinner at the small camp restaurant on our first night. The food was delicious and the conversation lively, as we chatted with an animated mix of park staff, volunteers, researchers, and visitors. One knowledgeable staff person told us that, due to its limited international flights, Suriname receives only 2,000 visitors a year, primarily from the Netherlands. We felt very privileged to be included in that group! When we finally got up from the table to go to bed, we turned to see a huge tarantula sitting right on the place where we had been eating. I made a mental note to check my shoes in the morning. As we walked back to our room, we were astounded at the huge number of frogs and toads all over the grounds. Their boisterous croaking serenaded us to sleep, and after a restful night, we awoke to the now-familiar sound

A monkey keeps an eye on us

of howler monkeys. We lay in bed, enjoying the harmonic chorus and joking about how afraid we had been when we had first heard them in the Bolivian pampas.

After the musical interlude, we prepared our own breakfast and then took several hikes along the well-marked walking trails around the park. Our favorite path involved a five-hour extensive walk through some dense brush where several types of monkeys passed us as they foraged for food. Usually very careful on the walking trails, my attention was briefly diverted by the monkeys at one point. "Look at the snake you almost stepped on, Mom!" Christopher pointed out the culprit. It was a very smooth, milk-chocolate brown color so I wasn't too worried. With all of our visits to serpentarios, I had learned that poisonous snakes were usually quite colorful or had some kind of distinctive design to ward off predators. However, later that night, we discussed our find with a local guide who had escorted another visiting family to the lodge. Based on our description, he wasn't so dismissive, indicating that it might have been quite poisonous after all. Eeek! Thank goodness one of us was paying attention. We spent two full days in the park, and as we were leaving on our last day, we were rewarded with a close-up view of a sloth. Hanging out in a tree near the camp restaurant, the sloth moved slowly but efficiently through the branches. As we watched it disappear from sight into the dense foliage, we sadly said goodbye to the exotic rainforest of the Amazon Basin.

Très cher!

For families trying to remain on budget, we strongly recommend Suriname over French Guiana. While the natural environment is similar in both countries, English-speaking travelers can access it much more affordably and easily in Suriname. However, we were determined to investigate the offerings of our final South American country, so we made a quick side trip. As we neared the foreign shore, I glimpsed the old Transportation Camp, serving as a grim reminder of French Guiana's history as a penal colony. In the 1930's, a Frenchman named Charrière, also know as Papillon, was wrongly accused of murder and exiled to French Guiana, passing through that very place. His story was made

Cayenne, French Guiana

A tribute to Daveed

famous in the Hollywood movie *Papillon*, starring Steve McQueen and Dustin Hoffman. After disembarking from our boat, we sweated profusely in a hot van for almost an hour until enough passengers had filled the vehicle and we were able to set off for the capital city of Cayenne. While we waited, we stared in dismay at the excessive fees advertised on a small sign in the van; the three-hour ride on a smooth, paved road was going to cost us close to US$100 (US$30 per person). The overpriced fare sharply contrasted with the US$40 we had paid earlier for the 12-hour trip from Georgetown to Paramaribo, which included two ferry rides, and set the standard for the exorbitant prices we encountered throughout this tiny country. Governed by France as a protectorate, French Guiana had recently converted to Euros, and their prices were comparable, or perhaps higher due to the cost of importing most of their goods, to those found in Paris. This relationship had provided its citizens with some services and amenities not found in the other Guianas, including good roads, nice restaurants, and banks with functioning ATM machines, but a brief survey of their dilapidated houses and worn clothing suggested that the locals could not afford many of these luxuries. Their quality of life appeared quite similar to that of their international neighbors.

Upon our arrival in the capital we were quite disappointed to discover that we had again arrived on Labor Day weekend. Everything was closed. After much searching, we found a small room at the clean Central Hotel, costing US$70 a night for only the basic amenities. We wandered around the town and the tranquil shoreline, collecting sea glass, those colorful bits of bottles washed smooth by the waves. In the evening, we indulged in a wonderful French meal complete with escargot and a snotty waiter. Christopher and I were so excited about sampling the snails that we each ordered our own plate and dived right in. Back at our hotel, Fran and I evaluated our budget, and we calculated that we had already spent over US$300 in two days. *Très cher!* (Very expensive!) We agreed that we had made the most of our experience in Cayenne, and we decided to return to less expensive Suriname on the following day. As we waited for passengers to fill the van leaving for the border, Fran snapped a photo of a monument dedicated to the French

Foreign Legion for Daveed. Proudly poised atop a tall concrete spike was a replica of a rooster.

A Decadent Caribbean Vacation at the End of Our Vacation

As our year-long adventure was coming to a close, we decided to ease the transition by splurging on a Caribbean vacation in the nearby islands of Trinidad and Tobago. Easily accessible by a short, inexpensive plane trip from Paramaribo, the islands offer beautiful natural scenery by way of tropical rainforests and white sandy beaches, diverse wildlife and abundant birdlife, scrumptious spicy seafood, and friendly, laid-back locals. Looking for more sea turtles, we headed to St. Riviere Beach on the northeastern coast of the larger island of Trinidad. Due to its remote location and limited public transportation, we had prearranged an airport pick-up service over the Internet through our hotel, Le Grande Almandier. Our hotel room was very comfortable, with large beds, a private bath, and a balcony overlooking the brown sandy beach that backs right up to the jungle. Tiny bats occasionally flew through the vents below the pointed roof, enhancing the native experience. A delicious breakfast was served every morning in the open-air restaurant overlooking the intersection of river and ocean where the leatherbacks emerge nightly to lay their eggs. The lovely setting was a perfect way to start each day.

Arriving after a major storm, we strolled down the beach and were distressed to see that the river water had unearthed some of the precious turtle eggs. Scraggly black vultures thrust their beaks into the gooey mess, taking advantage of the abundant meal. Christopher tried futilely to shoo them away, but they listlessly flew just out of his reach, eyeing the eggs hungrily until they could swoop back for more after we moved on. We diverted his attention with our first sighting of a leatherback baby. The white stripes against its greenish-black soft shell made it an easy target for the scavenging birds. Disoriented, the baby valiantly tried to swim along the river's shore through the debris dredged up by the storm. While delighted at our tiny find, we also feared for its survival and tried to direct it towards the ocean. We watched sadly as it drifted away, so small and helpless against the immense waves.

Further down the beach we encountered a grass-roots organization with similar concerns. The young volunteers collect the babies that hatch during the day, keeping them safely stowed in colorful plastic bins until releasing them at dusk to help them avoid land predators. We joined up with a volunteer and followed him down the beach in search of the tiny turtles. His keen eyes quickly picked out even the most subtle movements in the sand. He placed a moving turtle on top of one nest. Collectively the rest of the turtles also began paddling as they instinctively copied each other's efforts to burrow out of the deep hole. We watched in fascination as the wiggly bundle of 60 to 100 tiny babies struggled to emerge live from their sandy home. At twilight, several volunteers carried the plastic bins to the water's edge, spreading themselves out along the shore. In unison, they tilted their buckets and hundreds of tiny turtles sped across the sand towards the vast, perilous sea. We quietly cheered on our little friends in this incredibly uplifting evening ceremony.

Our hosts signed us up for a night walk to view the leatherbacks laying their eggs. Due to the large size of the group, we worried about the human impact on the turtles. After the guide picked up a newly-laid egg and began to pass it around the group, we decided to end our tour and return to the hotel. We shared our concerns with the hotel owner and arranged a more environmentally-friendly hike for the next day. A guide was essential in the absence of a marked path and for support when rappelling down slippery embankments. The trek through well-preserved jungle ended at a breathtaking waterfall surging through glittering emerald-green foliage and mosses. Glorious!

As we prepared to leave, we retrieved our valuables from the hotel "safe" which in actuality was just a locked cabinet in the often unoccupied office. The office was totally open to road traffic, and the cabinet key was casually tossed in a desk drawer next to the computer which provided Internet service for the hotel. We opened my small fanny pack and, upon comparing the remaining money with the amount written in our notebook, we discovered US$95 was missing. We had carefully recorded every dollar in the notebook just prior to locking it in the "safe," so we were confident of our calculations. We immediately spoke with the owner, who asked us to double-check our belongings and tried

Leatherback hatchlings on St. Riviere Beach, Trinidad

Christopher gives a helping hand to a new little friend

to assure us that no one had access to the "safe" except the owners. To me, it seemed very easy for someone to come in to use the Internet, come across the key in a drawer, and then take something out of the cabinet. We discussed some ideas about how to prevent this from happening in the future. The owner said that he would go through the valuables with the guests, documenting all the items to be stored. We also suggested putting them in a signed, sealed envelope as well. Ultimately, our host generously honored our loss and credited us with US$95 towards our bill.

To really soak up the relaxed Caribbean lifestyle, we decided to spend about a week on Tobago, the smaller, quieter, less developed island. The friendly folks at the Cocrico Inn cooked us up some amazing spicy greens with beans and rice, as we comfortably settled into two fully furnished rooms with kitchen facilities and checked out the very clean pool. Fran took a run on the dirt roads around the island and met a "Trini" woman who had grown up in Switzerland. She invited us to come spend some time with her and the other islanders, "liming," or hanging out, and downing cold Carib lagers on the corner block one hot, humid night. After hearing Fran rave about the delicious island cuisine, one of the locals offered to teach him how to make his own special, extremely hot sauce. Fran jumped at the chance for this unique lesson. While Christopher and I played in the hotel pool, the two of them slaved away in the kitchen. Two hours later Fran returned, dripping with sweat but happily waving a plastic pop bottle full of the fiery liquid. We even managed to bring it all the way through customs back home!

Our days in Tobago were a wonderful blend of "liming" and exploring the natural beauty of the small island. We rented a car and drove to Speyside, on the eastern tip of the island, where we boarded a glass-bottom boat. Through the Plexiglas flooring, our guide pointed out the myriad of coral formations, including brain coral, the largest in the world. We jumped off the boat to do some great snorkeling amidst the colorful growth and then hiked through the bird sanctuary on the nearby island of Little Tobago. Before heading home, we stopped at an absolutely magical restaurant called Jemma's Seaview Kitchen. Designed like a tree house, the restaurant overlooks the gorgeous turquoise sea and blends in so well with the environment that hummingbirds dart in and out of the open windows. As we returned to our hotel, we drove through the oldest national rainforest park in the world and stopped to enjoy the protected flora and fauna of the area. Following that delightful outing with another to the main town of Scarborough, we visited the Tobago Museum. Christopher loved the taxidermal local critters while Fran and I appreciated the spectacular view overlooking the Caribbean and the well-manicured, flowering gardens. As we took the scenic route along the southern coastline, we stopped at the Genesis Nature Park and Art Gallery in the home of Michael Spencer. We all enjoyed the wildlife, including monkeys, boas, caimans, and turtles, and were very impressed by Michael's artistic and gardening talents. However, we became increasingly uncomfortable when the conversation turned to religion. When Michael insisted that women are the weaker sex because God created them from Adam's rib, I had to draw the line.

Driving away along the northern coast, we discovered several private, picture-perfect beaches where palm trees swayed above pristine white sand. Perhaps a little too relaxed, Fran lost track of his wedding ring while swimming in the warm waters. Throughout our entire trip, the only four tangible items that we left behind were the gold band, the first aid kit, Fran's Leatherman tool, and the stuffed penguin. The symbolism of family, health, work, and wildlife seemed a fitting tribute and sacrifice for the journey. Pachamama (the Incan term for Earth Mother) would be satisfied.

After Tobago, we took a quick, inexpensive flight back to Trinidad for a couple days to enjoy the capital city of Port of Spain. The airport contained huge displays of the colorful costumes worn during Carnival, and we eagerly discussed returning to the islands for this seemingly amazing event. We organized a canoe trip through the Caroni Bird Sanctuary, a protected swamp full of mangrove trees. Lathered up with repellent against the hoards of mosquitoes, we were thrilled to see a medium-sized boa constrictor twisting around a tree branch like something from the Disneyland Jungle Cruise, as well as a small furry anteater curled up on a limb. We also sighted many waterfowl, such as storks and egrets. Climbing to the top of a wooden lookout structure, we watched brilliant pink scarlet ibises fly overhead as we gazed out over the vast stretches of marshland. Eventually, our guide called for us, and we scurried back down to the canoe with the bugs hot on our trails.

Too quickly it was time to leave Trinidad and head over to Caracas, Venezuela, to catch our flight home. Feeling despondent that our journey was coming to an end, we all tried to reach some closure on the experience by making two lists together (see Appendix D). The first list described all of the things that we would miss about South America. We had a wonderful time reminiscing about the great adventures that we had taken together, the wondrous things we had seen, and the amazing cultural diversity we had encountered on the continent. In an attempt to ease the pain of saying goodbye to all of those extraordinary events, our second list was comprised of all the things that we would NOT miss about South America to increase our appreciation of the comforts of home. We laughed as we ticked off some of the hardships and crazy mishaps we had survived on the road.

Our short flight from Port of Spain, Trinidad, into Caracas, Venezuela, went very smoothly. The political situation had calmed down there, and everyone we asked reassured us that our safety was no longer at risk. Over the Internet we contacted a hotel near the airport with shuttle service each way to ensure that we would catch our flight home without incident. Upon arrival, our driver helped us exchange money with a man in the airport before taking us to the hotel. The money changer gave us an excellent rate but tried to convince us to exchange more cash, insisting that we would need it for the airport exit tax. This time we had done our research in advance. We knew the exchange rate and the cost of our airport fees, and we had even located an ATM in the airport. We told him that if we needed the money in Venezuelan currency before our flight out, we would exchange it at that time. It turned out that the airport officials gladly accepted our U.S. dollars for the required taxes. Our clean room at the pleasant, reasonably priced Las Quince Letras Hotel overlooked the Caribbean, and being too far from the city center to justify a taxi ride there, we spent our last day relaxing by the pool and eating as many Venezuelan *arepas* as we could hold. As our plane lifted out of Caracas the following morning, we peered out of the window at the slowly receding South American coastline. In unison we chanted our farewell song, "Good-bye South America, we loved you!" Fran and I looked at each other in amazement over our accomplishment, and I hummed the immortal words of the late, great Jerry Garcia, "What a long, strange trip it's been!"

"I found out that I really like turtles!"

CHRISTOPHER'S COMMENTS

We went to see an opera in Manaus. It was the day before my birthday. The opera was all in some other language so I really didn't understand it. It was my first opera and it wasn't that fun. Kids and operas don't mix. When the opera was over, it was my birthday because it was past 12:00 a.m. I said, "Can I open my presents now?" Mom and Dad said, "First let's get some sleep, and then we will open the presents in the morning." Then I woke up and I asked Mom and Dad if I could open my presents. They had to get them out of the backpack. I opened my presents and one was a Game Boy game. It was Powerpuff Girls, Blossom. I also got some stamps and stuff. I started a stamp collection at the beginning of the trip. It was fun collecting the stamps because I liked how they looked. After my presents, we spent hours and hours and hours playing Harry Potter. We really liked the game, Harry Potter, and collecting Harry Potter cards. We probably played more Harry Potter than anybody else in the world. Daveed says that this is nothing to be proud of, but we were proud anyway.

I liked seeing all the fish in Manaus. In an aquarium as big as a swimming pool, there was a big fish that could eat a man whole. I loved seeing that fish because it was so huge. I got to use one of its scales as a fingernail file. Then we went to see the manatees. The manatees looked cool because they had a weird trunk to come and breathe at the top of the water. They were gray and brown. We also got to go to the fish market. One of the guys gave me these weird white little bones that were like the tonsils of the fish. He was nice.

Leatherback turtles are a protected species of turtles. At St. Riviere beach, I liked helping to collect baby turtles because it was fun to watch them climb out of the sand and around inside the bucket on top of each other. They were so cute! It was also cool to see all the baby turtles going out to the sea in huge mobs and the mothers laying eggs. I found out that I really like turtles!

TRAVELER'S TIPS

1. Get rid of your foreign money within or as close to the border as possible.
2. Air conditioning in the hot sticky tropics can be a very good thing!
3. Research exchange rates over the Internet before entering a new country.
4. Check the dates of all holidays and plan on everything being closed at that time.
5. Clarify volunteer expectations up front. Talk to the people who work at the site as well as other volunteers. Stress your family's skills and limitations to ensure a good fit.
6. When volunteering, identify your advocate or the person that you can go to when a problem arises. Make sure that person can speak your language or a translator is available. Communicate any concerns immediately.
7. Be punctual until you are absolutely sure of local norms.
8. Keep track of all of your daily expenses in a journal. Write down all of your financial information to monitor the amount that you have on the road, as well as to compare against your bank and credit card statements back home. The journal will also document names of hotels, restaurants, and sights as well.
9. Stamp collecting is an excellent way for your child to accumulate interesting and unique mementos of his or her trip. Seeking out post offices can be enjoyable for the entire family, and your child will love being able to select special stamps to commemorate the experience. Best of all, they are very lightweight and portable!
10. Put some closure on your extended time abroad by doing some transitional activities. We chose to make two lists: one of things that we enjoyed about South America and the other of things that we wouldn't miss (to heighten our appreciation of life back home).

RESOURCES

SÃO PAULO, BRAZIL

Hotel Joamar

Rua D. Jose de Barros, 187
Telefax: 221-3611

Inexpensive hotel in great location near the Praça da República. Clean double room with private bath, TV, and breakfast included. However, they later charged us for three people although we only had two single beds, so our price for a triple was US$16 per night.

Fun sights for the family include the **Japanese town and Sunday market** (Metro stop Praça da Liberdade), the **Memorial da América Latina** (Av Mário de Andrade 664, Metro stop Barra Funda, www.memorial.org.br) with colorful exhibits and fabulous handicrafts from all over Latin America, and especially, the famous **Instituto Butantã/The Butantã Snake Farm and Museum** (Av Vita Brasil 1500, Tel: 813 7222) where visitors see many poisonous snakes and spiders and learn how serums are produced.

MANAUS, BRAZIL

Plaza Hotel

Av. Getulio Vargas, No. 215 –Centro
Telefax: 55-92-232-7766/ 622-3314

Reasonable hotel in central location with small indoor pool, our room with private bath, TV, AC, and buffet breakfast cost US$32 a night.

Teatro Amazonas

Praça Sao Sebastião, s/n, Centro
Tickets: (92) 232-1768

Telefax: (92) 622-1880
www.ticketronics.com.br
teatroamazonas@visitamazonas.com.br

World-famous opera house built at the turn of the century with the finest materials from Europe in the middle of the rainforest. Tours and performances are highly recommended.

Green Planet Tours

Rua 10 de Julho 481, Centro (Near the Opera House)
Telefax: 55- 92-232-1398
www.planettours.com.br
info@planettours.com.br

Helpful brochure provides a wealth of information regarding local sights. Can arrange a variety of tours on the Amazon and in the rainforest; make sure at least to take a day tour to see the **Meeting of the Waters** (Rios Negro and Solimões).

Interesting family excursions include the fish stalls at the **Municipal Market**, the **Museu do Índio** (R Duque de Caxias 356 near Av 7 Septembro), and the **Museu do Homem do Norte** (Av 7 de Setembro 1385 near Av J Nabuco) with information on the culture and handicrafts of the local people. Take a bus out of town (towards Aleixo) to the **Instituto Nacional de Pesquisas da Amazônia (INPA)**, a beautiful botanical garden where visitors can see manatees, caimans, giant otters, monkeys, birds, agoutis, and sloths. Walk or take a taxi to the nearby **Museu de Ciências Naturais da Amazônia**, a natural science museum with a fascinating collection of fish and insects, including an aquarium with the largest freshwater fish in the world.

GEORGETOWN, GUYANA

We were concerned about our safety while in Georgetown, and the locals were worried for us as well. Unfortunately, we would not recommend spending much time here; in fact, we did not see some of the attractions due to safety concerns. If you do find yourself here, the **Botanical Gardens** are worth a look.

Guyana Tourism Authority

National Exhibition Center, Sophia
Tel: (592) 223-6351
Fax: (592) 223-6352
visitguyana@networksgy.com

Palace de Leon Hotel

32 Public Road, Kitty
Tel: 226-4374
Fax: 226-8329
palacedeleon2000@yahoo.com

Wooden Caribbean building with homey, comfortable, tropical décor and helpful management. Huge room with balcony, AC, and TV for US$40 a night. Don't bring any food into your room; ours attracted hundreds of ants!

PARAMARIBO, SURINAME

Eco Resort

Cornelis Jongbawstraat 16
P.O. Box 2998
Tel: (597) 425522
Tel: (597) 471500 (for reservations)
Fax: (597) 425510
Fax: (597) 411682 (for reservations)
www.ecoresortinn.com

This was a splurge but an incredible deal for the money. Beautiful tropical setting with gardens and terraces. Comfortable, well-furnished rooms with big beds, huge hot showers, full set of towels (including washcloths!), balcony, fridge, AC, TV, safety deposit box, and big buffet breakfast. Guests have full use of the facilities at the luxury hotel, Torarica, next door, which include a large pool, hot tubs, sports facilities, tropical garden with small zoo, and poolside bar and restaurant. All for US$78 a night!

STINASU (Foundation for Nature Conservation in Suriname)
Cornelis Jongbawstraat 14 (Next door to the Eco Resort)
Tel: 00(597) 476597/ 421683/ 427102/ 427103
Fax: 00(597) 421683
www.stinasu.sr
stinasu@sr.net

Fabulous government-run agency that will customize trips to the wide variety of nature reserves in Suriname, including Galibi Beach to see the huge sea turtles laying their eggs, and the pristine rainforests in **Raleighvallen and Brownsberg National Parks**. STINASU will arrange everything from completely planned guided tours to basic transportation and lodging for independent travelers for very reasonable prices that directly support conservation efforts. Volunteer opportunities are also available; check these out carefully before committing. Highly recommended!

La Bastille
Kliene Waterstraat 3
Across the street from Torarica

Great restaurant with a variety of spicy noodles and other Indonesian and local cuisine. Very friendly service.

Dr. Chang Fong Chu
Dr. Sophie Redmondstraat #250
(stichting bedryfs Gezondheidszorg)
Tel: 44 10 12

Professional, friendly doctor who was able to help me on a weekend!

Apotheek (Drug store)
Dr axwijkstraat 107
PO Box 12115
Tel: (597) 550644
Fax: (597) 551423

Drugstore open on the weekend.

If at all possible, make sure to check out the **bird song competition** on the lawn of the Presidential Palace (Gravenstraat) early Sunday mornings.

CAYENNE, FRENCH GUIANA

Central Hotel

Angle des rues Molé et Becker
Tel: 05 94 25 65 65
Fax: 05 94 31 12 96
centralhotel@wandoo.fr

Clean, modern room, with AC and TV for US$70 a night.

TRINIDAD

Tourism and Industrial Development Company

US: Travel Trade Hotline: 1-800-748-4224
http://www.VisitTNT.com
info@tdc.co.tt

Trinidad:
10-14 Philipps Street, Port of Spain
Tel: (868) 623-1932/4
Fax: (868) 623-3848
Information office: Piarco Airport, Telefax: (868) 669-5196

Tobago:
Unit 26, TIDCO Mall, 8-10 Sangster's Hill Road, Scarborough
Tel: (868) 639-4333
Fax: (868) 639-4514
Information Office: Crown Point Airport, Tel: (868) 639-0509

Le Grande Almandier

#2 Hosang Street, Grande Riviere, Trinidad
Tel: 670-2294
Telefax: (868) 670-1013

www.legrandealmandier.com
info@legrandealmandier.com

Adobe open-air hotel, restaurant, and bar located right on the beach where the leatherback turtles lay their eggs and local grassroots organization collects hatchlings to release at sunset. Comfortable rooms with fans, private bath, and balcony with hammocks for US$68 a night. Will arrange jungle hikes and night walks to observe turtles. Unfortunately, we discovered that some of our money stored in the hotel "safe" was missing; the owner took this off our bill and we discussed procedures needed to ensure that this is an isolated incident.

Alicia's House

7 Coblentz Gardens, Port of Spain, St Ann's, Trinidad
Tel: (868) 623-2802/ 624-8651
Fax: (868) 623-8560
www.aliciashousetrinidad.com
info@aliciashouse.com

Beautiful facilities include gardens, swimming pool, Jacuzzi, and clean, comfortable rooms with cable TV, AC, and fridge for US$58 a night.

Sweet Lime Restaurant

Corner French St. & Ariapita, Port of Spain
Tel: 624-9983

Fun atmosphere includes sidewalk seating with a great range of drinks and good food.

Veni Mangé

67a Ariapita Avenue, Woodbrook
Telefax: 624-4597
veni@wow.net

Restored Caribbean home with tropical décor and friendly waitresses, dressed in island wrap-around skirts, serving delicious local Caribbean dishes. Well worth the trip.

Caroni Bird Sanctuary

Tour Operators/Reservations:
#38, Bamboo Grove Settlement No. 1
Uriah Butler Highway, Valsayn P.O. Trinidad
Telefax: (868) 645-1305
nantour@tstt.net.tt

Organizes boat tours of mangroves with 168 species of birds (including impressive flocks of scarlet ibis), mammals such as anteaters, and reptiles. Wear mosquito repellent and cover up. Highly recommended.

TOBAGO

Cocrico Inn

North and Commissioner Street Plymouth, Tobago
P.O. Box 287
Tel: 1 (868) 639-2961
Fax: 1 (868) 639-6565
www.hews-tours.com
cocrico@tstt.net.tt

Hotel run by extremely nurturing folk, clean pool, and comfortable apartment with hodgepodge furnishings, full kitchen, and cable TV for US$70 a night. On-site restaurant serves up amazing spicy Tobagonian cuisine.

Carmen Duncan "Lady in Red"

Signal Hill, Tobago
Tel: (868) 631-8261
Home: (868) 639-6380
Pager: 625-5472
Cell: 678-1047

Within walking distance of Crown Point airport. Very friendly woman who rents cars inexpensively and will negotiate a satisfactory price.

Wayne's World Tours

Wayne Gray
#29 Top Hill Street, Speyside, Tobago
Tel: (868) 660-5495
Cell: (868) 780-7020
waynegray23@hotmail.com

Certified tour guide who accompanied our snorkeling and bird-watching trip in glass-bottom boat to the bird sanctuary on **Little Tobago**. Trips can also be arranged at Blue Waters Inn (Tel: (800) 742-4276, (868) 660-4341/ 6620-4077, www.bluewatersinn.com).

Jemma's Seaview Kitchen

(868) 660-4066

Just a short way down the street from the Blue Waters Inn, Speyside. In this "tree house" restaurant with a sea view, hummingbirds dart in and out of the open windows as you eat flavorful local cuisine. A very unique dining experience.

Genesis Nature Park and Art Gallery

Tel: 660-4668

Located right off the main highway on the east side between Bacolet and Roxborough, owner Michael Spencer shares his home and gardens full of art and interesting wildlife (e.g., monkeys, boas, and caimans). A delightful stop, although Michael's religious zeal may put off some visitors.

On Tobago we also enjoyed the beaches at **Store Bay** and **Englishman's Bay**, the nature hike and exquisite food at the **Arnos Vale Water Wheel Park** (Tel: 660-0815), the great view and taxidermal critters at the **Tobago Museum** (84 Fort King George, Scarborough, Tel: (868) 639-3970), and the drive through the **Tobago Rain Forest Reserve**.

CARACAS, VENEZUELA

Hotel Las Quince Letras

Av. La Playa Macuto, Sector Las Quince Letras
Estado Vargas.
Tel: (58212) 4151111
Fax: (58212) 2638067/ 5147515
webmaster@quinceletras.com

Clean, modern hotel close to the airport and overlooking the rocky coastline, with nice pool and restaurant on-site. Comfortable room with AC, TV, and ocean view for US$50 a night. Will provide transportation to and from the airport for an additional fee.

CHAPTER 11

EXTRANJEROS IN OREGON

Landing at George W. Bush Airport, we abruptly found ourselves thrust headfirst into American culture. It felt like ages since we had been in the United States, and I found myself singing another classic Garcia quote, "What a long, long time to be gone and a short time to be there." American English was spoken all around us, but everyone was talking a lot faster than we were accustomed to hearing it. We had to readjust to the pace of the conversations, and we struggled for word retrieval. Literature on second language acquisition describes a phenomenon called "subtractive bilingualism" in which the first language is lost while learning the second. Even though we often spoke English amongst ourselves, after a year of speaking slow, deliberate English with other foreigners, I definitely had difficulty communicating for a while upon our return.

The overwhelming visual assault of commercialism stood out as the most resounding first impression of the United States. Merchandise and advertising loomed everywhere, as far as the eye could see. European *viajeros* we encountered during our travels had shared how overwhelming it was to go into U.S. stores where the shelves were laden with several brands of the same product. "How do you choose?" they frequently asked. Enter the power of advertising. The constant barrage of images encouraging consumers to "buy, buy, buy" plastering most public places and coming from the media feels truly mind-numbing. I had to readjust to this sensory overload by making a beeline to a gourmet coffee stand. After I bought my first "black forest mocha half caff-half decaff nonfat no whipped cream" in a year, with no *la nata* in sight, I started feeling very happy to be back home.

My wonderful mood continued when I went shopping to purchase exactly the product I desired. My first day out I drove to Target in search of toothpaste for sensitive teeth. Initially I felt a touch of irritation because I couldn't find it in the distracting blitz of colorful boxes stretching across an entire aisle in the store. I compared this lavish display with our severely limited selection in South America, where we battled the challenges of seeking out a pharmacy that was open, explaining what we needed, and then accepting whatever they gave us. My frustration soon turned to delight to see an entire row of toothpaste devoted to us sufferers of sensitive teeth. I plucked my favorite brand joyfully off the shelf, giving silent thanks to the wonders of capitalism. I jumped back into my own, private vehicle and savored the freedom of being able to drive wherever I wanted, without having to follow any kind of bus schedule. Now simple errands could be done in a snap!

We also really enjoyed being back in our own home in Portland. Summers in Oregon are glorious, and the sunshine and dry weather were extremely comfortable after three months in the sticky tropics. Our house looked great, and it felt absolutely decadent to have the entire place all to ourselves after a year of living together in generally one small room. The air conditioning and electricity worked with the predictability that we lucky Americans have come to expect. I still marvel at the clear stream of piping hot water that emerges from the shower head just by a simple turn of the knob. Perhaps the best part of our return for Fran and me was the sheer luxury of sleeping in our own pillow-top California king-sized bed, well stocked with clean, smooth sheets and many plump, fresh-smelling, comfortable pillows. Christopher particularly delighted at having a ridiculous amount of toys to play with again. As we unpacked them, I stopped him about halfway through the process. "How many kids did we meet in South America who had this many toys?" I asked him. "None," he responded, quite humbled. The ability to truly appreciate the lifestyle that so many Americans take for granted is one of the biggest gifts we could have given our son. How many other children in the United States receive that kind of reality check? He had learned the lesson well.

We moved into our home over the July 4th weekend, and Fran jumped right into a project at work on the following Monday. I spent the next few weeks getting resettled, which was infinitely easier upon our return than our departure. My mother had done a great job maintaining our finances, and I spent some time updating those records. I met with our very good friend and insurance agent, Tom Quirk, who helped me change our accounts from renter to homeowner status. I reinstated our utilities, a process made easy because I had developed a list of company names and contact numbers before we had left. I called my employer, and due to my greatly improved Spanish skills, I was offered a position as school psychologist in Forest Grove, a small town on the outskirts of Portland with a high percentage of Spanish-speaking students. This opportunity was exactly the kind of job I wanted!

Fran and I also contacted Barnes Elementary, a public school in our home district of Beaverton, in the hopes of enrolling Christopher in their Spanish Immersion program. When Christopher was entering elementary school, we had applied to Spanish Immersion programs at Barnes and another elementary school in the district, but he was unable to attend due to lack of space. To our delight, the new principal at Barnes Elementary was enthusiastic about Christopher's experience in South America and agreed to enroll him in the 3rd grade of their program. I offered to show her the 2nd grade workbooks I had so diligently sent home as evidence of his home-schooling on the road, but she did not need to see them. Initially apprehensive about changing schools, Christopher met another child who was also new to the program on his very first day. The two quickly became best friends as he adjusted to his new classroom.

Time off had given all of us new opportunities, recharged energy, and a fresh perspective. What an incredible gift to have a year to really spend quality time together and learn about each other in an intimate, in-depth way. Despite the stresses and strains of constant family togetherness and in Christopher's case, social isolation, we would all do it again in a heartbeat. For every decision made, there are always pros and cons. We were very fortunate to have each other for help and support in transitioning back into American culture. *Viajeros* traveling solo can find it much more difficult to reintegrate back into society after an experience so foreign from their home. In contrast to our experience, Daveed felt depressed and isolated upon returning alone to the Netherlands. We couldn't wait to see our friends and family in Oregon and were very fortunate to have their support and interest in hearing about our life on the road.

However, we also felt the need to reach out to other travelers with similar experiences and perspectives to those we acquired in South America. I sought out travelogues and memoirs about foreign cultures in our local library and requested several books about South America. We received emailed updates about the animals at CIWY and inquiries from prospective students all over the world about the Canoa Spanish School through a quote that was posted on their website. At Bonnie Michaels' suggestion, I also subscribed to travel magazines, such as *Transitions Abroad*, and ended up writing an article for them. I found it vitally important to remain in contact over the Internet with the friends we made on our trip, including Daveed, Rich and Cyndi, Sven, and Bonnie, to share experiences about reintegrating back into society and reminisce about our travel experiences. During our first year home, we even enjoyed visits from Bonnie Michaels and Michael Seef while promoting their new book about taking a year-long sabbatical and from Sven, off again on another adventure. Long-term travelers should anticipate some difficulty upon reentry and develop some plans to ease back into daily life. Writing this book with Christopher and Fran was also my therapy and a permanent way to keep the memories alive. And of course, one of the best ways to get over the back-at-home blues is to begin planning your next vacation!

Christopher grew in many ways as a result of the experience. He became much more extraverted and communicative in both languages. Although he insisted on speaking English with us, his Spanish skills always impressed us when he needed to ask questions or engage other children through the *juegos en red* (games on the Net) in Internet cafés. Relying heavily on his auditory processing skills, he was able to recognize and remember Spanish words very well, and at times, translate spoken

Spanish better than I could. He connected with many different types of people and was fortunate to have many wonderful male role models, such as Alfonso and Daveed, enter into his life. He developed patience and acceptance of others with a variety of capabilities. His teachers continue to credit him with these characteristics and pair him with classmates that need a socially and behaviorally appropriate peer. Often left to his own devices, Christopher also cultivated the ability to entertain himself. We frequently watched him deep in fantasy play, and his teachers now report that his creativity is outstanding. Very important, Christopher learned about himself and his own preferences. By collecting stamps in each country, he indulged in a hobby that expanded his cultural horizons by enabling him to visit different post offices throughout South America and observe what the people choose to put on their stamps. He expresses an interest in different career choices based on his knowledge and exposure to experiences obtained on the trip, such as archaeology and working with animals. As he talked to other young adult travelers about their dreams and aspirations, he himself began planning for his own future, talking about places that he would like to live and things that he would like to do.

Christopher also experienced other cultures and civilizations in a way that he never could have learned in the classroom or from a book. History came vividly alive as he witnessed the Nazca lines from a helicopter and reveled in the mysticism at Machu Picchu. He saw how people in other countries make a living by watching subsistence farmers toiling in the fields on the Bolivian altiplano and milking cows on a Mapuche farm in Chile. He feels gratitude for the things we have at home and has an understanding of the limitations of material possessions. Perhaps best of all, Christopher has developed an interest in the world around him and a passion for exploration beyond our borders.

Long-term traveling also made me a better parent. As a psychologist I have always stressed the importance of stability and predictability, but I experienced first-hand the necessity of routines and structure, particularly for my son. I also learned the importance of including kid-friendly activities in every daily plan, which ultimately turned out to be fun for all of us as a family. Furthermore, ensuring that Christopher had adequate entertainment, in the form of books, video games, cards, and other types of toys, was essential in keeping him a happy traveler. I saw how to help my shy little boy establish friendships by creating opportunities to interact with other children. Together, Christopher and I discovered our similarities, including our need for routines and advance planning, and we also figured out how to work through our differences. We make an excellent team where each person plays a crucial part in the success of each adventure. Perhaps, best of all, as a direct result of Christopher's interests, I nurtured a wealth of skills and passions that I never knew that I had. Through my son I discovered exotic birds and animals, the tranquility of the rainforest, the magical Galápagos Islands, and Harry Potter cards. For all those things and more, I am eternally grateful. But as a mother, I'm still not perfect. Much to Alma's chagrin, I still refuse to throw a Harry Potter game!

As for our marriage, Fran and I have made it through something that most couples never experience. We lived joined at the hip for a year and survived to tell the tale! We developed a wealth of knowledge about travel in general and, specifically, South America. We learned how to accommodate each other's desires and compromise in a way that works for everyone. We became better short- and long-term travelers, and now we can put that knowledge about ourselves and the process to use in making future experiences more rewarding. Travel is also so much more fun as a couple, sharing the joys of each new discovery and buffering the stresses of living in unfamiliar territory by laughing over our bungled attempts to adjust. Perhaps best of all, I learned to appreciate Fran's calm, uncomplaining, flexible approach, his strength, and his handiness in being able to fix just about anything. And I daresay he learned a bit about the benefits of my micromanaging!

For myself, I discovered that I can push myself to my physical limits and emerge, perhaps without toenails, but victoriously at the summit. I can learn to speak a foreign language and come to recognize a variety of dialects. I can fend off aggressive touts and the false police, and I can hold my ground and assert myself against con artists. I can tell the difference between the call of an oropendola and a poison dart frog. Most important, I can conceptualize a dream, and with the support of the people I love, I can make that dream become a reality. With a little help, you can too. *¡Feliz viaje!*

CHRISTOPHER'S COMMENTS

Coming home, our plane kept getting delayed. I felt disappointed when I kept seeing "Delayed" on the board. When we were finally on the plane, I was super duper excited because I had been homesick for a lot of the time. Then Grandma and Grandpa picked us up and brought us back to our own home. That night we slept in our own bed!

On the trip I learned a lot of things. I learned about animals and how they live in South America. I learned that I like animals a lot, so when I came home I went to visit Dr. Kirk Miller at the clinic where he works. He is one of our friends who is a vet. I also learned that I like dinosaurs, so I decided to go to a camp to learn more about archaeology. I learned that Daddy likes to carry heavy things and Mom always remembers. No negotiating! I learned that I like home a lot, but I also want to go on a trip all over the world to see all of the friends that we made again. Next time we go on a trip, I also want to go to Africa to see the animals. I want to take two trips! Maybe more!

I have two recommendations for any kids that are reading this book. If I knew I was going to learn how to read on that trip, I would have brought a lot more books. Books for me in English were a pain to find on the trip. Also, you have to learn another language before you go to South America so that you can talk to other people. Learning Spanish wasn't that hard to do. Most of all have fun!

TRAVELER'S TIPS

1. Be aware that your return home will require some adjustment. Many travelers feel isolated and, possibly, depressed.

2. Take time to savor the advantages of your home town. If you are lucky enough to live in a developed country, enjoy the advantages of running hot water and having predictable electricity.

3. Seek out employment or volunteer opportunities that utilize your new skills.

4. Consider language immersion programs that will help your children extend their developing language skills.

5. Help your children investigate classes, camps, or outings that support new interests generated during their trip. Perhaps they would like to get involved in a cause that helps those less fortunate than themselves.

6. Reach out to other travelers via the Internet and stay connected to friends met on the road.

7. Read magazines and contribute articles to keep your experiences alive and help others benefit from them. Maybe you, too, will write a book!

APPENDIX A

TRIP BUDGET

Unless you are independently wealthy beyond your dreams, budgeting will play a large role in planning for your trip as well as making decisions en route. While it is simple to determine whether you have the financial capability to take short excursions, a firm budget is imperative for a longer journey. By establishing your financial parameters ahead of time, you and your traveling partner(s) can reduce and even eliminate arguments stemming from the insecurity of not knowing whether you have enough money to see a certain sight or do a once-in-a-lifetime activity.

Pre-trip Planning

Our initial budgetary work began in earnest about three years prior to the sabbatical. We had to determine whether we could afford to spend a year in South America and how much money we would need to cover traveling expenses as well as our ongoing commitments back in the United States (e.g., real estate taxes, mortgage payments, professional licensure fees, and other assorted obligations). In order to create our first budget, we developed a rough itinerary and used our guidebooks to estimate the average daily costs for food, lodging, entertainment, and public transportation. We then added a line item for travel between countries, and built in some spare days for miscellaneous use. Fran entered these numbers into an Excel spreadsheet along with our expected length of stay in each country. After calculating pre-trip necessities such as gear, airline tickets, and insurance, we generated a final estimated budget. We set monthly financial goals and began putting aside every spare penny towards the trip.

Financial Planning en Route

Throughout the sabbatical, maintaining a detailed budget served several critical functions. By comparing how much we had actually spent against our pre-trip budget, we could make well-informed decisions on what splurges (e.g., the Galápagos Islands, the Termas de Reyes Hotel-Spa in Argentina, flying to Rio for Carnival, and the Eco Resort in Suriname) we could afford. By keeping track of our expenses, we were able to analyze exactly how we spent our money and therefore could better predict future expenses (e.g., food, lodging, or transportation). We recorded each bank withdrawal and credit card charge, and emailed this information to my mother so that she could compare it with the statements received in the mail. We also used the budget as a tool to record our cash on hand so that we knew when and how much money to take out of the bank. By keeping such accurate records we determined that someone had stolen US$95 out of a hotel "safe" in Trinidad. Our excellent record-keeping caused the hotel to reimburse us this amount.

In order to keep track of our expenditures, we took a moment nearly every day to review and record every expense, including the cost of our hotel, restaurant meals, tours, and other special events. This ritual was actually a nice way to relive the day. For simplicity's sake, the expenses were typically entered in the local currency and then converted as needed. Every week or two we spent time tallying our cash on hand and comparing it to our expected amount based on our expense book. Generally, this process went fairly quickly and we discovered that we were pretty accurate recorders. Whenever we finished a particular segment of the journey (e.g., leaving a country or perhaps a city that we had stayed in for some time), we conducted a budget check. Fran calculated all expenses based on our cash summaries (so that miscellaneous items were included) and compared them to our pre-trip estimated budget. While at first Fran had expected to track our expenses based on the categories listed in the estimated budget, this quickly proved to be too cumbersome. Instead, he combined the costs for food, lodging, in-country travel, and entertainment together into a daily average for each country. As our itinerary changed, Fran became more creative in making the budget comparisons. For example, if we spent extra time in one country, he used all of the days allotted for that country and then borrowed some "days" from another comparable country or used our spare days. While he kept the line items for travel between countries, this expenditure typically involved just another bus ride and did not constitute a significant expense. At any rate, this tracking system served us quite well.

Looking back on the process, Fran suggests some changes for families when creating their own budget and tracking system. He notes that he would eliminate the line items for inter-country travel and build these costs into the daily expense budget instead. He would also have set aside a few more spare days at the high end of the average figure to use during the trip and have a budgeted slush fund to cover any incidentals that occur on the road or at home during the sabbatical. Readers are also encouraged to consider inflation and other changes due to shifting politics, so that initial estimates should always be conservative.

Below is the summary of our actual expenses incurred during our trip. Balancing somewhere above the shoestring budget but well below the luxury tour, our style of independent travel allows us to remain closer to the local people and off the beaten path while maintaining an acceptable standard of comfort and safety. In short, travelers can spend less than we did and still have a wonderful trip depending on their own personal preferences, interests, and resources. Consistent and accurate budgeting is the key.

The Numbers

Countries are listed in roughly the order that we visited them. When appropriate, we chose to group certain countries and/or regions together for ease of comparison. Again, the reader is encouraged to consider that these are costs incurred during 2002-2003. All prices are listed in U.S. dollars.

Pre-trip Expenses

	Total Costs	Costs Per Person
Health Insurance	$1,800	$600
Catastrophic Health Insurance	$1,800	$600
Hotel and Food at Airport	$102	$34
Airfare	$3,300	$1,100
Vaccinations	$855	$285
Medications	$900	$300
Travel Equipment	$600	$200
Travel Club, Maps, etc.	$260	$87
Total	$9,617	$3,206

Ecuador

	Spent	Days	Per Day	Per Person Per Day
Total	$5,971	85	$70	$23
Non-Galápagos Ecuador	$3,746	77	$49	$16
Canoa Subtotal	$1,202	19	$63	$21
Baños Subtotal	$1,051	29	$36	$12
Galápagos Islands	$2,225	8	$278	$93
Subtotals:				
Food	$1,066	85	$13	$4
Hotel	$1,795	85	$21	$7
Transportation	$1,430	85	$17	$6
Internet	$94	85	$1	$0.4
Mementos	$66	85	$0.8	$0.3

	Spent	Days	Per Day	Per Person Per Day
Entertainment	$1,158	85	$14	$5
Laundry	$50	85	$0.6	$0.2
Photos	$87	85	$1	$0.3
Mail	$66	85	$0.8	$0.3
Miscellaneous	$159	85	$2	$0.6

Summary: We chose to break out our expenses in Ecuador to provide the reader with a sense of the costs in each category. The amount noted for the Galápagos Islands includes airfare ($350 per person from Guayaquil), entry fees ($100 per person), a three-day boat tour ($625 total), and all other expenses. Staying on the island and seeing local sites cost as little as $50 per day for the three of us. We allocated eight of our spare days to this and therefore were over budget by $1,425. Well worth every penny.

The Remainder of the Trip

	Spent	Days	Per Day	PPPD
Peru	$2,166	37	$59	$20
Bolivia				
Rurrenabaque (Rurre)	$1,529	12	$127	$42
Non-Rurre	$2,258	55	$41	$14
Argentina Non-Patagonia	$4,403	61	$72	$24
Patagonia (Argentina and Chile)	$2,290	21	$109	$36
Chile Non-Patagonia	$1,315	19	$69	$23

	Spent	Days	Per Day	PPPD
Brazil				
Carnival	$3,520	14	$251	$84
Non-Carnival	$1,659	10	$166	$55
Uruguay	$462	9	$51	$17
Paraguay	$524	4	$131	$44
The Guianas				
Guyana	$267	3	$89	$30
Suriname	$2,401	18	$133	$44
French Guiana	$628	2	$314	$105
Trinidad and Tobago	$2,548	14	$182	$61
Venezuela	$110	1	$110	$37
GRAND TOTAL:	$41,668	365	$114	$38

Additional Notes:

Peru: Costs included two trips to the emergency room, shots, and medicine for Christopher, totaling $65.

Bolivia: Rurrenabaque, or Rurre, costs included Chalalán Lodge totaling $781 for 3 days.

Argentina and Chile: While at first glance Chile appears slightly cheaper than Argentina, we invested in a splurge at Termas de Reyes Hotel-Spa for six days at approximately $100 a day ($33 per person), purchased numerous mementos (including leather goods) and mailed them home, and prepared for Carnival.

Brazil: Costs for Carnival included $355 ($118 per person) for visas as the laws changed during our trip. Non-Carnival costs included two plane flights (São Paulo to Manaus, and Boa Vista to Georgetown, Guyana).

Paraguay: Costs included visas ($45 per person), shopping for numerous mementos, and doctor's visit ($45).

Guianas: Suriname prices included a splurge on the Eco Resort for US$78 a night and tours to Galibi Beach and Brownsberg National Park.

Appendix B

TRIP CHECKLIST

NOTE: We took these items with us, although we discovered the need for a few changes along the way. Our suggestions appear in brackets.

CHILDREN'S ITEMS

Travel Games to Go (Pressman Co.). Plastic magnetic toy containing several popular games (including checkers, snakes and ladders, etc.). [This was invaluable during our trip.]
Ungame
Playing cards
Polly pocket
Beads and string
Markers and papers
Spanish and English reading books [Bring along as many books in English as possible.]
Game Boy or some electronic toy [This was essential to the trip]
Snuggle toy
Baby blanket
Home-schooling workbooks
Index cards

CLOTHES

Sarong
Bathing suits
Workout outfit (sports bra and shorts)
Travel pants with zippered legs [These were essential in the rainforest.]
Jeans (not recommended)
Light sweats
Shorts (boxers and durable)
Short- and long-sleeved T-shirts
Sweatshirts
Socks
Tevas/sandals
Tennies
Hats
Jackets
Underwear
Sports watch

DOCUMENTS

Passports
Driver's license
Immunization cards
Credit cards
Travel account debit cards
Money (U.S. and foreign)
Traveler's checks
List of contact numbers and email addresses
Emergency numbers
Travel insurance information and hotline number
U.S. State Department Citizen's Emergency Center 202-647-5225
Copies of everything, including emergency numbers of cards
Copies of prescriptions
Guidebooks

Documentation, including email correspondence, of reservations (Spanish school, plane, hotels)
Maps and directions
Bus and plane schedules
Envelopes [These are useful to store valuables in hotel safes.]
Doctor's number/insurance card
Bloodtypes
Note allergy to sulfa
Identification for Christopher (to carry on him)
Passport photos
Exchange rates (www.oanda.com)
Location of ATMs (www.visa.com)

HEALTH CARE

First aid kit
Bandaids
Tweezers
Bactine/iodine packets
Allergy medications (inhalers, Claritin, Allegra, Nasonex, Rhinocort)
Antibiotics (mine and family's)
Malaria tablets
Immodium
Pills for yeast infection (Diflucan)
Aspirin
Tylenol
Advil
Tums
Benadryl
Ear drops antibiotics
Eye drops antibiotics
Afrin
Sudafed
Prescription decongestant (Guaifen)
Back Medication (Skelaxin, Neproxin)

Throat Lozengers
Dayquil and Nyquil tablets, cold remedies
Fioricet
Thermometer
Bonine
Antifungal cream
Iodine tablets to purify water [not needed]
Elastic bandaid

MISCELLANEOUS GEAR

Jackknife
Silverwear and plastic plate
Portable cup
Water heater [not needed]
Adapters
Mosquito net
Mosquito coils
Mosquito repellent (lotion and spray)
Sunglasses
Yoga mat
Inflatable pillow
Water and carrying tote
Snacks
Gifts for families/schools
Scissors
Sewing kit and patches
Bandana
Locks/chains and list of combinations
Travel alarms
Clothesline and detergent
Whistles and travel charms
Little flashlights
Headlamps [These were essential for many purposes.]
Wetsack
Notebooks

Spanish-English dictionary
Spanish-English electronic dictionary
Pens
Mechanical pencils
Highlighters
Books [Bring plenty of paperbacks to exchange along the way.]
Camera and film and battery
Travel recorder and cassettes
Inflatable life vest for Christopher
Binoculars
Money belts (waist, neck, bra, waterproof)
Water purifier [We never used this.]
Travel sheet
Travel umbrella
Batteries for alarm clocks, cassette, flashlights
Lighter
Universal plug for sinks
Backpack waterproof covers
Plastic rain poncho
Plastic bags

TOILETRIES

Deodorant
Razors
Facial products
Cottonballs
Qtips
Aloe vera lotion
Suntan lotion (SPF 4 and SPF 40+)
Small water bottle with squirt top [This was very convenient for brushing teeth.]
Nail files and clippers
Wet wipes
Toilet paper [Always keep a spare stash.]
Tissues

Hand sanitizer
Chapstick
Brush and pick
Hair supplies (ponytail holders and barrettes)
Shampoo
Conditioner
Washcloth
Liquid body soap
Body moisturizer
Glasses and spare pair, disposable contact lenses
Toothbrushes, toothpaste, and floss
Tampons [Bring a year's worth.]
Travel towels

Appendix C

AMAZONIAN BOAT TRIP FROM HELL

by Daveed (David de Jel)

I have a picture hanging on my wall with all the hammocks to remind me of the worst moment in my life. The boat trip, from Iquitos to Pucallpa, should have taken two or three days. But the first boat went very, very slow. It just crawled over the river. After a day and a half I heard that the boat was packed with sacks of cement below deck. The biggest part of the passengers was a team of construction workers, and they were going to build a new village in the jungle. The weight of the ship prevented its progress.

The next boat was passing by, and they laid out a plank between the two boats. One of the construction workers brought my baggage to the other boat, and I crawled on hands and knees over the plank. It was in the middle of the night; the plank wasn't even 17 inches wide, and I was terrified. If I would fall off, I would land in the river between the two boats and I would surely end up as fish food in one of the propellers. And every passenger of both boats was on the deck to watch that silly gringo on the plank. As soon as I was in reach they grabbed me and pulled me safely on board. Everybody was cheering and clapping when I was safely on the other side.

But the other boat was just as bad. A lot of people were transporting jungle animals to sell them in the city as pets. I had a box of screeching parakeets under my hammock. There were terrified monkeys on board that were calling out to each other. It was really, really sad.

The boredom was terrible. There was nothing to do. My book was finished on the first day. All passengers would spend about 20 hours a day just lying in their hammocks. Everybody was bored, and because nobody on the boat had ever seen a foreigner, they started talking to me. That sounds like fun, but I had the following routine with almost each passenger:

"Do you grow fruits in your country?" they would ask.

"No, it's too cold. We import our fruits."

"What, no bananas?"

"No, no bananas."

"No oranges?"

"No, no oranges."

"No mangos?"

"No, we don't grow our own fruits."

"No guava?"

"No."

"No pineapples?"

"No, nothing."

"Not even melons?"

"No, no melons, we import all our fruits. We have nothing."

"Surely you must grow papaya."

"NO! NO! NOTHING!"

"How about vegetables then?"

There were two toilets on the boat, and just in front of the bowl was a faucet in the ceiling. If you opened that, water would come out of a pipe so you could wash yourself.

The food was the worst part. I stopped eating after four days. They would catch fish by hanging nets behind the boat. Then they would cook the fish and rice in the brown river water. Everyone would get half a fish, some rice, and a cooked banana. Because it had been cooked in disgusting water, you really had to force the food down your throat and try not to breathe so you wouldn't taste anything. It was hard not to throw up while eating. Every little town along the river throws its garbage (and God knows what else) in the water so you can imagine what it would taste like. Half a fish means that half of the passengers received a big fish head. As I was the biggest guy on the boat, I always demanded to receive the back part. I'll be damned if I start eating a fish head. And the cooked banana...I only had it once. I ate half of it and threw the rest away. During the other meals, I skipped the banana. It was extremely dry, hard, and had a horrific taste. Most passengers threw away the bananas for the fishes.

And the trip took forever. After three days I started to get the feeling that we were not there yet. Not by a long shot. So I asked the captain politely what our estimated time of arrival would be. "Tomorrow, we will arrive," he told me. All the other passengers would be standing around and repeat to me, 'Tomorrow, we will arrive, mister." The day after, he told me, "Tonight, we will arrive." "Tonight, we will arrive, mister," all passengers would repeat. That changed to, "Tomorrow morning, we will arrive." That little routine went on for three more days. I only asked him the question of our arrival once. All the other 'updates' he gave freely. They were useless. He had no clue, and I was going insane.

Everyone would call me 'mister' on board. "Good morning, mister." "Mister, I wanted to ask you...do you grow coconuts in your land?"

One day we stopped at one of the bigger towns along the route. One of the guys told me he had family on the island. An aunt of his lived there and he was going to visit her. He asked me if I would like to go with him. Of course I jumped to the opportunity. She had a little wooden store and we sat there chatting with coca-cola and cookies. And it tasted delicious! I informed to the possibilities of traveling over land to the city. The riverboat is the only mode of transport they have. Then we sat near the water and the guy had bought us some local food wrapped in banana leaves. I could cry with joy.

But suddenly we heard the engine of the boat starting...we quickly looked up and I saw the damn thing PULLING AWAY!!! Oh, lord... that would be bad. So we started running like the Devil was chasing us. Everyone on board was shouting "Mister! Mister! We forgot the mister!" when they saw us running like mad. The guy jumped first and made it. Then I jumped and I barely made it. Everyone pulled me in. "We almost lost the mister!" they were shouting.

At one moment the captain again told me, "Tomorrow morning we will arrive." This time it sounded different. It also sounded different when all the passengers repeated it to me. Something was in the air. I could feel it. I believed that we finally were starting to come near our destination....and then the boat broke down.

The motor broke. There we were...on the river. After a couple of hours little motor boats would come and transport the ones with money to the city. At least that meant that we indeed were near! Of course I had no money on me, and I was doomed to stay on the boat.

It took a day to have the engine fixed. By that time the first boat I took had passed us by, and I was stuck on a boat that could not go forwards or backwards. In the end the engine started up again, the whole boat was vibrating, and everyone was cheering. A couple of hours later we pulled into the harbor of our destination. The trip of two to three days had lasted almost a week.

I met a guy at Macchu Picchu and I told him about the boat trip. "Pfff, that's nothing," he told me. "I was on that boat for two weeks."

Appendix D

TRANSITION LISTS

Things We'll Miss about South America:

- Andes
- Rainforest
- Capybaras
- Penguins
- Dolphins and whales
- Ecuadorian beaches
- Travel buddies, especially Daveed, Alfonso, Rich and Cyndi, Bonnie and Michael, and all of our friends at CIWY
- *Caipirinhas* with our American buddies, George, Mark, Brenda, Dilip, and Raj
- Freedom
- Vast unspoiled areas
- Salt flats
- Argentine *asados*, Uruguayan *parrillas*, and *tenedor libres*
- Wines like Sean Connery and Mel Gibson
- Brazilian Bahian cuisine (including *moquecas*)
- Crystal clear oceanic waters
- Quality family time
- Speaking and hearing Spanish
- Argentine *maté de coca*

Sleeping in
Chorus of howler monkeys
Groans of leatherbacks laying eggs
Growl of a baby puma
Rush of water at Iguazú
Crunch of pebbles under penguin feet
Peeping of a poison dart frog
Whoop of Suriname toad
Roar of two elephant seals play-fighting
Primal scream of a penguin
Distinct call of an oropendola
Andean pipe music
Samba in the Sambadrome at Carnival
Hypnotic drumbeat of Bahia, Brazil
Spanish dialects
Christopher speaking Spanish and singing "Somewhere over the Rainbow"
Swish of sand from the green turtle
A capybara chewing grass
Noisy macaws
Screech of loros waiting for breakfast
Passion of the Argentine tango
Singing "*¿A donde va la lancha? A Keawe va.*" with Bonnie and Michael
Songs by Ketchup and Shakira

Things We Won't Miss about South America

Overnight bus rides
Roosters
Pollo, papas, y pan
Polvo (dust)
Outstretched hands
Sweat
False police
Pickpockets

Sand flies
Aggressive and deceptive sales tactics
Apagó la luz (*y agua*) (Off went the lights [and water])
Saggy beds, thin mattresses
Shared bathrooms
Unexplained delays for days
Long lines
Portuguese
Guyanese English
No kitchen
La nata and instant coffee
Lack of floor space for stretching
Bolivian roads

Appendix E:

WHICH COUNTRY IS FOR YOU? A QUICK COMPARISON FOR FAMILIES

Country	Family-friendly?	PublicTrans-portation	Language	Cost	Hassles	Highlights
Argentina	Yes	High quality, excellent roads	Spanish dialect can be difficult	Affordable	Usual	Iguazú Falls, Buenos Aires, Iberán Marshes, wine-tasting, Lake District, Patagonia, Cafayate
Bolivia	Very challenging	Poor quality, poor roads	Spanish is easy to understand	Very inexpensive	False police, beggars, recent kidnapping reported	Lake Titicaca, Rurrenabaque, CIWY, Sucre, Salar of Uyuni, Tupiza
Brazil	Somewhat	Good quality, good roads	Portuguese	Affordable	Petty crime, pickpockets, robbery at knifepoint, very insistent beggars	Rio, Salvador, Manaus, Project TAMAR in Praia do Forte
Chile	Yes	High quality, excellent roads	Spanish dialect can be difficult	Somewhat expensive	Usual	Chiloé Island, wine-tasting, Lake District, Patagonia
Ecuador	Yes	Variable quality, variable roads	Spanish is easy to understand	Affordable	Usual, but crime does occur in cities	Galápagos Islands, Baños, Canoa/Sundown Inn, Montañita, Tena, Otavalo Market

Country	Family-friendly?	PublicTrans-portation	Language	Cost	Hassles	Highlights
French Guiana	Yes	Inconvenient vans, excellent roads	French	Very expensive	Usual	None that we can recommend
Guyana	No	Inconvenient vans, poor roads	English dialect is very difficult	Expensive	Very insistent beggars and touts, violent crime	None that we can recommend
Paraguay	No	Poor quality, poor roads	Spanish is easy to understand	Affordable	Very corrupt, dangerous	None that we can recommend
Peru	Somewhat	Variable quality, variable roads	Spanish is easy to understand	Affordable	Insistent and dishonest touts	Machu Picchu, Cusco and the Sacred Valley, Chan Chan, Arequipa, Colca Canyon, Lake Titicaca, Nazca Lines
Suriname	Yes	Variety of transportation options, decent roads	Dutch is the official language, English is widely spoken	Affordable	Usual	Galibi Beach, Brownsberg National Park, Paramaribo
Uruguay	Yes	Excellent quality, excellent roads	Spanish is easy to understand	Affordable	Usual	Colonia, beaches, hot springs
Venezuela	Unclear	Good roads	Spanish is easy to understand	Affordable	Unclear	None that we can recommend

Spanish-English Glossary

Agouti	Large rodent with spindly deer-like legs
Agua	Water
Aguardiente	Distilled liquor made from sugar cane
Almuerzo	Lunch
Amigo	Friend
Apagó la luz.	The lights turned off (the term used for the electricity shutting down).
Arepa	Venezuelan fried bread
Asado	Argentine barbecue
Bahía	Bay
Baños	Baths, or bathrooms
Blanca	White
Bodega	Wine shop
Bote salvavida	Life preserver

Brujo	Witch
Caiman	Crocodile
Caipirinha	Brazilian drink made with aguardiente, ice, sugar, and limes
Caliente	Warm, also used for spicy
Campesinos	Indigenous subsistence farmers
Campo	Country
Caña	Sugar cane
Capybara	Largest rodent in the world, lives around water
Casi	Almost
Casillero (Casillero del Diablo)	Cellar (Devil's Cellar)
Cava	Cave
Cementerio	Cemetery
Cena	Dinner
Cerro	Hill
Choclo	Tough corn popular in Ecuador
Churrascaria	A Brazilian all-you-can-eat buffet in which waiters bring skewers of grilled meats directly to the table
Ciudad	City
Coati	Raccoon-like animal with a long snout
Cochineal	Tiny grey bug with bright red blood used as a dye

Cómodo	Comfortable
Con dolor	With pain
Conquistador	Conquerer (typically referring to the Spanish who colonized much of Latin America)
Corazón	Heart
Cordillera	Mountain range
¿Cuántos cuesta?	How much?
Curanto	Chilean seafood and meat stew
Cuy	Guinea pig
Dados	Dice
Desayuno	Breakfast
Día (Día de los Muertos)	Day (Day of the Dead)
Diablo	Devil
Donde	Where
Ejército	Army
Empañada	Fried bread stuffed with sweet or savory fillings
Entre	Between
¡Espera!	Wait!
Esquina	Corner
Esteros	Marshes
Extranjero	Foreigner
Faro	Lighthouse

¡Feliz viaje!	Happy trip! (Have a good trip!)
Finca	Large farm
Gallo/Gallina	Rooster/Hen
Gané. Yo gané.	I won.
la Garganta	Throat
Gaucho	Argentine cowboy
Gratis	Free
Guanaco	Llama-like animal with tan coat and tuft of white fur on chest
Hacienda	Ranch
Hechicería	Witchcraft
Helado	Ice cream
Huaca	Temple (especially in Peru)
Huecos	Holes
Isla	Island
Jardín	Garden
Juego (juegos en red)	Game (games networked on the computer)
Lago	Lake
Lancha	Boat
Leche	Milk
Libertador	Liberator
Luna	Moon

Mediodía	Noon, a time when most South American businesses close for siesta
Mercado	Market
Mestizo	The offspring born to a native person and one of European descent
M'hija	Affectionate term for my daughter
Milagro	Miracle
Mirador	Lookout point, view point
Mitad del mundo	Middle of the earth (equator)
Mono	Monkey
Monumento	Monument
Muerto	Dead
Museo	Museum
la Nata	Cream that forms a skin on top of heated milk typically used for coffee
El Niño	Literally "the boy," weather changes associated with Pacific Ocean currents
Norteamericanos	North Americans
Nubes	Clouds
Ñandú	Ostrich-like bird that is also known as a rhea
Olivo	Olive
Oropendola	Weaver bird found in rainforest with distinct call
Pampas	Plains, typically flat with only grasses

Pan	Bread
Pantalones	Pants
Papas	Potatoes
Parque (Parque Nacional)	Park (National Park)
Parrilla	Uruguayan barbecue
Peligroso	Dangerous
Peña	Impromptu get-together with live music, also a work crew
Pescadores	Fishermen
Pisco	Peruvian brandy made with distilled grapes
Pollo	Chicken, most commonly refers to cooked chicken
Polvo	Dust
¡Por supuesto!	Of course!
Rapidito	Jeep used for transport out of Uyuni, Bolivia
Recuerdos	Mementos
Rico	Rich, often used as "tasty" for food
Ruta	Route
Santos	Saints
Seguro	Safe, sure
Semana	Week
Semana Santa	Sacred week leading up to Easter

Serpentario	Snake museum
¡Siéntate!	Sit down!
Siesta	Nap, break taken in the middle of the day
¡Silencio!	Silence! (Be quiet!)
Sol	Sun
Suecos	Swiss people
Taller	Workshop
Te toca.	Your turn.
Teleférico	Cable car
Tenedor libre	Free fork (all-you-can-eat buffet)
Terminal terrestre	Land terminal (Central bus station in many Ecuadorian towns)
Tierra colorada	Red earth of Argentina
Tinajas	Large earthenware jars
el Tío	Uncle
Todos	All
Torino	Type of black dolphin with white spots on top
los Torres Gemelos	Twin towers
Tortuga	Turtle
¡Tranquilo!	Calm down! Relax!
Trencitos	Little trains (a row of several drinks in Cochabamba, Bolivia)

Trés cher	French expression meaning very expensive
Unos pocos pasos	A few steps
Vale la pena.	Worth the pain (worth the effort).
Vendimia	Harvest festival
Viajero	Traveler
Vicuña	Llama-like mammal similar to a guanaco, but smaller and more delicate
Vienen.	They are coming.
Vino	Wine
Viña	Winery, vineyard
Virgen	Virgin, meaning Mary, mother of Jesus
Viscacha	Rabbit-like rodent with long tail
Yaceta	High altitude plant that grows very slowly and is dome-shaped.
Zoológico	Zoo

Index

A

B

G

H

I

J

L

M

P

Q

R

S

T

U

V

W

Y

Z

About the Author

Psychologist and travel enthusiast Robin Malinosky-Rummell, Ph.D., has been working with children and families in a variety of settings for over 20 years. She has written articles for professional psychology journals as well as travel literature. Her background affords an in-depth look at the psychological processes and emotional extremes of adapting to various cultures as well as a year spent intimately with family members on the road. While journeying through six continents and over 60 countries around the world, she and her husband, Francis, have cultivated their own style of budget traveling, with a higher level of comfort and safety than bottom-end hostels yet more affordable and authentic than expensive luxury resorts. They are actively passing on their passion for travel to their son, Christopher. By founding Rumsky Travelworks, they hope to help other families nurture a social awareness and compassion in their children through travel as well.

For the most updated information about obtaining this book and other Rumsky Travelworks publications, please see the website at www.rumskytravelworks.com, or contact the author at rumskytravellers@yahoo.com.